Management
An International Perspective

Irwin Perspectives in International Business

Series Coeditors

James E. Harf   *The Ohio State University*

Robert R. Miller   *University of Houston*

B. Thomas Trout   *University of New Hampshire*

Management
An International Perspective

R. Hal Mason
Robert S. Spich

Both of
Graduate School of Management
University of California, Los Angeles

1987

IRWIN

Homewood, Illinois 60430

© RICHARD D. IRWIN, INC., 1987

ISBN 0-256-05631-5

Library of Congress Catalog Card. No. 86–82592

Printed in the United States of America

1 2 3 4 5 6 7 8 9 0 ML 4 3 2 1 0 9 8 7

PREFACE

This book is written for readers with an interest in understanding how managing abroad differs from managing at home. The book takes a general management view point by focussing on how the nature of managerial work changes when a firm decides to become more involved in international business. The perspective is both strategic and operations oriented. The strategic addresses the issues of how factors in country and international business environments affect decisions on the why, where, when and how of moving company business activities abroad. The operations focus describes how the implementation of the decision to go abroad requires adjustments to basic operations and business functions. The objective is to draw distinctions which identify how the management task differs in an international setting.

This book does not claim that international business is a set of conditions so unique that standard management theory and practice at home do not apply. It supports the idea that management practices need not be altered when business environments in different countries are similar. However, since conditions in international business environments usually differ in important ways, adaptations in major management practices need to be considered. Furthermore we have focused only on major themes and topics rather than provide a detailed treatment of all the ways managerial activities and processes can be affected by country business environments.

This book is targeted for use in a business policy or strategic management course. It could also serve as a means to internationalize the basic management course through assignments of chapters that complement standard text topics. Company personnel departments and international divisions might find this book useful to include in a training program for employees who are about to be assigned abroad. Finally, this book can be used as a stand-alone text for an introductory course in international business or international management. For these uses, the book offers a core text around which flexible case and reading supplements can be used.

HOW TO USE THIS BOOK

We would like to suggest the following as one way to use the text materials in a strategic management or business policy course.

Chapter 1.   This is an overview of the nature of contemporary business with an emphasis on how international issues are an integral part of the strategy question. It should be assigned at the first class session.

Chapter 2.   This chapter addresses the process of strategic decision making and describes the rationales and methods by which businesses get involved in the international business arena. It can be used with course materials on competitive analysis where strategy options are identified.

Chapters 3 and 4.   These chapters cover the nature of the international business environment and would go well with the strategy topics of environmental and industry analyses.

Chapter 5.   This chapter would go well with the internal strengths and weaknesses analysis topic because it ties the firm's opportunities for engaging in international business with its capabilities. It emphasizes an analysis of domestic business practices with an eye for where they can be transferred to a foreign setting and where they need to be adapted or developed.

Chapters 6, 7, 8, and 9.   These chapters are designed to show how decisions in the functional areas such as marketing differ from purely domestic business considerations. These chapters could be assigned to cases that have strong content in any of these functional areas. They could also be assigned with implementation chapters and cases to show how the manager who faces similar decisions in an international context may need to adapt to the environmental conditions of a particular country.

Chapter 10.   This chapter deals with the management problems of design of the organization and control. It could be assigned with an implementation-type case or with a strategic options analysis where the design of the organization may act to constrain the choices available.

Chapter 11.   This chapter is about the nature of managerial work abroad. The emphasis is on the role that a manager plays abroad and how that role requires paying attention to headquarters demands, subsidiary needs, and host country partner and government expectations. It might be assigned earlier in the course to give the student a flavor for the complexity of the international manager's role.

Chapter 12. This chapter deals with the interdependence theme that was introduced in Chapter 1. It emphasizes how the destinies of nations are tied together and the key role that the multinational corporations play in economic development. In particular, the past stormy and ambiguous relationship of the MNC to the host country government is discussed and resolved with an emphasis on a new realism between the two. This chapter is probably best used as an overview or summary chapter on the nature of the international business environment and the role of the firm in the international transfer of resources.

Each chapter is introduced with a summary statement of the major themes to be covered. Discussion questions are provided to both review major points in the chapter and allow for application of ideas to different situations. A general bibliography is provided at the end of the text. In addition, News-Boxes, excerpts of international business articles from the major U.S. newspapers, are included to provide examples and give perspective to chapter topics.

Finally, we have attempted to write in a clear, direct and simple style. We think there is merit to reducing the academic complexities to an understandable exposition of an international manager's point of view. We hope you agree.

R. Hal Mason
Robert Spich

CONTENTS

Social and Cultural Differences: *Attributes of the People.*
A Guide to "Cultural Wisdom". Management Response to
Foreign Cultures. The Two-Way Nature of Cultural
Adaptation. Achieving Effective Cultural Management.
Political and Regulatory Factors: *Sources and Settlements*
of Disputes. Resolving Conflict. Risk Analysis
Negotiations.

CHAPTER ONE

The Internationalization of Business: What This Book Is About

The purpose of this book is to provide an understanding of how business firms manage their affairs across national boundaries. Our focus is on how the role of the manager changes when he or she must make decisions and manage the affairs of the enterprise once its activities go beyond a single national market. International activities bring additional dimensions that are distinctly different from those of purely national firms. These major differences arise as a result of having to:

1. Conduct transactions in more than a single currency.
2. Deal with more than a single country's economic, political, and legal system. These differences translate into policy changes in interest rates, inflation, taxes, and growth rates, which both create and constrain business opportunities.
3. Overcome language, social, and cultural differences that strongly influence human values and behavior and, hence, the methods managers can employ in fulfilling their leadership and decision-making roles.
4. Integrate and coordinate a firm's business activities extended time zones and greater geographical distances.
5. Face a wider variety of competitors including public enterprises where government is often an active partner.

Firms engage in international business for one primary reason: profit opportunities. Firms in different fields have different capabilities that make it attractive to do business in more than one country. Some banks and insurance companies do business abroad while others do not. The same can be said of manufacturing firms, mining firms, and petroleum firms. However, not all firms find it profitable to engage in international business. Those that do generally have a specific competence or advantage not universally shared by other firms.

These firms tend to have some advantage in skills, resources, or organization that other firms in the group either do not have or fail to recognize in themselves. One of the keys to whether or not a firm develops international activities is the ability and willingness of the senior management group to use and develop a firm's specialized competencies in an international strategy.

Strategy is not easily described but it usually is defined as the set of objectives and underlying managerial motives that define and establish what the enterprise is attempting to do and the actions it intends to take to reach the objectives set by its managerial leaders. Most internationally oriented firms include in their objectives the desire and commitment to serve more than a single market or to take advantage of superior resources outside of one's own national boundaries. Without such a decision by management, few firms would ever venture beyond their home country. We would all tend to live in isolation from peoples of other lands. Through their decisions, business firms have thus helped make possible a broader perspective for each of us by their willingness to venture abroad.

Throughout this book, we will be discussing the role of the managers in fostering this international business process. Through their efforts to generate profits, managers discover new raw materials, pools of skills, new markets, new products, and new methods and technologies. Managers' actions have changed the world from being a set of relatively isolated independent countries and cultures into a world of countries and cultures that is interdependent and relies to a growing degree upon international trade and investment.

In the following sections of this chapter we highlight some aspects of the growing impact of international transactions.

The Internationalization Process

Two of the most salient characteristics of today's world economy are the increased internationalization of domestic economies and the resulting interdependence among nations. This is particularly true for the United States and its major trading partners. Internationalization refers to increased foreign influence on national trends and policies. For example, the increased flow of goods, investment capital, and technology from Japan to the United States has had a profound "foreign" influence on U.S. consumption patterns and manufacturing operations. U.S. citizens not only consume larger amounts of foreign made goods, they also work for U.S.-based foreign firms using technologies that are often brought in from abroad. Thus everyday North

American buying and work behavior has become internationalized, less provincial, and more open to outside influences.

The internationalization process, however, is not without its cost. With increased foreign influence comes an increased dependence on the goods and services available from abroad. Since trade and investment flow among many countries, mutual dependencies grow over time. Eventually they can lead to interdependence of national economic and political sectors. This in turn *reduces* the autonomy of national governments to make independent policy. The rise of the European Common Market and present U.S.-Japanese trade relations demonstrate these points well. In the latter case, U.S. dependence on Japanese goods and Japanese dependence on U.S. markets restricts both nations from setting policy on the basis of pure national self-interest. The resulting political and economic struggle of the United States with Japan highlights the problems of managing strategy in an interdependent world. More will be said of this in the last chapter.

It is widely recognized that the national borders of market-oriented countries are generally more open to international transactions than ever before in modern history. This openness is due to a number of important developments. First, there are international institutional developments such as the General Agreement of Trade and Tariffs (GATT) and the International Monetary Fund (IMF) both of which provided post–World War II guidance and rules for international trade and payments practices. These institutional developments were strongly supported by the United States in its aim to develop liberal, market-oriented Western economies in the 1950s and 1960s. The activities of GATT and the IMF, among other things, facilitated business transactions by reducing the risk and uncertainty with respect to restrictive government policies and practices.

Secondly, as incomes rose and tastes changed after World War II, the ability and willingness of domestic consumers of all countries to buy foreign goods increased. This naturally led to increased trade and foreign direct investment as businesses saw opportunities to meet market demand in a variety of ways.

Thirdly, developments in trade technology, services, and legal protection, which facilitated international transactions between nations, greatly contributed to globalization of demand and supply for various goods. Shipping developments such as container cargo, bulk carriers, and port infrastructure have vastly reduced the costs of shipping, handling, and storage of goods. Information technology created a true "world market" as better and more timely information was made available to more people. The barriers of time and distance were reduced by developments in information transmission, reception, and collection via telex, air mail, and satellite. A further contribution to internationalization was provided by such bank services as financing of trade, collecting of payments, and managing foreign exchange. Finally, the development of insurance protection such as that offered through the Export Import Bank, investment guarantees, the handling of investment disputes by the Bank for International Settlements, and reciprocal patenting of technology all have helped reduce the risks involved in international business by identifying rights and responsibilities of transacting partners and by providing an institutional forum in which to settle differences.

The extent of this internationalization process can be demonstrated by examining the various trade and investment transaction patterns of the major developed countries. Table 1–1 shows the relative importance of exports and imports among the economies of major developed countries. The figures in Table 1–1 indicate that there is a general growth in U.S. exports as a percentage of economic activity from 1960 to 1980. This is seen in the growth of exports and imports as a percentage of GNP. A second trend, not shown in the table, is the significant increase in the percentage of exports of manufactured goods. There has been nearly a fourfold increase in imports and a more than doubling in the exports of manufactured products from 1960 to 1980. Since the manufacturing of goods is an important source of employment, all countries are continually sensitive to fluctuations in this area of economic activity.

The figures in Table 1–1 also highlight the significance that trade plays in the economies of United States major trading partners. These partner countries have experienced an internationalization of their own economies for a longer period than the United States. As a result, we can expect them to be more sensitive to the impacts that trade fluctuations have on their economies. This helps to explain why countries with similar shared economic and political systems can differ significantly over policy issues. As an example, the Federal Republic of Germany was very keen on completing a natural gas pipeline agreement with the Soviet Union in the early 1980s, despite strong U.S. objections. West Germany's external dependence on trade requires it to look at business opportunities less from an ideological view than from an economic view.

Table 1–2 provides other indicators of the internationalization of domestic economies. On seeing a declining percentage for most countries (22.8 to 12.8 for the United States), the reader may presume that less economic activity is occurring. However, trade data shows that there has been a long-term trend of expanding U.S. trade, with exports increasing from $43 billion in 1970 to $200 billion in 1983 while imports went from $40 billion to $260 billion in 1983. This trade growth

TABLE 1–1 Importance of Merchandise Exports and Imports to GNP (for major western developed economies)

Period	United States Export*	United States Import	France Export	France Import	Germany (West) Export	Germany (West) Import	United Kingdom Export	United Kingdom Import	Japan Export	Japan Import	Canada Export	Canada Import
1960	4.0	3.0	10.3	11.2	15.9	14.1	14.4	17.6	4.4	10.4	14.1	14.3
1966	4.0	3.4	10.2	11.0	16.4	14.7	13.7	15.5	9.6	9.3	16.7	16.3
1970	4.3	4.1	12.8	13.5	18.5	16.1	15.8	17.7	9.5	9.2	19.6	16.3
1976	6.7	7.1	15.9	18.4	22.8	19.7	20.8	25.1	11.9	11.5	20.1	19.6
1980	8.2	9.3	17.6	20.5	23.6	23.0	20.9	22.0	12.5	13.6	25.7	23.4
1981	7.8	8.8	18.5	21.1	25.7	23.9	20.2	20.4	13.3	12.5	24.7	23.4
1982	6.7	7.9	17.8	21.3	26.7	23.5	20.1	20.6	13.0	12.4	23.7	19.0

*Exports/imports as percent of GNP.

SOURCE: This table was compiled from data taken from *International Trade Indicators*, 1975, 1978, 1980, 1984 U.S.D.C.-International Trade Administration.

TABLE 1-2   Percent Shares of Free World Exports*

Period	USA	France	Germany (West)	United Kingdom	Japan	Canada
1960	22.8	9.1	18.2	15.2	6.5	4.5
1966	19.6	6.1	11.1	8.1	5.4	6.3
1970	15.4	6.4	12.1	7.0	6.9	5.9
1976	12.8	6.3	11.3	5.2	7.5	4.5
1980	12.1	6.3	10.5	6.0	7.1	3.7
1981	13.0	5.9	9.8	5.8	8.4	4.0
1982	12.8	5.8	10.6	5.8	8.3	4.3

*This does not include Soviet bloc, China, and several Asian allies.

SOURCE: *International Economic Indicators and Competitive Trends*, USCD-International Trade Administration, 1976, 1978, 1980, 1984.

indicates that while the percentage shares of U.S. trade going to major industrialized economies has declined, the expanding volume of trade means that U.S. trade is probably more diversified. We now trade more with more countries.

There is some evidence that the U.S. economy is becoming more diversified. One recent study shows, for example, that U.S. market shares have increased for such relatively new trading partners as Mexico, Saudi Arabia, China, Korea, and other Pacific rim trading nations. This expansion of partners has occurred at the cost of trade share among the more traditional European partners. Thus, because a larger number of countries now share in its trading activity, the U.S. economy has become increasingly internationalized. Despite having a smaller share of the pie, the fact that the pie is much larger translates into absolute gains in trading activity.

Finally, the data in Tables 1-3A and B indicates that increased economic activity among the major world trading partners has occurred in more than just the area of import/export trade. Two aspects of this increased activity are seen here. First, there has been an increased flow of investment capital both in and out of the major economies. Generally there is more direct investment than ever before in history. This, no doubt, reflects the early successes of the post-war liberal economic system.

However, interpretations of country specific trends are more risky. For example, the increased investment into the U.S. economy from $140 million in 1960 to $22 billion in 1981 is no doubt due to multiple causes. One interpretation might be that the size and homogeneity of the U.S. market made it mandatory for foreign firms to consider investing directly in U.S.-based manufacturing and marketing to be

TABLE 1-3A Trends in Investment and Income as Indicators of Internationalization of the U.S. Economy. Foreign Direct Investment Outflows and Inflows (value in billions of dollars)

Period	USA		France		Germany (West)		United Kingdom		Japan		Canada	
	Out	In	Out	In	Out	In	Out	In	Out	In	Out	In
1960	1.7	.14	.05	.14	.15	.16	.46	.20	.08	.006	.05	.67
1970	7.6	1.5	.37	.62	.87	.60	1.3	.87	.36	.09	.30	.86
1973	11.3	2.7	.91	1.2	1.7	1.9	3.9	.90	6.9	-.42*	.77	.73
1976	11.9	4.3	1.7	1.1	2.5	1.1	3.8	1.3	2.0	.11	.60	-.30
1980	19.2	13.7	3.1	3.3	4.1	.24	8.0	6.0	2.4	.28	2.7	.50
1981	9.7	22.0	4.6	2.5	4.5	1.2	10.3	1.8	4.9	.19	4.9	-3.8

*This probably reflects the oil shock of 1973 where Japan was nearly 100 percent dependent on foreign oil.

SOURCE: *International Economic Indicators* 1976, 1978, 1980, 1984, USDC-International Trade Administration.

TABLE 1–3B   U.S. Income, Fees and Royalties from U.S. Direct Investment Abroad (billions of dollars)

| Period | Investment Income | | | Fees and Royalties* |
	Receipts to U.S. Owners of Foreign Firms	Payments To Foreign Owners of U.S. Firms	Net	Net 1
1971	9.5	− 4.9	4.6	2.6
1973	21.8	− 9.7	12.2	3.2
1975	25.4	− 12.6	12.8	4.6
1977	32.1	− 14.2	18.0	5.3
1979	64.1	− 32.9	31.2	5.7
1080	72.5	− 42.1	30.4	7.3
1981	86.4	− 52.4	34.1	8.0
1982	83.9	− 56.1	27.8	8.3
1983	77.0	− 53.5	23.5	8.7

*Fees and royalties from U.S. direct investments abroad or from foreign direct investments in the United States are excluded from investment income and included in other services, net 1.

SOURCE: Economic Indicators—1984, 1980, 1978, 1975. Council for Economic Advisers based on data provided by the Department of Commerce, Bureau of Economic Analysis.

close to markets. Another cause might be that the uncertainty in European investment climate led companies to consider putting their assets into a safer U.S. economic and political climate. This has been especially true of the United States since 1980. Finally, the high interest rates, lower inflation, and reduced regulatory climate no doubt provided further impetus for investment flows into the U.S. Similarly, the investment rates into Canada may reflect resistance to the Canadian governmental review process over foreign investment as well as general economic conditions. Whatever the specific country trend, generally speaking, there has been an increase in foreign direct investment throughout the world economy.

The second aspect of international capital flows is seen in the growth of the income from foreign investments in Table 1–3B. This income mainly represents profits earned on investments that are allowed to be "repatriated" or sent back to the parent company. However, these flows of income occur slowly and thus have a lagged effect on the investment cycle. Today's income from abroad represents the results of investment decisions that have been made over a long historical period. The expansion of foreign investment into the United States will inevitably result in the expansion of outflows of payments to foreign-based firms. As a result of these expanded flows, individual country balance of payments are being influenced more and more by economic trends that are the result of historic investment decisions. Firms and governments alike no longer depend solely upon their own domestic economies to provide for economic growth opportunities. As the opportunities and requirements for growth go beyond the capability of a domestic economy, the search for investment opportunities beyond national borders also increases. The result is a further internationalization of investment decisions.

In summary, the increased magnitude of international trade and investment has led to greater interdependency among individual national economies. Consumers and producers alike are finding that opportunities have been broadened by international transactions and accordingly, these transactions have become a vital part of economic decision making. As a result, international perspectives have been incorporated into everyday economic life. This is the real meaning of the "internationalization of domestic economies."

THE ROLE OF MULTINATIONAL CORPORATIONS IN THE GLOBALIZATION OF THE WORLD ECONOMY

Internationalization has been made easier by institutional reform and technological advances that have facilitated the flow of goods, services, people, and information. However, increases in economic activity are most directly the result of private firms' decisions to engage in international business. Thus, attention should be paid to the role of the multinational corporation (MNC) in the international economy. In transmitting resources between geographic regions having different supply and demand conditions, the MNC has become a major force in internationalizing national economies. One group of authors notes,

> The multinational corporation is probably the most visible vehicle for the internationalization of the world economic system. As the economies of different nations have become increasingly linked and functionally integrated, the multinational corporation seems to have been the institution most able to adapt to a transactional style of operation. Indeed, multinational corporations are a major result of and a prime stimulus for furthering the number and complexity of transnational interactions and relationships.[1]

---

[1] Daniel H. Blake and Robert S. Walters, *The Politics of Global Economic Relations*, 2nd ed. (Englewood Cliffs, N.J.: Prentice-Hall, 1983), p. 83.

In their search for new markets, cheaper raw materials, efficiencies in production, or friendly business environments, the MNCs have readily extended their economic activities across national borders. Whether motivated by new opportunities for improved operations or by fears of competitor's actions, each new venture represents an extension of economic activity into a foreign business environment.

Given the uncertainty and risks involved, a firm's first venture abroad is likely to be a limited commitment. As experience and success in foreign markets grow, a firm may gradually decide to invest abroad and produce some of its products in other countries. The fact that many firms have increased their proportion of sales and investment activity in foreign markets is the result of an ever-increasing involvement and dependency on foreign markets and resources which, in turn, strengthens the linkage between the interests of the MNCs and national governments. Sometimes these interests are mutual; other times they are conflicting. Whatever the general state of relations, both find themselves involved in a widening web of interdependence.

The reader should be aware that this process of internationalizing a firm's operations is neither inevitable nor characteristic of all industries. If we look at the total number of firms of all sizes in an economy, the largest percentage are domestically oriented; that is, they buy from and sell in regional or at most national markets.

Several factors are important determinants of a firm's probable involvement in international business. The first is size in terms of roles and operations. With size comes an increased need, interest, and capability for engaging in international business. For example, the top 50 U.S. exporters were represented almost exclusively by MNCs. Secondly, the need for specific resources or markets has been an important determinant in a firm's decision to go abroad. Until the early 1950s the dominant multinational firms were found in the extractive industries such as petroleum, mining, and agriculture. Their status as multinational firms was a matter of absolute necessity. It was necessary to gain direct control over supplies and crucial primary materials. To do so the firms had to establish foreign-based operating facilities where such materials were located. However, since the early 1950s, the number of multinational business operations in nonextractive industries has grown dramatically. For example, in Table 1–4 we see that among the firms considered most internationalized (i.e. foreign sales are a high percentage of total sales), food, drugs, machinery, chemical, and electrical industries have a near equal representation to the extractive industries among the ranks of MNCs.

A review of some selected statistics on multinational companies will give us better insight into the nature of these firms. By 1980 more

---

TABLE 1–4   Mix of Industries Represented in the Top 50 of the Most Internationalized Firms

Food/Drink	6	Metals	6
Drugs	6	Tobacco	3
Machinery	6	Building materials	2
Chemical	5	Textiles	1
Electrical	6	Rubber	1
Oil	6	Miscellaneous	1

SOURCE: Based on Table C, "Most Multinational Directory Firms, 1981" in John U. Stopford and John H. Dunning, *The World Directory of Multinational Enterprises 1982–83* Vol. 3, (Gale Research Company: Detroit, Michigan, 1983).

than 10,000 enterprises could be characterized as multinational with equity ownership interests in foreign affiliates or subsidiaries. These firms control over 90,000 foreign affiliates, with almost three fourths of them located in the industrialized countries, and one fourth in the developing countries. Although over 10,000 existing firms can be characterized as multinational, the 500 largest firms control almost 80 percent of all assets invested abroad and account for about the same percentage of total sales by multinationals. The large majority of multinationals are headquartered in the industrial countries. However a small and rapidly growing number of multinational firms are headquartered in the newly industrializing countries. Of the more than 10,000 firms in 1980 considered to be multinational, about 22 percent were based in the United States; Germany and the United Kingdom accounted for 14 percent each; Switzerland for 7 percent; France, Japan, and the Netherlands for about 6 percent each; and Canada for 4 percent. These eight countries account for nearly four fifths of all the multinational firms.[2]

It is important to keep in mind that all firms, in some form or other, engage in daily business that has international aspects to it. They may buy foreign-made parts and equipment or sell to distributors with foreign clientele. They may also hire foreign nationals. However, for the most part, this international activity is occasional and intermittent. The real measure of internationalization is the commitment of a firm's strategy and resources to business opportunities in foreign markets. The willingness to accept the many risks and to persevere

---

[2] These figures come from the sources noted in Table 1–4. John U. Stopford and John H. Dunning, *The World Directory of Multinational Enterprises 1982–83*, Vol. 3, (Gale Research Company: Detroit, Michigan, 1983).

through the challenges presented by foreign business environments is a commonly accepted hallmark of success. In this book then, we are concerned with the strategies and operations of firms that have made those commitments and undertaken those risks.

ORGANIZATION OF THIS BOOK

This book consists of 11 more chapters. In Chapter Two we explore the reasons firms engage in international business. The several methods they employ are discussed along with the reasons for choosing one method or combination of methods in preference to another. Chapters Three and Four describe and analyze the environmental conditions firms encounter when they conduct business beyond their home borders. The economic, technical, sociocultural, and political aspects of these conditions are discussed. Chapters Five through Ten examine how operational decisions of the firm are altered when the firm operates outside its national boundaries. Chapter Five provides an overview to the next five chapters which examine the firm's challenge in managing the marketing, production, human resources, finance, and management functions. The focus is on matching the company's capabilities to the demands of international business environments. Likewise, there is an emphasis on the relationships between parent firm and overseas subsidiaries and between governments and enterprises. Chapter Eleven discusses the manager's various roles abroad. The focus is on how these roles must respond not only to the socio-cultural environment abroad but also to the organizational problems that result from attempting to integrate and coordinate a complex set of operations across national boundaries. Finally, Chapter Twelve examines of the future prospects for multinationalism and for continued growth and change in international business.

DISCUSSION QUESTIONS FOR CHAPTER ONE

   1. What factors have contributed to the internationalization of the U.S. economy over the last 40 years?

   2. What are some good indicators or measures of the impact of international economic flows on the U.S. economy?

   3. In what ways do foreign competition affect domestic business decisions? Give examples.

TWO VIEWS OF INTERNATIONALIZATION

NEWS BOX 1–1
"Internationalization of U.S.Banks Falters after Decade of Expansion"
M. R. Sesit and D. Hertzberg

The internationalization of the U.S. banking system, which has been building for more than a decade, has started to falter. In the face of the Third World debt crisis, U.S. banks are making fewer loans abroad. And, foreign investors are becoming skittish about depositing funds in American banks. . . . But the changes could hurt U.S. banks because they come at a time when some banks have grown more dependent on foreign sources of money.

The internationalization of U.S. banking won't disappear; the process has been going on too long and makes too much economic sense. From 1960 to 1983, the international assets of U.S. banks and their foreign branches grew from about $5 billion to about $410 billion, according to a Federal Reserve Board economist in Washington. At the same time, U.S. banks were raising lots of funds abroad; such foreign funding grew to an estimated $260 billion last year from miniscule amounts in the early 1960s.

Additionally, banks have many business reasons for lending and borrowing overseas, including the need to service their multinational corporate clients. Overseas, U.S. banks aren't subject to many federal and state regulations that restrict both their geographic expansion within the United States and the products they can offer.

They can also make big money overseas. The top 10 U.S. banks earned as much as 50 percent of their operating profits from 1977 through 1981, according to Salomon Brothers, Inc. In addition, tapping money from foreign depositors allowed banks to borrow at lower costs and diversify their funding base.

But that internationalization has started to worry U.S. banks—on both the asset and liability sides.

Banks are stuck with billions of dollars of troubled Third World debt. At the worst, banks could be forced to write off a large portion of those loans, sharply reducing or even wiping out their capital. At the very least, having to postpone some loan payments by as much as nine years represents an opportunity cost to banks. They can lend those funds to another, more creditworthy borrower. Furthermore, market reaction to the international debt problem has reduced the stock prices of the largest U.S. money-center banks.

The combination of uncollectible Third World debt and fickle overseas funding sources has changed some banks' asset-liability strategies. When banks do lend abroad, they are often returning to basics: making loans that are collateralized or designed for a specific project or for trade. All three kinds reduce risk. Banks are also emphasizing lending in the country's local currency, eschewing the risk that the borrower won't be able to get the dollars needed to repay the loans.

SOURCE: Excerpted from M. R. Sesit and D. Hertzberg, "Internationalization of U.S. Banks Falters After Decade of Expansion," *The Wall Street Journal*, August 7, 1984, p. 24.

NEWS BOX 1–2
Around the Globe, La Dolce Burger

As the United States fills up with more and more McDonald's the fast-food giant is looking increasingly overseas for growth. One reason, says Fred L. Turner, the chairman, is "there are more people in Europe than in the United States.

In Europe, the big news is the opening of Italy's first McDonald's. The restaurant in Rome, which nearby boutique owners have complained about because it isn't chic enough, is doing so well, that it may be the number one McDonald's in sales worldwide this year. Although American McDonald's restaurants average higher sales per unit than their overseas counterparts, a McDonald's in Singapore now has the greatest sales in the chain.

Italy, however, remains far behind England and West Germany, both of which have more than 200 McDonald's. France has just 28 because growth there was paralyzed by a bitter dispute, now ended, with the original franchisee there.

Asia is the company's fastest-growing market, adding almost 100 McDonald's a year. The number of Asian units will exceed 700 at the end of 1986, up from 328 in 1981. Japan has more than 530, with more than 100 each in Tokyo and Osaka. "People in Asia seem more receptive to try new things, and there is great growth in the middle class," said Steven J. Barnes, chairman of McDonald's international operations.

South Korea is scheduled to add its first McDonald's next year, and the company is also working to open its first outlets in Hungary and Turkey. China has invited McDonald's in, but Turner said the company is holding off there because it wants to wait until China's middle class expands. Meanwhile, the company is helping to teach Chinese farmers how to grow potatoes, which can be used in french fries—imitating similar work it did in Brazil.

McDonald's hopes to conquer many more hearts and palates in Latin America, where the company has 72 restaurants. "The potential for growth is great in Brazil and Argentina," said Jack M. Greenberg, the chief financial officer. "But those countries are having a slow time of it right now. If they grow faster, then we'll grow faster too"

SOURCE: T. Wise, "The Rise and Rise of McDonald's," The *New York Times*, June 8, 1986, Section F p. 1.

---

4. Does a small U.S. manufacturer that sells all of its products in the U.S. market need to concern herself with international business issues? Why or why not?

5. "The internationalization of domestic economies has always been a reality for most of the smaller countries in Europe." Why would this tend to be true for them and not the United States?

6. While it may be obvious how increased trade makes an economy more internationally minded, the same is not true for capital flows. How do you think capital flows contribute to the internationalization of an economy?

7. The more internationalized an economy becomes, the more interdependent it may find itself with other national economies. How do the internationalization process and interdependence relate with one another?

8. Why is the interdependence theme in business and government policy so important to a country like Japan?

9. Increased interdependence suggests that the position of the U.S. economy in the world is changing from a position of dominance to one of shared power with other major economies. Why might this be happening?

10. What are the implications for U.S. business of a relative weakening of the U.S. economy vis a vis its major trading partners?

_____

CHAPTER TWO

Engaging in International Business: Motives and Methods

INTRODUCTION

In this chapter we explore the reasons that firms engage in international business and discuss the various methods they use to do so.

The process by which a firm becomes international involves both strategic and operational decisions. The occasional export sale is probably the first operational decision that all international firms experience initially. Eventually, a series of such sales may result in a growing commitment to international markets. As success in foreign sales increases, the firm may set up a foreign sales office, hire local staff, and invest in a foreign-based warehouse and inventory system. Eventually this process of incremental increases in international business transactions may require installation of production facilities and redefinition of the firm's mission. At this point the firm has moved to a strategic commitment to international business. International business strategy requires a conscious allocation of resources, tasks, and responsibilities to activities abroad.

In the following three sections we address three questions:

1. Why do firms engage in international business?
2. What methods do firms use to engage in international business?
3. Why do firms choose one method over another?

WHY DO FIRMS ENGAGE IN INTERNATIONAL BUSINESS?

This question cannot readily be examined separately from the nature of the firm and the nature of the industry of which it is a part. It is interesting that some industries have a large proportion of firms that become internationally involved while certain other industries have a relatively low international participation. For example, virtually all of the automobile manufacturers in the free market economies are engaged in international business. Most of these firms have significant investments abroad and a global organization of manufacturing and assembly operations. At another extreme, most firms in the food industry never venture beyond their own national borders. Of the thousands of food manufacturing firms worldwide, perhaps only about 25 can be considered to be multinational in scope. Thus, the nature of the firm's industry influences the degree to which the firm will be motivated to engage in international business.

There are five key considerations for firm's deciding to engage in international business. These are:

1. Economies of scale.
2. Economies of scope of the firm.
3. Access to superior resources.
4. Specialized assets of the firm.
5. Degree of commitment and personal preferences of management.

A firm may be able to reduce its costs by increasing the size of its market through export to markets in other countries. This increased volume makes larger lots or production runs possible (larger lots) and reduces unit costs. Lower unit costs allow for improved price competition. The lower costs result from what are called economies of scale and, hence, one reason for entering overseas markets is to obtain additional efficiencies, or in economic terms, "economies of scale."

Secondly, a firm may be able to achieve reduced costs or increased margins of profit by broadening its product line or by integrating business processes such as producing its own raw materials rather than buying them from someone else. This expansion allows the firm to build upon its existing business to generate new types of business, or, stated differently, it can broaden the range of business activities in which it engages. When this occurs, we say that the firm can achieve "economies of scope."

In some cases, both economies of scale and economies of scope occur simultaneously. For example, suppose a firm has a well-developed distribution system through which it sells shaving creams and lotions to drug stores. It currently does not sell disposable cigarette lighters but decides to sell an imported line of such lighters because a sizable portion of these lighters are sold through drug stores. In so doing, the firm utilizes its distribution system more effectively, and thus it achieves economies of scale. But, it also has changed its scope because it has taken on a new product line that has little to do with its original products except that they are all sold through drug stores. Thus there is interaction between economies of scope and economies of scale.

The third motive for becoming international is to obtain "superior resources." In some instances necessary resources may not be available in the firm's home country and it thus becomes necessary to do business across one's national border to obtain needed resources. For example, Japan has very little in the way of natural resources such as iron ore or crude oil. Thus, it must obtain these resources from abroad either by importing them from foreign-owned firms or by establishing its own operations abroad to extract, process, and ship the resources. It should be noted that natural resources are not the only resources that firms seek from overseas locations. Increasingly, labor skills and technology are significant factors in the decision to establish overseas operations. For example, in the biotechnology field firms from Japan and Europe are now investing in the United States in order to gain access to technology being developed here. Firms from advanced countries are investing in developing countries in order to obtain access to low-cost labor. U.S. companies are setting up manufacturing operations across the Mexican border to gain such benefits. While the existence of superior resources overseas may be a necessary condition for investment abroad, it is usually not a sufficient condition for investing in foreign facilities. In addition the firm must have a special competitive advantage that is not possessed by locally owned firms in the host country.

Perhaps, the most important reason then for engaging in international business is to exploit some specialized or unique asset owned by the firm. Specialized assets provide the firm with the means to achieve a competitive advantage. Indeed, it can be argued that firms that do not possess such an asset or advantage will not invest abroad. If a firm has no special advantage, it cannot succeed when it attempts to compete against locally owned firms. This is true because locally owned firms already have an advantage in terms of their knowledge of the language, social customs, local business regulations, markets, and resources available in their own country. A foreign firm that attempts to compete with local firms must incur the costs of learning these things. If it has no special advantage to offset these costs, it will be the high-cost producer in competition with local firms and hence probably will not survive. Thus, the foreign firm must have special advantages not available to local firms such as economies of scale and scope; specialized technological, financial, production, and marketing know-how; or superior management systems. And this will be true even if the costs of production for the foreign entrant are lower abroad than at home because the costs of production for the local foreign firm would be lower still.

This brings us to the fifth reason for engaging in international business. Without "personal commitment" on the part of senior management, a firm, even if it has all of the other necessary characteristics, will not engage in international business. Commitment from the top is important because personal leadership and resolve from top management is required to deal with the difficult changes and decisions that result from international business activity. Without such commitment, the international strategy will most likely falter and fail.

The willingness to undertake foreign ventures arises from the experiences and backgrounds of senior managers. The absence or presence of this quality is why firms of the same size, in the same industry, and possessing similar resources differ so markedly in their degree of international activity. For example, in the farm equipment industry International Harvester Company had a wide variety of overseas activities for decades whereas Deere & Company did not enter the European market until the 1960s. The move from being primarily a domestic firm to becoming an international firm was a major decision for Deere and Company, and the commitment did not occur until senior management was willing to change its values and perceptions of international business risks and opportunities.

WHAT METHODS CAN A FIRM USE TO ENGAGE IN INTERNATIONAL BUSINESS?

There are a variety of methods firms use to accomplish transactions across national boundaries. As seen in Figure 2–1, these transactions are grouped under two major headings: (1) export and import of goods or services and (2) investment in foreign assets.

The variations in business methods that can occur within these two basic business groupings forms depend on three important criteria: the location and characteristics of the market, the transferability of management control to foreign operations, and the economics of the resulting costs and benefits. For example, a firm may be able to serve a foreign market by exporting from its domestic home base. However, if the firm sees that it can serve a foreign market better by locating its business activities abroad, it can invest in foreign assets. In other instances, it may choose to sell access to its production technology and let a locally based firm serve the market. Japanese investment in U.S.-based manufacturing, using both wholly owned and joint venture forms of business, exemplify how these elements enter into the decision to go abroad.

We should note further that these methods are not mutually exclusive. Companies can simultaneously export some products and directly invest in production operations for other products. The main guiding

---

FIGURE 2–1   Two Major Methods of International Business

Exporting and Importing of:	*Examples*
Goods:	
Raw Materials	Iron ore, agricultural commodities, crude oil, coal, bauxite.
Semifinished Goods	Automobile parts, textiles, leather, chemicals, semiconductors, sheet metal.
Finished Goods	
Consumer Goods	Television sets, prepared foods, clothing, automobiles, refrigerators, furniture.
Capital Goods	Tractors, airplanes, machine tools, computers.
Services:	Insurance and financial services; technology licenses; franchises; transportation, lodging, tourism, communications, and legal services; consulting services.

Foreign Investment:	*Examples*
Portfolio Investment	100 shares of Olivetti stock, $10,000 worth of Bank of England notes, purchase of a mortgage on a Swiss chalet. No operating control is involved.
Direct Foreign Investment*	Joint ventures, with more or less than 50 percent ownership.
	Consortium ventures with multiple partners including governments.
	Wholly owned subsidiaries and branches (100 percent ownership).

---

*NOTE: By definition, direct foreign investment means that the foreign investor has enough of an ownership share to guarantee operating control of the enterprise. If there is not operating control, then the investment would be considered to be a portfolio investment. In many instances, a minority ownership position is sufficient to provide operating control and minority positions are therefore often considered to be direct foreign investment.

criteria for the firm is how best to serve their chosen markets— whether by export or direct investment.

EXPORTS AND IMPORTS

Exporting means the selling of something outside one's borders that has been produced inside one's borders. When Caterpillar Tractor Company produces a tractor in East Peoria, Illinois and sells the tractor in Egypt, it has exported a product. When Pan American Airways sells a ticket to an Italian who goes as a passenger from New York to

Rome, Pan Am has exported a service. When Motorola, Inc. licenses a Japanese firm to use one of Motorola's patents to produce semiconductors in Japan, Motorola is paid a fee by the Japanese firm. Motorola has exported a service.

Exporting is the simplest form of involvement in international business. Risks are minimized because the firm continues to operate in its own business environment. Even risks in foreign exchange can be controlled through hedging services provided by banks. In exporting, the commitment to internationalize internal operations can be nearly avoided by contracting with export management companies to represent and sell the firm's products abroad. Or the firm can make stronger commitments by setting up an export department, hiring and training export management specialty skills, and using resources for market research.

There are numerous types of contracts that result in fees being paid by the foreign-based operation to a home office. These contracts result in either a good or a service being exported or imported. Examples of contracts that deal with exports or imports of goods include bills of lading, long-term supply contracts, and resource concessions. Contracts which deal primarily with the export or import of services include licensing agreements, technical aid agreements, maintenance contracts, consulting contracts, management contracts, financing agreements, and contracts related to communications, transportation, and insurance. Any of these contracts may or may not be accompanied by the ownership of business assets in foreign countries. The important point is that contracts merely spell out the obligations of various parties to particular types of business transactions.

INVESTING ABROAD

Before we examine the meaning of foreign investment, let us review some basic propositions about the production of goods and services. One way of looking at international trade and international investment is as follows: we assume that the competitive situation requires that a firm be only interested in achieving the lowest cost of serving markets and have various options for doing so. Let us further assume that the firm itself can either produce a particular product or have someone else produce it either at home or abroad. In fact, many firms do not produce the products they sell. Sears, for example, does not own the manufacturing plants in which many of the products bearing the Sears brand name are produced. Indeed, most large manufacturing firms do not produce everything they sell. General Motors Corp. buys many of the components that go into its cars from firms which are not located in the countries where the cars are assembled. Finally, we assume that all firms conceivably have these same options.

The location where products and services will be produced obviously can differ from the location where they will be consumed. This, then, provides multiple options for international investment. Choice allows free consideration of where these goods (or services) will be produced and sold, who will own and therefore control the facilities in which goods (or services) are produced, and what economic benefits and costs result from these choices. The options are depicted in Figure 2–2.

Virtually every type of contract could appear in Figure 2–2, including licensing agreements, supply contracts, technical aid contracts, and turnkey projects. While the relationships may seem somewhat complicated, the actual relationships among firms usually are even more complex. One example of a more complex arrangement could be a licensing agreement whereby the producing firm produces the product for our firm based on one of our firm's patents. The more complex the arrangement, however, the more difficult it is to manage.

WHY DO FIRMS CHOOSE ONE METHOD RATHER THAN ANOTHER?

Firms seek to use the least costly method to serve markets. These costs are measured not only in terms of production, transportation, and marketing costs, but also in terms of risks. For example, while it may cost less to produce a product abroad than at home, the potential of losing one's assets may be too great to warrant installation of a plant in a foreign location. Some of the more common risks include:

1. Plant expropriation by the country's government.
2. Plant shut-down due to labor strikes or interruptions in supplies of raw materials.
3. Goverment regulations and development goals which lead to the imposition of price controls, local content requirements, job creation requirements, and ownership sharing requirements.
4. Imposition of tariffs on critically needed imported components.
5. Imposition of foreign exchange controls so that profits cannot be sent back to the parent company.
6. Loss of proprietary information and rights due to licensing, industrial espionage, or piracy.

These risks are associated with installation of production facilities in foreign locations. However, these same risks could also occur in the firm's own home country. Thus, the crucial difference is between the likelihood of these events happening abroad or at home. Even for the

FIGURE 2–2 International Business Options

Who Owns the Production Facilities	Where Are the Production Facilities Located?					
	In Our Country			In Some Other Country		
Our company	We make the product and sell it at home	or	We make the product and export it to other countries	We make the product in another country and import it for sale in our home country. We export from our subsidiary.	or	We make the product in another country and sell it there or to other countries. In the latter, we export from our subsidiary to third countries.
Some other company	We buy the product from them and sell it at home	or	We buy the product and export it to other countries	We buy the good in another country and import it for sale in the home country.	or	We buy the good for sale either in the host country or third country markets.

firm whose home base is in an unstable country, foreign investment may be highly attractive because other countries are less risky than its own.

Sometimes investing abroad is perceived as less risky than not investing at all. For example, suppose a firm has developed a foreign market by exporting from its production facilities at home. Suppose also that the foreign country's government imposes a tariff on the products this firm has been exporting. If the firm does not invest and set up production facilities abroad to serve its foreign market, it risks losing the market to firms that are willing to deal with government policy and invest. Thus, different methods of engaging in international business will result in different types and levels of risk. This means that managers must assess the trade-offs associated with different risks—the outcome ultimately determines the choice of method. Generally, management applies major decision criteria, such as those in Figure 2–3, to its choice of methods. In making those choices, the following questions need to be considered:

1. Does the method require substantial amounts of key resources?
2. Does the method involve economic and political risks that cannot be justified by the expected rate of return?
3. Does the method develop new more efficient resources or does it improve the efficiency of existing resources?
4. Does the method provide the desired operating control?
5. Does the method allow us to use our specialized assets to full advantage?
6. Does the method provide a reasonable level of protection to our specialized assets and guard against loss of competitive advantage?

Importance of Intangible Assets

Firms own intangible assets such as technological know-how, patents, brands and trademarks, corporate image, reputation, and access to distribution systems. It is these intangible properties that distinguish firms from one another. They can choose to exploit these specialized firm-specific assets either by applying them in production facilities they own or by selling or renting out the right to use these assets to one or more other firms. The licensing of Coca-Cola is an example. Thus, what we are concerned about is the degree to which firms will allow other firms to have access to their tangible and intangible property rights.

It is the intangible assets that distinguish the purely national firm from the international firm. The Sears brand name, Apple's patented DOS system, or Fluor Company's project management system demon-

---

FIGURE 2–3 Decisions Criteria and Choice of Methods

Decision Criteria	Decisions Leading to Choice of Method
Size of market	Product to be sold
Rate of market growth	Country market choice
Market share attainable	Location of production facilities
Size of investment	Plant size
Competitive advantage	Technology to be used
Costs of production	Make or buy the product
Level and type of risk	Own or rent facilities
Need for operating control	Control assets or not
Efficiency gains attainable	Choose an organization
Rate of return required	structure and management system
Protection of specialized assets	

---

strate such intangible assets. Many firms might well be able to accumulate the physical facilities required to produce a product, but this alone does not guarantee that the product can compete internationally or that the firm would be able to operate similar physical facilities outside its own borders. As we have noted, the international firm must be able to offer a superior alternative to the purely national firm simply because the purely national firm has an inherent advantage through knowledge of its own country's environment.

If the firm is willing to share its intangible assets it can:

1. License other firms to use the assets, in which case these firms pay a fee.
2. Sell the intangible assets outright to another firm, and thereby divest itself of the assets.
3. Share ownership with one or more firms by engaging in joint ventures in which it can hold either a minority, an equal, or a majority ownership position.

The degree to which the firm will allow access to its specialized assets depends upon the value of the assets in terms of their ability to generate profits. Many factors, of course, determine the value of an asset. In general, the uniqueness of the asset and control over its use are the main determinants of value. This can be seen in special formulas for products, technical processes, product designs and image, established relations in distribution systems, and client relations. Since these assets may not be readily available from alternative sources, their relative scarcity increases their value. It is the objective of most firms to see that scarcity and control continue to be the case.

A highly profitable asset is more likely to be protected against access by others than is an asset that is not so profitable. For example, a firm that has developed a superior technology to produce a product is more likely to either export the product from home or, produce the product abroad in a wholly owned facility. This limits competition's access to the assets that are critical to the production of the product. It is often the case that where the product is produced abroad, the firm will attempt to staff key jobs will personnel from the firm's home country. This reduces the likelihood of a foreign national gaining understanding and know-how about an intangible asset.

The less valuable the asset, however, the greater will be the likelihood that the firm will sell the asset, rent access to the asset, or share ownership rights in the asset. This follows from the fact that its uniqueness or control over it have diminished. Thus, the choice of method of engaging in international business largely depends on the value of intangible assets possessed by individual firms.

There are still other considerations that affect the choice of method. Part of the intangible assets firms may possess include knowledge of foreign country environments and markets. A firm that has engaged in business in one foreign environment is likely to be more willing to venture into another foreign location than is a firm which has never operated outside its own country. Gaining such experience seems to be a function of firm size. Large firms are more likely to accumulate such knowledge than are small firms. Thus, even if a small firm has a distinctive competence in producing a product, it may fail to expand into foreign markets because it does not know how to make such a decision.

Government policies also influence the asset-use decision. For example, many countries place prohibitive tariffs on the importation of certain goods. Foreign firms then must invest in physical facilities, or "hop over" the tariff wall in order to produce the product locally. But some governments may also insist that foreign firms share ownership with local investors. In this situation the firm cannot export from home into the foreign market and it cannot use a wholly owned facility if it wishes to produce the product in the host country. Thus, the foreign firm may have few choices if it wishes to participate in a particular national market. IBM's refusal to share its intangible assets with the Indian government is said to be one of the main reasons for the company's decision to leave the Indian market until government policy changed.

Finally, some projects are so large and/or so risky that no single firm would want to undertake them. Nuclear power generation, R and D in the development of airplane technology, and the privitization of space flight are examples of such projects. In this case the mode of entry may be dictated by the nature of the project itself. Thus, a joint venture with one or more other firms or even with a government would be required. However, such joint efforts usually require considerable sharing of information which undermines the ability to protect the firm's unique assets.

Competition and Choice of Methods

The choice of method is not made with only market characteristics in mind. Firms differ in their ability to compete not only with local firms in the host country, but also with other multinational firms in their chosen fields of business. Thus the nature of competition becomes an important determinant of methods.

For example, firms sometimes appear to pursue a follow-the-leader strategy. If an industry leader sets up a manufacturing plant in Germany, others follow making similar investments. This investment decision is often made out of fear of being preempted in a market. Thus, following a leader becomes a way of not losing a competitive edge. Several factors determine the degree of competitiveness:

1. The resources available to the various firms.
2. The intensity with which each firm competes.
3. Industry characteristics and the relative competitive positions of the firms.

Resources include not only physical assets such as manufacturing plants, but also intangible assets. Ultimately it is the combination and strategic use of these resources that determines how well or how poorly a firm will be able to compete. The intensity of competition is determined by the number of products a firm offers, the market and market segment it chooses to sell in, and the resources it invests in its marketing efforts. The intensity of competition becomes magnified in international business because multinational firms must compete with one another. Thus, General Motors not only competes with American, European, Japanese, and now Korean auto firms in the U.S. market, they also must compete with these same firms abroad in addition to local firms. Some firms attempt to compete by having a full product line while others seek to develop niches within an industry that they can defend vigorously. For example, Caterpillar Tractor Co. competes in virtually every segment of the construction equipment industry. It produces and markets crawler tractors, graders, scrapers, forklifts, wheel loaders, and several other items. It is noted for the excellent quality of its products and post-sales service. On a worldwide basis its market share in this industry is nearly 50 percent. However, it is not necessary to compete in every segment of the industry to be successful.

For example, Clark Equipment Company concentrates on forklift trucks and front-end loaders and does very well. It, too, is known for the high quality of its products and service. What determines how well these firms can compete is not only the availability of resources, but also how effectively they apply these resources to the assessment of customer needs and to the production of products or services at a cost which allows high value for the prices charged (see News Box 2–1).

Lastly, the degree of competitiveness of a company's market is determined by the characteristics of the industry and the relative position of a firm within that industry. The industry's characteristics include the number, size, age of firms, their degree of forward or backwards integration into markets or suppliers, and the concentration of market power. The relative position of a firm within a given industry is determined by its market share, size of asset base, technological capabilities, quality of products, and effectiveness of its management systems.

Large firms are usually involved in more than one business and thus are often competing in several industries at the same time. This complicates the managerial task, because it requires constant industry analyses to keep abreast of trends and sudden changes in competitive advantage. Breakthroughs in technology or development of new markets are examples of such changes.

The true strategic nature of international business comes out under these circumstances. The complexity of multiple-industry analysis combined with multi-country environments creates strategic opportunities on a global scale. Thus, the strategies that a multinational firm will or can pursue depend very much upon the capabilities of managing a multiple-industry conglomerate firm of its rivals. Periodic divestment cycles, that is, times when firms sell off various businesses, show this task is not always successfully managed.

From a management viewpoint, what happens in one country may have a major influence on the competitive situation in other countries. Firms, because of the resources they have available in various countries, are able to establish distinctive positions on a worldwide basis. For example, if Michelin Tire Company is going to compete effectively in the United States, it must guard itself against loss of markets in Europe because it needs the strength in Europe to generate the resources necessary to enter, develop, and hold a sufficient share of the U.S. market to be efficient. It needs market share to obtain economies of scale in production and to achieve costs that are low enough to compete with Goodyear Tire & Rubber Co. and Firestone Tire & Rubber Co. in the United States. These latter firms are vying for similar markets. They compete by developing and differentiating their products, by developing certain market segments that allow them to exploit their distinc-

NEWS BOX 2–1
Caterpillar: A Test of U.S. Trade Policy
James Risen

Heavy-Equipment Maker Gains the Edge Against Japan's Giant Komatsu as Dollar Falls Against Yen

Here in this modest, oft-stereotyped city by the Illinois River, there's a new pastime—dollar watching.

No matter what other image Peoria conjures up, this is simply a bedrock, blue-collar company town, with its fortunes tied inextricably to the corporation that overshadows all others here—Caterpillar.

And right now, it's hard to find an American firm with more to gain than Caterpillar from the recent dramatic decline in the value of the dollar—and the simultaneous run-up in the Japanese yen.

Four years, Caterpillar, the nation's biggest construction equipment maker, has been locked in a global, one-on-one struggle with a single Japanese giant—Komatsu Ltd.

That competition has forced Caterpillar to slash costs, eliminate jobs and cut prices in order to hang on to its number one position in the worldwide earth-moving equipment industry. To avoid getting swamped by cheap machines from Komatsu, Cat has not increased prices since 1981. At the same time, many of the smaller American and European equipment makers have quit the business after getting caught in the Cat-Komatsu cross fire, leaving the field open for the giants to battle.

But until recently, no matter what Cat did to remain competitive, the strong dollar kept battering its worldwide market share.

The weakness of the yen against the American currency over the last few years gave Komatsu a huge cost advantage. It produced its equipment in Japan with parts and labor paid for with cheap yen and then exploited the yen's weakness by keeping prices low overseas. That edge helped Komatsu steal sales away from Cat around the world—and in the United States.

Traditionally one of the nation's premier exporters of manufactured goods, Caterpillar suddenly found its foreign markets shrinking just as it was being severely tested at home. The results were plain to see on Cat's bottom line—combined losses of $953 million from 1982 through 1984.

But since the yen has appreciated nearly 40 percent against the dollar over the last few months, the ground rules for Caterpillar's fight against Komatsu have suddenly changed—in Cat's favor.

SOURCE: The *Los Angeles Times*, June 8, 1986, Part IV, p. 1.

tive competencies, and by concentrating on those countries where these advantages can be most effectively applied. They are not always accurate in their assessments and, accordingly, they sometimes lose out to another firm. However, they have the objective of establishing a competitive position that draws on their strengths while shunning situations where they are weak. Firms thus seek "relative competitive position" which will preclude one firm having a superior position in each and every country.

Commitment and Corporate Culture

Recent management literature has focused on organizational excellence, foreign corporate models of success, and the internal working environment of effective organizations. One characteristic of excellence that merits the attention of international managers is organizational commitment to success (see News Box 2–2).

A firm's response to foreign business opportunities depends on the level of management commitment to going international. A firm whose management has shared goals and consensus in its top ranks is more likely to direct management time and attention toward these goals of internationalization. Commitment can be seen in the decisions management makes: to hire or not hire internationally oriented staff; to reorganize the firm to include organizational units which are specifically designed to handle international business transactions; to create international consciousness through travel, training, and forward planning; and to invest in production facilities abroad. The results can be measured by the number of countries where business is done, foreign sales volume, profits generated abroad, and the forms of involvement the firm pursues.

By internationalizing its operations, a firm opens itself to a decrease in managerial control over many business decisions. Time and distance make international business decisions more difficult to implement, monitor, and evaluate. Even with today's highly developed communications systems and speedy air travel, this remains a problem. The development and diffusion of corporate culture represents one effective method of integrating and controlling far flung foreign operations. Managers and staff personnel who are trained and socialized into a firm's values and methods are more likely to make decisions consistent with corporate strategy. Culture, in effect, represents an internalization of control in the individual. Through the placement of staff in key positions abroad, control over operations improves.

The second theme from commitment regards the effect of corporate culture on success. The idea is that successful firms seem to have distinctive and effective organizational cultures. Organizational culture

NEWS BOX 2–2
Apple in Japan

Alexander D. van Eyck, 44, a former MCI Communications Corp. executive, is the third president that Apple Computer Japan, Inc. has had in less than three years, a fact that has made the firm appear "unstable," he says. At a news conference he called to declare that Apple intends to turn over a new leaf in Japan, he said he personally intends "to stay here indefinitely to demonstrate that we at Apple Computer are committed to this market and that I am committed to this market."

* * * * *

Van Eyck refused to disclose what results Apple had achieved here since it set up a subsidiary in June 1983, but he did not dispute a Japanese reporter's assertion that sales had been poor. He also admitted that Apple has created an "image of instability."

"We had had an image of having an unstable organization in terms of management that we've had here. . . . Our distributors and dealers have felt rather uncomfortable. So I believe it is important now to smooth over this feeling of unstableness and reiterate as firmly as we can our commitment to them and our commitment to the Japanese market," he said.

In 1983, Apple in the United States had not made a sufficient commitment in international markets, van Eyck said. "It was a technology-driven company, concentrating very much on the United States and giving very little attention to markets in the Far East," he added.

"Our policies were short term [in 1983], and we were managing on a short-term basis. To be a success in Japan, management along those lines cannot continue," van Eyck said.

New International Strategy

Asked why Apple took nearly three years to realize what nearly all American businessmen have widely recognized—that a long-term commitment is necessary to succeed in Japan—Fred Sherrer, sales and marketing director, replied: "The question hits the mark."

Sherrer said Apple had merely followed the "easiest" course—of adapting its personal computers to fit the needs of languages using Roman characters while ignoring development of software for use in the countries of Asia that use Chinese characters.

Now, the firm has adopted a new strategy in which it aims to expand the proportion of its revenue from international operations to 35 percent from 22 percent "in the next few years," van Eyck said.

"Japan is the world's second-largest personal computer market, and, to be a truly international company, we must make a success here," he declared.

Apple, van Eyck disclosed, will announce what he called "a localized Japanese product" in the "late spring or early summer" and focus new attention on selling computer systems instead of "stand-alone" personal computers that are incapable of communicating with other computers.

SOURCE: The *Los Angles Times*, April 4, 1986, Part IV, p. 3

is similar to attributing personality traits to corporations. Top management leadership style, flexible problem-solving approaches, extensive employee sense of participation, and open channels of communications and information flow appear to be the more important traits contributing to an effective culture.

At issue is whether or not corporate culture can be translated or not to a firm's operations in another country. Can the Control Data Corporation's corporate culture, which was uniquely devised and successful in the U.S. Midwest, be kept intact and effective when Control Data sets up operations in Spain? This question is important because many managers and management researchers believe that the development of a corporate culture can be a deliberate process. If resources are invested in such an effort, then the impact of national culture on the organizational culture needs to be better understood. Furthermore, if the development of an identifiable culture is important to organizational success, as is suggested, then we need to understand how their linkage is affected by a second country culture. Presently we do not have answers to these questions.

SUMMARY

In this chapter we have explored the motives and methods firms use to engage in international business. From the general motives to solve problems, avoid pressure, or seek opportunities, we reviewed the specific reasons why individual firms engage in international business, what rationales they use, and what forms their business options can take. As we have seen, there is a variety of answers to these inquiries. There is a range of methods firms can use in their pursuit of market opportunities, sources of raw materials, finished goods, skills, technology, and other production inputs. They can export and import or they can buy and sell ownership rights in operating enterprises through transactions across national boundaries. We have seen that to compete effectively, firms in international business usually must have a distinctive ability which local firms do not possess, an advantage which offsets the costs of doing business in a foreign culture and economic system.

Multinational firms compete not only against local firms, but also against one another in a global system of national markets for goods and services and for resources. They use different approaches in this competition. Which approach each chooses depends on their individual strengths and weaknesses within their chosen industries. Much also depends on management commitment to being internationally involved. How intensive this commitment is and the orientation pursued ultimately depends on management's philosophy and the personal values of management that are reflected in the firm's corporate culture.

DISCUSSION QUESTIONS FOR CHAPTER TWO

1. Are some industries more internationalized than others? (See Table 1–4.) If so, why might that be true?

2. Firms engage in international business either because they have some specific competitive advantage or they seek to develop one by going abroad. What are some important competitive advantages that are needed to successfully engage in international business?

3. What are the two main methods a firm can use to engage in international business? How do they differ in terms of serving market needs?

4. What are the risks involved in international business that differ from a purely domestic business?

5. How do the various methods of international business (e.g. exporting, licensing, joint ventures, etc.) affect the types and levels of risk involved in international business?

6. Suppose you were manager of a ceramics dishware subsidiary in the midwest. Except for an occasional export order that is handled by a local export management firm, sales are all domestic in the U.S. market. Suppose you are looking for the first time for an opportunity to expand internationally. What are some strategic questions that need to be asked and answered before you go abroad?

7. "The choice of method of engaging in international business largely depends on the value of intangible assets possessed by individual firms." Explain.

8. Government policy is often the crucial factor in determining the success of a business venture abroad. Cite two examples where that might be true.

9. Suppose two managers from different companies are at a convention cocktail party. They each are boasting about how "committed" they are to international business. As a third party to this conversation, what questions would you ask them to determine the true level of their commitment?

10. If a successful corporate culture is key to the success of a domestic business, can that culture be successfully transferred to operations abroad? Speculate as to the success of such a transfer.

CHAPTER THREE

Environmental Conditions in International Business: Economic and Technological Environment

INTRODUCTION

This chapter addresses the issues connected with the varying environmental conditions facing firms when they move across national borders. As one might readily expect, national economies differ from one another along many dimensions, some of which are not always apparent. While people may dress and behave similarly, they are usually quite disparate in their attitudes, beliefs, and economic status. A casual stroll along the beaches of Southern California and Rio de Janeiro might suggest that the people are alike. They are tanned, comparably attired, and often handsome. There the similarity ends. The food differs; the language differs; the culture and systems of beliefs differ even though both Brazil and the United States were settled largely by immigrants of European stock. Similarly, national economies are described in common ways when inflation rates, growth trends, and employment patterns are reported. Yet, the underlying fundamental economic conditions and the technology that produces them may differ quite significantly. In this chapter we shall discuss some of the ways in which economic and technological systems vary across countries and how these differences can represent either opportunities or constraints for firms doing business internationally. See News Box 3–1.

INSTITUTIONAL DIFFERENCES IN ECONOMIC ENVIRONMENTS

Whether the environmental conditions represent an opportunity or a constraint depends very much upon the resources the firm brings with it when it decides to move abroad. As we noted in Chapter Two, there are firm-specific resources which, if they are to be utilized effectively,

NEWS BOX 3–1
Why Investors Are Sour on China
John F. Burns

Many Doubt its Market will Open or that They'll ever Turn a Profit

To many people, the opening of China to foreign investors at the outset of the 1980s seemed like one of the most promising political and economic developments since World War II. But now, fresh on the heels of the American Motors Corporation's well-publicized problems with its jeep-making venture here, (Peking) there is a growing sense among Americans and Chinese alike that the lure of investing in China has dimmed.

In public, at least, the Chinese continue to stress their successes. According to Chinese Government statistics, 2,300 joint ventures between foreign companies and Chinese state enterprises had been approved by the end of 1985, drawing $6 billion in foreign equity investment to China. Of this, about $1.4 billion was American, including investments by such Fortune 500 corporations as McDonnell Douglas Corporation, A.M.C., Pepsi-Cola, Coca-Cola Company, Atlantic Richfield Co., and Occidental Petroleum Corporation.

But now—despite the Chinese decision to meet A.M.C.'s threat of a pullout with concessions that at least temporarily resolve the problems—there is widespread doubt among foreign investors whether their efforts to establish a foothold here are worthwhile. Many are increasingly doubtful that their dream of gaining access to the vast Chinese market will ever materialize. All but a handful of them remain plagued with the same foreign exchange problems, disputes over contract interpretation, inflexible bureaucracy, and high costs that have shadowed A.M.C.

*   *   *   *   *

The Chinese, clearly worried, have intensified their efforts to reassure investors, particularly Americans.

*   *   *   *   *

Still, skepticism persists, partly because of a growing awareness that China and its foreign partners are seeking contradictory ends. Ever mindful of foreign depredations in the century before communist power, Chinese leaders have always said that foreign investment is a tool to be used for the shortest time necessary to effect a transfer of technology and managerial skills. Their declared purpose is to help China modernize in a manner that ultimately will make it possible to manage without a major foreign investment presence in China.

Until recently, executives making investment decisions, usually far away, have tended to minimize this stated concern for sovereignty and to assume that China—in the manner of many of the noncommunist nations in Asia—is embarking on a path that will make it progressively more receptive to multinational corporations. But recent events are forcing a re-assessment.

Confronted with a chronicle of such problems, Chinese officials are inclined to point out that few joint ventures have collapsed, indicating at least minimal satisfaction. But many foreign executives say that this is a false standard, since their head offices have made a strategic decision to stick with their investments here for the time being, regardless of cost. It is a demoralizing situation, and the turnover among expatriates—A.M.C. had three chief executives in a year—is high.

*   *   *   *   *

A briefing paper prepared by the American Embassy for the visit put the situation starkly: "In every case, U.S. partners are paying a very high price to be in China now because their parent corporations have made a strategic decision to enter the China market for the long term. They have taken a great commercial and potential political risk, and, for most, the potential payoff is still years away."

SOURCE: The *New York Times*, June 8, 1986.

must be matched with the location-specific resources of individual countries. Some countries are well endowed with resources and this fact alone makes it easier for firms to operate there than in countries less well endowed. The manager in a multinational firm faces many economic complexities not normally encountered in firms which serve a single national market or regional market. Not the least of these are the differences in the way economic activity is organized. Despite surface economic similarities, it is unwise to assume that what characterizes one's own country is true of all other countries. For example, while Germany, the United States, and Japan have economies based on private enterprise, freedom to own property, and the free exchange of goods, there are distinctions among these countries in how business is transacted. Some of these differences stem from cultural features that establish the underlying values of the population; some are the result of historical events; Some result from the availability of resources or other economic constraints on the ways in which businesses can operate.

ROLE OF THE FIRM IN SOCIETY

To illustrate the point already made, let us look at the role of the enterprise as a social institution. In Japan it is very common for the business enterprise to assume responsibility for the employees not only while they are on the job, but also for many of their social and economic needs away from the work place. The worker and his or her family are valued as part of a much larger corporate family that includes all of the other employees and managers. Much if not most of these employees' social life is structured around the organization for which they work, including choices for where they live, where their children go to school, with whom they associate, and how they behave. In addition, a much wider array of total social and economic needs are cared for by the Japanese employer than is true for employers in the United States. In large Japanese firms lifetime employment is the norm. This means that when employees are first hired, it is expected that they will spend most of their working lives with that firm. Thus, the multinational firm headquartered in the United States and establishing a business in Japan will need to alter its normal way of doing business to accommodate these differences since lifetime employment is not typically assumed to be part of the employment relationship in the United States. Social and cultural norms can be constraints or additional responsibilities to the firm's primary economic function.

ROLE OF THE PRIVATE SECTOR
AND THE MULTINATIONAL FIRM

Countries differ significantly from one another in terms of how they perceive the private sector to function in the country's economic life. Some of the socialist countries such as the Soviet Union see little role for a private sector. In the Soviet Union the means of production, marketing, and distribution are owned and operated by government agencies. The state plays an overwhelmingly dominant role in such countries. Linkages between the Soviet state agencies and Western private firms are usually tied to specific national goals and purposes. However, in the Western capitalist and socialist democracies, the role of the private sector is much more significant. Obviously, multinational firms regardless of their home country prefer to operate where they can own the plants and other properties that are critical to the production of the products or services in which they specialize. The argument is not so much about whether or not ownership is permitted under a particular economic system, rather it is a matter of whether the firm is allowed to freely engage in transactions and managing the firm's operations as it sees fit. Moreover, if the firm is successful, the disposition of profits becomes an issue: will it be allowed to accumulate profits and repatriate them to locations outside of the host country? It is the degree of freedom to conduct business in a self-determined way that is important. Where that freedom becomes so constrained by governmental rules and regulations that the firm cannot exploit its unique capabilities, the firm will seldom invest or choose to remain.

Where the constraints are so prohibitive that firms cannot operate effectively there still may be opportunities to undertake certain types of transactions. While it is true that the Soviet Union and China do not allow foreign firms to own property, there are nevertheless some firms that enjoy lucrative contracts with the governments in these countries. For example, PepsiCo, Inc. has helped establish plants in the Soviet Union to produce soft drinks. Pepsi-Cola does not own or operate these plants. It merely advises the operations, assists with quality control, and supplies the syrups used in flavoring the drinks. For this service it is paid a fee, in both currency and bartered goods, based on a contract with the Soviet Union government agency in charge of producing soft drinks.

Government policy and regulation is a concrete expression of the underlying attitudes toward private enterprise in general and toward foreign firms in particular. Firms that are multinational are often seen as more threatening to a country's economic interests. This results from the fact that only part of an MNC will be subject to state control. The subsidiaries of multinational firms represent only a part of the total firm; consequently, parent firms are less dependent on a single subsidiary in any host country. This gives the firm increased bargaining power in seeking government concessions. However, the host countries may be quite dependent upon these subsidiaries for certain goods. Host countries in turn may see themselves in an ambiguous situation in which they seek the benefits the multinationals can bring while simultaneously seeing themselves as being dependent and lacking control over firms operating within their borders. Even if this is an overstated fear, there still is in most countries a nationalistic desire to have locally owned firms be dominant in key sectors. It often angers nationalists when they see many of their manufacturing sectors dominated by foreign firms. For example, Canadians have recently been expressing nationalist concerns over U.S. dominance in the publishing industry. Similar patterns have long prevailed in the developing countries. This sector domination affects attitudes toward foreign firms. When serious enough, it is expressed through restrictive national legislation.

On the more positive side, countries hope foreign firms will bring in new technology in the form of products and production processes. Given a set of national economic and social goals, national leaders often see modern technology as the means to development. Since much of modern technology is developed by MNCs, they become the twin object of envy and respect. Thus, countries want the benefits that MNCs can bring without the costs. They attempt to do this using incentives and disincentives to guide MNC activity. It is out of this situation that investment rules and regulations have emerged.

GOVERNMENT INVOLVEMENT IN THE ECONOMY: MARKET ECONOMIES VERSUS CENTRALLY PLANNED SYSTEMS

Economies differ in the degree to which there is government involvement in the economic decision-making process. Governments become involved at many levels in establishing the rules under which business firms operate. In the United States the federal government is responsible for attempting to assure full employment, price stability, open competition, and equal opportunities to education and employment. State-level governments also regulate economic activity within their own jurisdiction. Within the rules established by law, however, business firms generally are free to make their own decisions regarding what products they will produce, where these products will be sold, at what price they will be sold, and how the products will be produced. Open competition in the market largely determines who will succeed and prosper, for it is households and customers who decide which products to buy. Competition assures that there will be several firms supplying similar products since if one firm is very profitable, other firms will be enticed into imitating this success by bringing similar products to market. Most economies in Western Europe, North and South America, Japan, and several other areas have this characteristic.

In contrast the communist countries of the Soviet Union, China, and Eastern Europe do not allow private ownership of the means of production. Decision making is highly centralized in the hands of government agencies rather than in the hands of privately owned firms. The consequences is that firms from countries having market economies must cope with state-owned agencies when they wish to do business in these countries. Thus, the way in which various countries have chosen to organize economic activity acts as a constraint on whether and under what conditions private firms can undertake business activities across national boundaries.

Between the extremes of free enterprise and free markets on the one hand and the highly centralized systems of Eastern Europe on the other, there are many variations in the kinds of roles and size of government activity. The developing nations in particular have turned to government-directed planning as the guiding means to economic and social development. In many cases, the local business institutions are too inexperienced to undertake major economic development roles, or the capitalist class is too limited by tradition and privilege to provide useful leadership. Thus, government, often led by nationalist military leaders, fills the leadership vacuum with varying degrees of success.

Even among the so-called market economies, the degree of governmental involvement varies. For example, in the United States government all levels are responsible for the allocation of about 35 percent of total economic activity. This economic activity results from defense expenditures, welfare payments, and the like. In the Netherlands the percentage allocated by government is in excess of 50 percent of economic activity. Thus, we see that across all countries, there is a spectrum of roles that both the private firm and the government play in economic activity.

UNDERLYING TECHNOLOGICAL CAPACITY OF COUNTRIES AND RESOURCE AVAILABILITY

The economic aspect of a country's business environment that is probably most important to international firms is the resources available in each country. What goods and services can be produced in a country depends on the resources available. For example, a developing country that has a low level of per capita income is not able to invest in enough education to provide an ample supply of high level skills. If transportation and communication systems are limited, it will not be an attractive place for a high technology firm to invest and produce a product such as computers. This is simply so because the needed skills are not in ready supply. Thus, the level of development of a country and its ability to offer various resources are going to determine what types of business activity take place and the degree to which multinational firms will be interested in doing business there. Most developing countries are heavily reliant on basic industries such as mining, agriculture, and simple manufactured goods. This is a part of the definition of *underdevelopment*, i.e., the resources to produce more sophisticated goods are in short supply and hence it is not feasible to produce the wide range of goods produced in the industrialized countries. The level of development of the country then acts as a constraint on the participation of multinational firms in various countries.

We have already noted that firms have specialized resources in the form of tangible and intangible assets such as technology in the form of internally developed processes. These are considered proprietary, that is, private property owned by the firm. These resources alone represent potential for creating wealth. To be economically useful, these proprietary resources invariably require other resources to go with them. These other resources include such things as raw materials, human skills, reliable sources of energy, communications and transport systems, marketing and distribution systems, and financing institutions. In other words, a foreign firm cannot apply its own capabilities if these resources are not available. While it is true that firms may be able to create some of these resources—a trained workforce for example—it cannot create all of these. For example, firms that specialize in the extraction of minerals cannot create the minerals themselves. If the minerals are not present in a particular country, there is no role for such firms to play. This brings us to consideration of the economic constraints firms face when going abroad.

ECONOMIC CONSTRAINTS

The economic constraints facing firms include the availability of resources, the size of market and its rate of growth, and the organization of markets and distribution systems. Resources include raw materials and intermediate goods like parts and components, labor and skills, financing, and infrastructure such as transportation and communication systems. Market size depends on population size, income levels, and economic growth. Market organization refers to the ability of the distribution system to serve different market segments, availability of media such as television and magazines, and the role of government in the regulation of marketing and other economic activities.

The data in Table 3–1 are indicative of many of the economic differences among countries. As can be seen, low-income countries are heavily involved in the production of primary commodities. Industry structures change as countries achieve higher levels of income. Also, income levels increase as the level of education and literacy increases. As countries become more urbanized, the services sector becomes increasingly important and the types of exported goods move toward the more technologically sophisticated. Also, the more advanced countries have a lower rate of population increase even though life expectancy is higher. While there are other indicators we could examine, the trends would be much the same. As income levels rise, the ownership of telephones, radios, television sets, automobiles, books, and other similar goods increases more than proportionately to income. Income and education levels are usually good indicators of other things as well, such as the skills of the labor force, the relative size of the market, and the consumption patterns of the population. In addition, high-income countries invariably have a much more developed infrastructure than do low-income countries. The economic constraints that lead to low levels of income are the same constraints which make it difficult for firms to operate efficiently in many countries.

TABLE 3-1 Some Basic Indicators of Economic Status

Indicator	Low Income Economies	Middle Income Economies	High Income Economies
Population (millions)	2,161	1,139	714
Population growth rate per year 1970–80	2.1%	2.4%	0.8%
Urban population as percent of total	17%	45%	78%
Life expectancy (years)	57	60	74
Population per physician	5,810	5,840	820
Adult literacy in percent	50	65	99
Percent of 20–24 year olds in post high schools	3%	11%	37%
Per capita GNP (1980 $)	260	1,400	10,320
Per capita GNP growth percent per year 1960–80	1.2%	3.8%	3.6%
Structure of production percent by sector in 1980			
Agriculture	36%	15%	4%
Industry	25%	40%	37%
Services	29%	45%	59%
Composition of exports 1979			
Fuels, minerals, metals	14%	40%	10%
Other primary products	42%	28%	15%
Textiles and clothing	19%	8%	5%
Machinery and transport equipment	3%	8%	36%
Other manufactures	20%	16%	34%

AVAILABILITY OF RESOURCES

As has been noted above, countries differ from one another in terms of the resources they have available. No two countries are alike. For example, the United States has an abundance of land in comparison to the European countries or Japan. It is also well endowed with highly trained scientists and engineers. Thus, we might expect that many of the firms operating in the United States would produce products that use the abundance of these resources. Abundance, we must note, means a larger supply and probably cheaper costs to the firm. That is exactly what happens. When we look at the data on the products exported by the United States we find that a sizable proportion of the exports is made up of land-intensive agricultural products and skill-intensive products such as jet aircraft and computers. These fundamental resources become the basis on which firms build their expertise. When firms invest abroad to produce products similar to home country products, these products will usually be very much like, if not identical to, those produced at home. In turn, the products produced abroad will have much the same resource requirements as those produced at home. In this case, a firm that produces milk products will more likely invest in New Zealand than Algeria.

This does not mean that firms will not invest in countries having vastly different resources than the home country. Firms do invest there, but when they do, they have to be prepared either to alter the methods they use at home or to alter the resource base of the host country. For example, in many developing countries the skills needed are in short supply if they exist at all. Thus the firm may have to create the skills through training programs or sometimes they change the production method to accommodate to the lower skill levels available. Of course there are limits on how far firms can go in doing the latter. The cost of irrigating Algerian land to turn it into cow pastures would be prohibitive. Many of the higher technology products thus simply cannot be produced in some countries.

FINANCING AND INFRASTRUCTURE

Among the resources needed are not only raw materials and skills, but also financing and underlying infrastructure. Firms generally attempt to finance as much of the needed capital as possible within the host country's economy. This is especially true for the financing of debt. Thus, it is important that there be a viable and reasonably capable banking sector that can assist with these needs. However, not all countries are desirous of financing foreign firms' entire debt requirements simply because locally generated financing is sometimes very scarce. Countries see multinational firms as being competitive with local firms in terms of the available financing capacity of the banking system. The consequence is that foreign firms are sometimes forced to borrow abroad rather than in the host country if they are to establish themselves or expand already existing operations. This is much more the case in developing countries than in the industrial countries. Developing countries usually have lower savings rates and less well-developed banking sectors. The result is that the scarce savings may end up being allocated by government rather than on the basis of market-determined terms and interest rates. Under any circumstance, the banking sector tends to be one of the most regulated industries in virtually all these countries. This represents a constraint on the foreign firm's access to financial resources to the extent that the firm may not be able to operate in its preferred way.

Firms also prefer to finance long-lived assets by using long-term financial instruments such as mortgages or other long-term loans. In many countries, however, the underlying economic conditions are so unstable that it is not feasible to obtain such contracts. For example, in Brazil most financing is in short-term instruments or, if not, in instruments that index the interest rate to the current rate of inflation. Unlike in the United States or Europe where there are well-developed financial markets, firms are not able to sell long-term bonds in local currencies in a large number of countries. Thus, they often must borrow in currencies other than that of the host country. By so doing, they expose themselves to greater foreign exchange risk because the repayment of the debt must be done in another currency. Lack of well-developed local financial markets then can act as a major economic resource constraint on the firm operating abroad.

Another element of resource availability is the degree to which there is a well-developed economic infrastructure in the form of transport, electrical and other energy, communications, health, housing, and educational systems. Generally, in most countries it is expected that these systems will be provided by the government. In many countries, however, not all of these systems are in place such that all firms wishing to locate there can be accommodated. Indeed, in many countries it is largely the responsibility of the firm to provide some of these infrastructural systems for itself. And it is generally true that this is more likely to be the case in developing countries than in the already industrialized countries. Thus there must be offsetting advantages if firms are to locate in developing countries. These advantages can include rich natural resources, inexpensive labor, or a particularly suitable climate. For example, much of the infrastructure in parts of Latin America and the Middle East has been developed by privately owned foreign firms in the mining, petroleum, and agricultural industries. This is the exception rather than the rule however. If a well-developed infrastructure is not present, most firms are loath to invest simply because the additional costs of providing the infrastructure can be prohibitive. Firms only provide infrastructure if most of the benefits of doing so can be captured by the firm itself and this is seldom the case.

MARKET ECONOMICS

One of the key considerations in any decision to serve foreign markets is the size of the market. Market size can and does represent a major constraint on foreign operations. If the market is small the firm may prefer to serve it by exporting from the home country. This preference, however, is not always an option. Some, if not most, countries use various trade barriers to induce local production of a wide range of products. Foreign firms that have been exporting to the country prior to the imposition of barriers must then decide whether they wish to serve the market by investing in the country. But if market size is small and there are several potential competitors, investment may not be economically attractive. Even if there are no barriers to trade, the firm must constantly reassess its position because as market size increases it may become less costly to produce locally to serve the market. Timing then becomes very important because there are always potential competitors who are gauging the market. If the firm does not move swiftly when market size becomes large enough to support an efficient plant, then the competition, if it moves first, can establish a dominant position. Thus market size and growth act both as constraint and opportunity.

Market size is determined by the size of population, the level of per capita income, the rate of growth of both of these, and the degree to which the population expresses a preference for the particular product or service the foreign firm has to offer. In addition, the age distribution of the population may have a major impact on whether there are market segments that will express a preference for these products or services. For example, if the birth rate is low and there are few children under the age of two years, the market for items aimed at satisfying the needs of infants and toddlers will not be large. In many developing nations the population distribution between urban and rural locations is also a factor in market size. Thus firms that concentrate on these products face a market size and growth constraint.

MARKET ORGANIZATION

Another aspect of market constraints is the degree to which the market is or is not organized in a way that is beneficial to the needs of the firm's marketing methods. For example, in the United States many consumer products rely heavily on television advertising to build not only product awareness but also brand image. We take it for granted in the United States that there are well-developed media systems, readily identifiable market segments, and readily accessible distribution systems. This is not the case in a large number of countries—even among the other advanced countries. In Japan, for instance, there is a highly complex, multilayered wholesale distribution system that is almost unfathomable to non-Japanese firms. This acts as a constraint on foreign firms that are attempting to gain access to the Japanese market. Also, in many countries television ownership is not great so that television advertising is not a useful medium through which to advertise and demonstrate products. And even where television set ownership is common, as in France, the television transmission system is regulated and advertising on television may either be greatly restricted or denied entirely. Under these circumstances firms that rely heavily on this medium are confronted with serious constraints on their ability to gain access to potential consumers. These constraints either force firms to adapt their marketing programs or make it impossible for them to adequately serve some national markets.

SUMMARY

To summarize, economic constraints are many and varied and they differ from country to country. This vastly complicates doing business abroad as compared with doing business in one's own country. Resource availabilities, market size differences, and the organization of markets require that firms be prepared to adapt to changing circumstances when operating in the international marketplace. How well firms do this depends upon the resource requirements they have and their past learning that enables them either to adapt their resource requirements or to create the resources they need. That they differ in their abilities to do this explains in part why some firms become international and why others do not and why those that do become international tend to locate their activities in some countries and not in others.

Economies differ in terms of the degree to which private enterprise is allowed. Socialist countries place heavy emphasis on public ownership of the means of production. This limits the ability of firms to locate production facilities around the globe. However, as was noted in Chapter Two, it is not always necessary to have ownership of foreign facilities to obtain many of the benefits of overseas production.

Firms seek access to markets and/or raw materials when they go abroad. All seek to take advantage of their firm-specific assets. However, if there are economic constraints such as inadequate markets or inadequate resources, the firm may not be able to find a match between its own resources and the economic and technological environment in some countries. When this is the case it has fewer options. It may find a partner that has complementary resources and together they may then operate a joint venture. The firm may also simply sell or rent its rights to proprietary advantages to another firm. If the proprietary rights are highly valuable, however, the foreign firm may simply export to the overseas location and refuse to own operating assets there.

Countries also differ in terms of what is expected of privately owned firms. As we note, firms in Japan and throughout much of Europe are expected to undertake a broader variety of activities than firms in the United States. Here these activities would be viewed as ones that should be undertaken either by the individual or by government agencies. It is evident that multinational firms face environments in which adherence to home country policies and attitudes may in fact be detrimental to enterprise performance in local national settings.

DISCUSSION QUESTIONS FOR CHAPTER THREE

1. What do "location-specific" resources refer to? From a strategic viewpoint, how do they interact with "firm-specific" resources to give the firm a strategic competitive advantage?

2. "Free enterprise is free enterprise! If Germany or Chile or Canada has a free enterprise system, then we can count on their offering the same business environment as here in the United States." Comment on the wisdom and assumptions of this statement.

3. What, in your opinion, is the role of the private firm in U.S. society? How might that role differ in a developing economy like Cuba, the Philippines, or Nigeria? Why?

4. What are some general strategic implications of doing business in a centrally planned economy? What opportunities and constraints does this form of economy offer?

5. From a firm's point of view, what three basic economic conditions does one country's economy offer compared to another? Consider a German electronics firm that is investigating setting up a manufacturing assembly plant in Taiwan, Mexico, or Australia for sale to that domestic market.

6. In what ways would Silicon Valley in Northern California be considered a "technological infrastructure?"

7. "The comparative advantage of one country over another in the production of any specific product is fixed by the availability and cost of resources. However, the movement of capital, technology, and market information can change relative comparative advantage. Thus Malaysia can produce high quality surgical equipment, Korea can manufacture cars, and the United States could become a major exporter of rice." In what ways does the movement of factors of production like capital and technology affect the comparative advantage of an economy?

8. The banking sector represents a financial infrastructure of a country. Why does the level of development of this sector in developing countries often present a problem to foreign firms?

9. "Hi-tech industry can only be located in highly industrialized countries like Japan and Germany." Do you agree? Comment.

10. How would high technology automation of manufacturing (e.g., robots, computerized production processes) allow companies to continue locating production in key country markets rather than locating it outside of the country?

_____

CHAPTER FOUR

Environmental Conditions in International Business: Sociocultural and Political Regulatory Aspects

INTRODUCTION

In making sales, investment, and production decisions, firms tend first to seek information about the economic and technological aspects of the target country and its markets. They do this because the feasibility of decisions is based on quantifiable economic and technical criteria. However once they determine the initial possibilities of success, the analysis that supports the decision often moves on to include more qualitative aspects of the business environment. The two most important of these qualitative aspects are the sociocultural environment and the political-regulatory environment.

The sociocultural environment refers to the characteristics of a country's or region's people. It includes facts and observations about the people: their demographic and ethnic profile, their social behavior and structure, their particular cultural adaptation to local conditions, and their languages. From this information businesses get a better sense of the market to be served and the kinds of changes in business products and practices that might be required. The political-regulatory environment describes the historical, institutional, and intergroup power relations within a country. The nature of the political system, how decisions are made and implemented, largely determines the kind of support or restrictions a private firm can expect to find. A country's set of policies and resulting regulations demonstrates how its government sees the role of the firm in contributing to economic, social, and developmental goals.

This chapter discusses how differences in sociocultural and political-regulatory environments directly affect decisions about the firm's products and operations.

SOCIAL AND CULTURAL DIFFERENCES

Attributes of the People

Managers abroad must acknowledge that their host people differ from those at home. While economic contrasts can be seen in the various indicators of economic and technical development, the sociocultural differences are at the same time both more obvious and more subtle. To the casual traveler arriving in a strange land, the focus is on "how different" it is from home rather than "how similar" it is. We notice distinctions in physical things such as the size of the airport or the condition of the buildings. But our attention focuses more on the people in terms of their mode of dress, skin color, language, and social activities. As time passes, these surface dissimilarities tend to disappear as we become more accustomed to the new environment.

At this point more nuances are noticed in behavior. We begin to acknowledge that the local people really are not the same as people at home. As travelers, we may think that this is merely interesting or even amusing, but for the manager in the international environment these differences need to be taken more seriously. This perceptual adjustment process may be the greatest challenge to international managers, as managerial effectiveness is measured by an intelligent and sensitive approach to the sociocultural environment. We should note that having knowledge of the factual content of the culture and having an interpretive knowledge of that same culture are not the same thing. The former deals with the obvious expectations and taboos that must be learned in order to function in the society, like driving on the left side of the road in New Zealand. The latter depends on the ability to fully appreciate and understand the subtleties of cultural traits and patterns, like the deemphasis of individual as opposed to group work in Japan. There is a fine balance that managers need to develop in making decisions requiring a respect for cultural mores. At the same time, decisions also must not deny the integrity of the organization's purposes and processes. One does not change just to fit in the culture. Cultural empathy requires an ability to be respectful without being patronizing, sympathetic to special circumstances without being judgmental, and intelligently accommodating without being slavish or ideological in adherence to cultural practices. This is a major challenge for the manager and too often comes as a gift of hindsight—after the "blooper" has been made.

A Guide to "Cultural Wisdom"

There are a few ways of arriving at a satisfactory level of "cultural wisdom." One way of guiding thinking in this matter is to ask three operational questions that set the stage for our understanding: (1) What are the key dissimilarities between peoples from different cultures (ours and theirs)? (2) How did these differences come about? (3) What are the implications of these differences when people of different cultures interact?

The first question addresses the factual knowledge or elements of culture. From the science of cultural anthropology we can identify at least seven areas in which people differ:

1. Physical attributes—physical size, eye, hair, and skin color.
2. Material attributes—income, wealth, tools, economic development.
3. Demographic attributes—sex, race, age, social organization.
4. Systems of beliefs—religions, ideologies, sense of relations between humans, nature, and the universe.
5. Aesthetic attributes—arts, music, folklore, fashion, dress, architecture.
6. Language—written and spoken language, nonverbal expression.
7. Institutions—political, economic, legal, defense, and education functions.

These areas represent major differences at the most general level of culture. Even though international managers have neither the time nor capability to develop a comprehensive view of every specific culture in which they may work, these categorizations can be useful in aiding managers to conceptualize the overall cultural distinctions. From this initial awareness of culture, managers can develop a checklist of cultural distinctions to aid them in some of the business situations they face.

The second "wisdom-raising" question deals with how cultures develop. While there are various theories about cultural development, anthropologists generally agree on some common definitions. Some anthropologists define culture as "the socially inherited assemblage of practices and beliefs that determines the texture of people's lives." Similarly the noted anthropologist Clyde Kluckhorn, who reviewed 150 definitions of culture, defines culture as "patterned ways of thinking, feeling, and reacting, acquired mainly by symbols. . . . Constituting the distinctive achievements of human groups. . . ; the essential core of culture consists of traditional (historically derived) ideas, values, and practices." These definitions suggest that culture is the sum total lifestyle and experiences for an identifiable group of people that evolves over long periods of time and is passed along to succeeding generations. It is the result of a people's interaction with a particular social and physical environment and demonstrates the ability of a people to deal with constraints and opportunities provided by the environment. Thus, for the manager, culture is best seen as:

1. Living—where culture is seen as a dynamic, active adjustment process that is learned and uses language and symbols as the primary vehicle of transmission.
2. Ecological—where groups develop ways of life within the confines of a physical and social environment where the relationships among the peoples in that environment can be both cooperative and competitive.
3. Rational—where culture can be seen as a rational response of commonly accepted adjustments to the environment as it has come to be known by a people. While not always understood or acceptable to people from another culture, the cultural practices are explainable within the context out of which they develop.
4. Integrative—culture holds people together. It gives a people a touchstone with the past and offers something larger than individual experience with which to identify. It gives cause for celebrating one's own cultural identity even while residing in another culture.
5. Nonmonolithic—while general cultural practices may be shared by a group, it is important to note that variations exist within the general culture that create diversity. Dominant cultural practices can be modified by minority groups. Faddish changes instituted by the young often become a permanent part of the cultural mores and ethos.

An applied example of the above theory might be seen in the differences between American and Japanese cultures. The United States's cultural development might be characterized as one in which succeeding waves of emigrating peoples seeking to escape religious, political, or economic contstraints settled a very large, rich, and relatively friendly physical and social environment. One result of this interactive process of mutual adjustment among peoples from differing cultures might be seen in the United States's social and cultural values. These might be characterized as individualism, openness, and candor in social situations accompanied by an ingrained suspicion or even hostility toward authority. By contrast, the Japanese have been a physically isolated people (perhaps purposefully) on an island nation with a racially homogeneous population. The constraints of an island would seem to have led to a somewhat different set of social adjustments and cultural practices where the emphasis is on group behavior; where consciousness of status and differences leads to restrained expression of self; where authority is generally revered and respected. While this comparison is necessarily simple, it does emphasize the dynamic adjustment process to a specific environment as the engine that drives cultural development. Thus managers can better understand a new cultural setting if they understand it as an adaptive response of humans to their environments. With this perspective, a cultural empathy may be developed and respect for the difficulties of changing culture may be appreciated.

Management Response to Foreign Cultures

The third guiding "wisdom" question addresses the issue of business response to the business environment in foreign cultures. We know that managers' responses to a culture will be the result not only of what they think about that culture, but also of their prior conditioning based on experiences from their own or other cultures. What they think depends upon their factual knowledge of the culture, what they believe regarding how the culture functions, and the attitudes they have developed towards various aspects of culture. These elements determine the general decision-making intentions a manager will have in the context of a particular culture. What managers actually do in a specific situation is influenced by their own prior experience in that particular culture, their assessment of the inherent risks of acting "wrongly," and the expectations regarding the outcome of decisions and actions. Table 4–1 is suggestive of the tension between managerial attitudes, beliefs, values, and behaviors and the potential impact of business decisions on culture.

The individual manager may experience conflict because his or her beliefs and attitudes do not conform to the acceptable beliefs and attitudes within the host culture. For example, time is perceived very differently among cultures. In the United States it is expected that appointments will be kept on time; in Latin cultures the norm is to be late for appointments. In fact, being on time in Latin America actually means being several minutes late. Being early could be considered insulting under certain circumstances. Furthermore, attitudes toward work, schedules, productivity, and responsibility are often different in Latin cultures. Thus, the manager who brings an Anglo-Saxon attitude without adaptation will not only be frustrated but may be ineffectual in dealing with the business environment in Latin America. As one author puts it, "When one becomes aware of the possibility of cultural differences and the probable consequences of failure to adapt, the seemingly endless variety of customs can become overwhelming. Where does one begin, what customs should be absolutely adhered to, what others can be ignored?"* This same author suggests a device for

---

*Philip R. Cateora, *International Marketing* (Homewood, Ill.: Richard D. Irwin Inc., 1983), p. 185.

TABLE 4–1   Cultural Impact and Business Operations

Individually Held	*Business Elements Involved*
Beliefs about	Role of work and status of occupations
Attitudes toward	Decision making and authority formal organization, and productivity
Values regarding	Verbal and nonverbal communication
Behaviors in	Conflict and its resolution, Competition, achievement, and wealth.
	The future, progress, and time
	Relations with co-workers—trust, cooperation, honesty, loyalty, responsibility, equity

---

separating the needed adaptations into three categories to simplify the complex problem of choice. They are:

1. Cultural imperatives—business customs and expectations that must be met and conformed to. (For example, engaging in small talk before "getting down to business" is a general requirement in Middle Eastern cultures).
2. Cultural adiaphora—business customs and expectations for which conformity or nonconformity is neither beneficial nor harmful. One can be indifferent if one chooses without being right or wrong in one's actions. Most dress, eating, and greeting customs are of this type.
3. Cultural exclusives—business customs and expectations from which a foreigner is excluded, such as regligious practices or political influence peddling.

Knowledge of the cultural practices then will assist in guiding adaptive decisions so that they are consonant with the expectations and practices of the host culture.

The Two-Way Nature of Cultural Adaptation

While focusing on the adaptations a firm makes in response to a foreign culture, it is important to note that not all of the adaptation needs to be borne by the firm alone. A firm has three basic choices when engaging in international business. First, it can decide not to enter a country. Second, it can engage in a process of adapting its business activities to conform to the customs and business community expectations in the new culture. And finally, it can attempt to influence and change the cultural environment in the host country to be more compatible with the firm's own methods of operations in terms of the way it produces and markets its products and the way it manages the people in the workplace. Thus, the adaptability of the national culture itself and its ability to accept and assimilate change is another factor in determining management response to the culture.

The change process, like most social processes, is a two-way street. Culture is not a fixed phenomenon. Although cultural change tends to be slow, it does occur. Modern communications, travel, trade, and education abroad are strong influences which inevitably affect a culture. The increase in foreign investment and ownership of business abroad points to further external sources of influence. Thus, managers should be aware of the possibilities that they may become change agents in ways that may alter cultural practices through their own business practices. To attempt change without an understanding of culture is not only risky but also not smart. The *beliefs* a manager has about the flexibility of a culture's practices, the manager's own *theories of change* and personal *aversion towards risk* of change will codetermine the manager's willingness to attempt change. The quality of their knowledge of a culture, in turn, will determine the probable success of any innovation they may wish to introduce. News Box 4–1 shows some examples of common cultural knowledge.

Achieving Effective Cultural Management

Cultural empathy is rarely achieved in the short run because there is a necessary maturing process that the manager must experience over time. Cultural assimilation is a function of time spent in the culture, the variety of contacts made in the culture, the intensity of the experience, and the quality of preentry cultural training which provide the basis for expectations and future learning about the culture. The suggestion here is that managers can go through a conscious learning process that can affect their thinking about cultures in general as well as about specific cultures. Most large multinational firms are well aware of this and make strong efforts to see that managers and their families are provided some formal preparation before entering a new cultural setting.

Apart from formal training there are two activities managers can perform to aid in their effectiveness in foreign settings. First, a thorough assessment of one's own culture is useful as a means of sensitizing oneself to the underlying characteristics of culture. "Know thyself well" is especially good advice in this context. Seeing how one's own culture works provides a basis for extending that learning process to the study of another culture. While this task seems simplistic, few of us ever really spend time analyzing the cultural basis for our own behavior. In the event of conflict, the manager will at least have some

---

NEWS BOX 4–1

What Kind of Things Unique to Indonesian Behavior Should Foreigners be Attuned To?

Shown below is a list of do's and don'ts outlined by the American's Women Association of Jakarta on "Introducing Indonesia":

Briefly stated, the following is a guide to cultural do's and don'ts:

In traditional Javanese culture, a lesser person does not have his head above that of a more senior person, which has given rise to the Javanese habit of ducking their heads as they greet people and walking stooped over through a room with other people in it.

A Jakarta custom is to shake hands with everyone in the room when arriving and leaving a gathering. When meeting a person for the first time, say your name clearly. He will respond.

In Indonesia, as in the rest of the Muslim world, the left hand is used for personal sanitary functions and is therefore considered unclean. It is offensive to give or receive things, particularly food or money, with the left hand. To strict Muslims, dogs are also unclean so that most Indonesians are acutely uncomfortable around them.

The area of empty space each Indonesian needs around him is much smaller than that necessary for an American or Northern European to feel physically or psychically comfortable. This is a "touching culture" with much acceptable casual body contact. Therefore, there is always room for two on a chair or for one more person on a bench or in a bus. While much touching is acceptable, do not pat people on the top of the head, or touch people of the opposite sex.

Generally, Indonesians do not hit or spank children but rather use a strong pinch. They also often pinch children, not always lightly, as a sign of pleasure. This is not usually easy for Western children to accept gracefully but parents should explain this to their children so they will not react negatively.

Indonesians are generally not comfortable alone and will often take a friend along on errands. They do not like to sleep alone in a room at night and prefer sleeping with the lights on and the windows shut. There is general concern about drafts, breezes, and electric fans for fear of catching cold (masuk angin). Keep this in mind when seating Indonesian guests.

It is considered rude to point at other people with the finger. One may point with the thumb or gesture with the chin. To point one's toes is also considered offensive, especially if you use your foot to point at goods displayed on the ground.

Indonesians are extremely courteous. Not offending other people, not making them "malu," is of primary importance. Therefore, disagreeable or unpleasant things are not said directly. People will often say what

they think someone wants to hear, rather than what actually is. A flat
negative is rarely used. The more important the subject under discussion, the quieter the voice. Loud voices are offensive. In delicate or
important matters, a go-between is often used to avoid the embarass-
ment of direct confrontation.

understanding of his or her own half of the problem. It also provides a
basis on which the U.S. manager abroad can help explain to foreign
colleagues or employees how to get along with Americans when doing
business with them. This helps to smooth the way for better relations
by clarifying expectations and norms. Thus, the manager is a teacher,
a change agent, and a manager all at the same time.

Another action managers can take is to assess their own capability
for personal changes. It is not necessary to "go native" to be effective
abroad. Nor is it possible to be just "a pure American" and to rely on
some intuitive notions such as "all people are basically alike" as a
guide to one's behavior in foreign cultures. An understanding of how
comfortable one is with change, one's ability to learn languages relative to the level required for job effectiveness, and one's own curiosity
and willingness to learn about other cultures; all are important determinants of potential effectiveness. If the gap between the requirements for change and the abilities of the individual to adapt is large, a
personal decision not to go abroad may be the best decision. A decision
under these circumstances to avoid exposing oneself and family to major change would be appropriate. To do otherwise, even for reasons of
career advancement, could lead to personal unhappiness and lower
performance for the firm.

If, after having completed an analysis of one's own abilities to adjust a manager still wishes to move abroad, that decision will probably
represent the greatest challenge of the manager's career. Few managers who have worked abroad successfully have ever regretted the experience. Most remember it as a career high point. However, they also
emphasize that sensitivity to culture and an understanding of the opportunities and constraints were a necessary prerequisite for success.
Thus, for the individual as well as the firm, an understanding of host
cultures and their processes is a necessary condition for business success in the international arena.

POLITICAL AND REGULATORY FACTORS

Having discussed the key economic and cultural factors in the international business environment, we now turn to a discussion of the politi-

cal and regulatory factors of the foreign business environment. Part of what firms may think of as political or legal constraints can simply be attributed to the fact that countries differ in terms of their political/ legal systems. All countries have rules about the ways in which business may or may not be conducted. Some of the differences are explicit and obvious and can be learned directly by reading the written laws and regulations. Other differences can be detected only after one has lived within the particular culture. Certain rules and laws can be superficially adhered to or ignored. However one needs to be careful in deciding the degree of adherence required or expected. Often there are double standards so that a host country citizen can get around a law but a foreigner is required to obey. This is especially true in the payment of taxes. The high visibility of a foreign firm makes creative adherence to the law a risky tactic.

An example of how legal-political environments differ can be seen in the contrast between the U.S. and Chinese firms. The United States has an increasingly legalistic business environment and many business transactions involve the use of written contracts. Moreover, the contract is looked upon as nearly sacrosanct. In many countries the written contract is looked upon at best as being only indicative of a continuing relationship. For example, in China a contract is looked upon as a living document which must yield to changing conditions. Should economic conditions change one or the other parties to the contract may simply say that the contract is no longer acceptable. But rather than go into litigation, as is often done in the United States, the Chinese may simply seek to amend the contract; this may be done with a handshake and will not require a written amendment to the contract. Thus, merely knowing what the law says does not fully prepare firms to conduct business in a new setting. It is probably as or more important to understand local business customs and to know who within the government and its bureaucracy has the power of decision.

The political and regulatory climate for business follows from the fact that a country has a set of goals to achieve. These goals may change as governments change. However most countries share a nearly universal set of common goals with regards to the economic and social development of people within its borders. Most would prefer to be self-sufficient in energy, food, and key resources; to have high employment rates; and no balance of payments problems and of course, safe borders.

To achieve these goals governments develop policy areas that define national interests in terms of specific development areas. For example, governments develop policies with regard to industrial development, agriculture, and technology. Policy areas represent statements by governments of their intentions to achieve a national goal—to encourage growth, redirect emphasis, or stop an activity. Furthermore governments have a set of policy tools they use to implement national goals and administer policy areas. These include monetary and fiscal policies, export/import promotion policies, and government procurement policies. These policy tools in turn become the government's laws, regulations, and programs that directly affect a firm's operations. A representative list of these country goals, policies, and tools can be seen in Figure 4-1.

The laws of most nations cover similar areas of national interest. The forms of business, the sole proprietorship, partnership, and company forms are all recognized as the basic legal structure of business. In the command economies of the socialist bloc they differ in the area of restriction on property rights and the degree of direct government participation in the operations of a business. Similarly many nations have regulations regarding environmental degradation, worker safety and benefits, consumer protection, and the nature of competition. This last area is of particular importance to the firm because it determines the degree of competition allowed in an economy. Competitive policy also influences the ways in which a firm is allowed to compete. Controls in pricing, advertising, and labor force reduction often reduce the firm's ability to introduce a competitive edge it may have gained in another economy. For example, the Japanese distribution system often restricts the ability of U.S. firms to reach final consumers.

While nations may share a set of similar goals, they differ in the means and methods they use to achieve these goals. A key area of differentiation between national governments is the role they see for the private firm in achieving national economic and social development. In the United States, for instance, the role of the private firm as a means to national goals has traditionally been paramount. In contrast, France has seen the role of the private firm as important but in recent years has restructured and restricted that role to conform more closely to a conscious national plan. Thus, for instance, the French banking system has been effectively nationalized, the computer industry has received strong political and economic support, and growth in basic industries is being deemphasized.

The political and regulatory environment of a nation, then, represents a series of opportunities, threats, or neutral conditions for the firm. In response, the firm has a number of options open to it. It can avoid an environment by choosing not to enter a country or it can leave a country by selling or abandoning its plant or other assets. Most firms tend to opt for making internal adaptations to political regulatory environments. They change the characteristics of a product, add a business operation required by a government (as in pollution control), or violate their own long-standing principles (hiring a joint venture partner's family members, for example). Those that neither leave nor adapt may choose instead to resist—by attempting to influence the

FIGURE 4-1   Country Goals, Policies, and Policy Tools

Country Goals	Policy Areas	Policy Tools
Autarky/Self sufficiency	Price stability	Tariff controls
Economic welfare	Economic competition	Nontariff controls
Border integrity and control	Free trade	Export promotion
(National security)	Industrial and basic resource	Import substitution
Employment stability	development	Foreign direct investment:
Financial performance	Infrastructure development	disincentives/incentives
of economy growth rates	Technology transfer	Official grants and loans
and in balance of payments	Defense	Fiscal and monetary policy
Economic development	Foreign aid	Exchange rate adjustment or
through technological	Ecological Balance	control
(Development)	Agriculture/food supply	Design of Governmental
Economic/political relations	Labor/employment	organization
External assistance	Consumer protection	Government procurement
	Education/science	programs
		Cross national agreements

regulatory environment in ways that make conditions more favorable to the firm. "Koreagate," the attempt by Koreans to buy influence of U.S. Congressmen, is an example of this.

Multinational firms are often accused of "playing politics" within host countries. However, it should be remembered that the subsidiaries of multinational firms are incorporated and domiciled in the host country. While it is true that the headquarters of the multinational firm are located elsewhere, this does not mean that the subsidiaries are immune from the rules, regulations, and laws of the host country. The subsidiaries generally must behave at least as well as the better local business firms. At the same time this is not to say that foreign subsidiaries should never get involved in politics within the host country. Since they must compete with local firms that seek government favors, they may well decide to engage in promoting specific policies and even supporting certain political candidates who offer positions that are compatible with the firm's specific needs. Doing so however can be risky, not to mention potentially unethical and illegal. Thus, an understanding of the political system and the legal constraints in host countries is a necessary precondition not only to business success but also to being a "good corporate citizen." And being a good citizen is essential if the firm is to develop a long-run presence in the country. News Box 4-2 demonstrates how culture and politics can create a business environment that makes effective management a nearly impossible task.

Sources and Settlements of Disputes

We have shown that governments and firms each pursue their own goals. Society, through law, grants the firm permission to pursue cer-

NEWS BOX 4–2
Coup in Uganda that Removes Obote is Rooted in the Problems of Tribalism
Lee Lescaze

Again this weekend citizens of an African nation—this time Uganda—turned on their radios and learned that their government had changed.

Africa has endured coup after coup, but they are less remarkable for their frequency than their similarity. Whatever the nation, whoever the new leader, whether civilian or military, colonel or sergeant, they are launched in the name of progress, justice, human rights, or prosperity and they deliver little, if anything, of what they promise.

Tribal Divisions

Other nations—Burundi, Rwanda, Equatorial Guinea—have suffered postindependence tribal massacres, brutal sortings out of the artificial coalitions of tribes left behind by departing colonial rulers. Yet nowhere have tribal divisions so hamstrung government and prevented a coalescing toward nationhood as in Uganda.

Even in countries that have escaped bloodbaths, tribalism remains an obstacle to merit-system government. At its most basic level, tribal loyalties burden every African with a large extended family that expects to share in his good fortune. "As soon as a man would get elected to Parliament, 26 cousins moved into his house, and since he couldn't feed them on his salary, he took bribes or they took bribes in his name," a Ghanaian remarked recently of the days when Ghana's political system was a paradigm of patronage.

One way or another, tribalism shackles the African nations even 25 years after independence. In Kenya, loyalties are so important you can't tell the political players without a tribal scorecard. Tanzania bent so much effort to insure that no tribe advanced at the expense of another that they all slid backward together.

Indeed, Brigadier Okello's coup was reportedly sparked by tribal resentment that his fellow Acholi were being passed over in favor of officers from the Langi tribe of President Obote. The Acholi-Langi alliance had always been an uneasy one and now it has split wide open, partly because of Uganda's economic decline, which has left the army and government with less money to spread around.

* * * * *

African coups are mostly a transfer of power within an elite group of soldiers and civilians. The bulk of the population's lives are little affected by who is in power unless there is widespread economic gain (rare) or decline (too common). Uganda has lived through horrors under Obote or General Amin. In a nation so tragically divided into tribal, religious, and political factions it will be a major accomplishment if the new regime can end the brutality and bring respect for law.

SOURCE: Excerpted from *The Wall Street Journal*, July 29, 1985, p. 16.

tain goals. When business firms are unable to serve these goals as optimally as society in general or as groups within society would like, conflict arises. There will be conflicts between host and home firms, between business firms and labor unions, and between the business sector and other groups in society.

Possibilities for conflict within a firm or between a firm and its host country can often be traced to three role problems: role ambiguity, role overload, and role conflict. Role ambiguity arises when a firm operates with an unclear charter from a government. Problems arise out of expectations that may not have been discussed in prior negotiations, out of newly created demands for specific economic performance, and out of putting modern organizations in traditional roles. The result is that neither the firm, the governments (host or home), nor general society understands clearly who ought to be doing what. For example, the role of the private firm in China is not completely clear. Private initiative is allowed but still distrusted. Capitalism is treated as a means and not as an end.

To exemplify: the 1985 Bhopal accident in India can be traced to the failure to assign safety control to a specific part of the organization or to define who had lead responsibility in the first place. Was it the responsibility of the Indian local government, the federal government, the subsidiary, or the home office of Union Carbide Corporation? Similar conflicts arise over lack of clarity regarding the roles of firms in providing nonemployment-related services for workers, such as housing, or in transferring technology, such as setting up research and development centers in host countries, and in being an exporter of national products.

The problem of role overload occurs when too many roles have been assigned to the firm that are beyond its organizational resources and traditional domain of activity. In this situation the firm finds itself attempting to be too many things to many people. Because of the MNC's local economic impact, many claims on a firm's time and resources are seen as legitimate because of the firm's size, experience, and national identity. The more diverse and complex a set of roles becomes, however, the less well resources can be focused to achieve important economic goals. Furthermore, the firm's identity then becomes less clear, making it possibly more vulnerable to challenges. In the end role overload hurts both the firm and the country of location. Finally, role conflict arises when the expectations held by governments or private parties differ from those held by the multinational firm. For example, while the host government may expect the MNC to export products with high local content, the MNC may be looking for strong local market growth with little emphasis on exporting.

As part of the broad expectations of the business sector, foreign firms in particular are expected to fulfill a specific set of roles in many countries. Accordingly they are in some ways treated differently than are purely local firms. How this set of roles is to be structured depends on host government attitudes toward foreign investment. A growing number of countries have established investment regulations that often treat foreign firms differently than local firms. Under these schemes foreign firms must negotiate entry into the country and may be denied entry depending upon the stipulations of the investment regulations. Some countries deny foreign firms access to certain resources, or if they are to use these resources, they must behave in a specified manner that is different from what is expected of locally owned firms. And finally, there is the issue of the government itself.

Governments represent the political philosophy and interests of the groups that control, by election or force, the policy-making and enforcement powers of the state. Governments are usually based on a formal constitution that details the structure of rule-making bodies such as the legislature and judicial procedures used by a society. However, the informal power relationships among elite groups also determines how government policy is conducted.

Furthermore, Governments can be both the source and settlement mechanism for a dispute at the same time. One branch of government, say a mining ministry may be part of an international consortium of investors in a minerals development project. As consortium member it may be the target or initiator of a suit against other partners. That conflict may bring other government sectors into the issue as mediators or courts of law. This confusion of roles makes dispute settlement a critical skill in international business.

Resolving Conflict

Firms have a series of options open to them to deal with disputes. These include litigation in domestic courts; arbitration for commercial disputes through the International Chamber of Commerce in Paris; the use of conciliations, legislative intervention, and other third-party consultants; and of course negotiations. The methods chosen will depend on the stage of the dispute, the importance of the issues, the parties involved, the time frame for settlement, and the past history of successful dispute settlement.

It is important to direct attention to two aspects of the conflict situation that very likely will influence the methods chosen. The first concerns the nature of the parties involved. Given the fact that host and home governments, country interest groups, as well as firms can be parties to international business transactions, the number of parties in any one conflict can be large. Usually conflicts between firms are private affairs. For example, simple export transactions may involve disputes over quality, payment, packaging, and the like. These issues, if not resolved privately, can be taken to local or designated third country courts. When government is a party to conflict, the issue can quickly become politicized and more costly to resolve. The Union Carbide Bhopal accident is again a case in point.

Disputes also arise between governments over the activities of a firm. For example, the U.S. government in the 1970s protested to the headquarters of Ford Motor Co. over a decision by Ford's Argentinian subsidiary to export trucks to Cuba. In this case two governments and two related business entities became involved in a dispute where the application of one country's laws to the activities of a domestic firm in a foreign country occurred. This is a form of extraterritoriality (literally, outside of the territory), which always is a source of potential conflict. Note however that some major disputes between nations are handled in the World Court. There is at present no equivalent World Court for business disputes. The International Chamber of Commerce is as close an equivalent as exists. This suggests that a firm needs to be aware of ways to avoid conflict before it arises because no simple one-stop shopping exists for legal resolution.

The second aspect of the conflict situation is the prevention of conflict. Conflict can be managed through a reduction of risk and uncertainty in business transactions. This reduces the possibility for misunderstanding, the source of most conflict. For example, an exporter by requiring prepayment on a letter of credit reduces the potential conflict over payment. There are two generally effective ways of preventing conflict: risk analysis and negotiations.

Risk Analysis

The first risk that firms face is the economic risk that ventures will fail. The firm also faces the risk of losing its proprietary advantages because a unique product or process may be copied by others without proper compensation for using these proprietary rights. There are foreign exchange or currency risks. A currency devaluation may reduce expected economic returns and make ventures less attractive than originally thought.

A second type of risk is political and regulatory risk. Political risk involves the threat that a change in government will lead to a loss of control of ownership and/or management control over foreign operations. The strongest form of this is the threat of expropriation and nationalization. The more common form of regulatory risk is exemplified by the imposition of new requirements on a business such as imposition of export requirements, local content requirements, and job creation requirements. Regulatory risk can also involve changes in the interpretations or enforcement of existing laws.

Risks are inherent in all business decisions. Assessment of these risks involves the identification of the types and probabilities of risks present in a business decision. For example, a decision by a French firm to locate an R&D center in the Silicon Valley may involve the risk of U.S. government restrictions on the access by the foreign parent firms to the research developments of the U.S. subsidiary. The chances of that restriction becoming a reality determines the "riskiness" of the decision.

Firms try to control their exposure to risk in a variety of ways. Obviously an effective analysis of external environmental factors (political, economic, social, cultural) is a first step. There are two common ways to identify the relevant environmental factors. First, firms can buy the risk analysis services of consultants. Since the radical changes in Iran in the late 1970s caused many firms to experience serious losses, political risks analysis has been a growing business service to international firms. This analysis involves the identification of trends in key factors critical to political change, (e.g. development of opposition political parties), an assessment of probabilities of the occurrence of important events (e.g. loss of an election), and the development of multiple scenarios that describe possible alternative future political conditions. Such an analysis allows a firm to make comparisons among different country investment sites.

Secondly, firms can develop their own internal capabilities for risk analysis. This usually involves hiring exdiplomats and political economic experts as well as using internal employees with significant foreign country experience. The large multinational corporations tend to go the route of developing their own internal capabilities that is then both used by the firms subsidiaries or sold to third-party users.

Risks and opportunities are not just a function of external environments however. They also are determined by the capability of a firm to succeed. Evidence of a well-developed market opportunity may exist in a foreign market. The failure to exploit it successfully, however, is not the fault of the market. If the firm does not have the capabilities to attack foreign markets in terms of experience, resources, good leadership, and sound product concepts, it probably should avoid these markets. However, firms often find themselves forced, for strategic reasons, to compete in a foreign market. In such cases the risk analysis is essential to the decision-making process.

Negotiations

Negotiation is a second method used to avoid conflict. Thorough prenegotiation preparation allows the firm to discover its own needs and capabilities more clearly. In the bargaining activity mutual interests are made more explicit and clarified. Furthermore, a negotiated agreement can specify the process for resolving any future disputes.

FIGURE 4–2   Negotiations Issues in Foreign Investment

---

1. Amount of capital involved and how it will be financed as between foreign and local sources and between equity and debt.
2. The products to be produced and the annual capacity of production.
3. The level of employment involved and new jobs created.
4. The estimated amount of foreign exchange required for importation of capital equipment and annual import requirements for production inputs.
5. The amount of output to be exported annually if any.
6. Training plans for the development of skills.
7. The employment of nationals in key managerial and technical positions if any.
8. Identification of any licensing or other contractural agreements calling for the payment of service fees to the parent firm or other collaborating firms— especially for purposes of identifying uses of foreign exchange.
9. Prices and costs of products and expected profits to be repatriated annually.
10. Ownership shares as between the foreign firm and local interests.
11. Location of R&D facilities and transfer of technology.

One of the key decisions to be negotiated is that of entry into a country. This usually involves a foreign investment decision and serious commitment of resources. In this case the need to reduce conflict (and risk) makes negotiation a paramount business activity. Foreign firms now must negotiate with governments in many countries whenever they wish to undertake a new investment even if the investment is but an expansion of an already existing plant rather than an entirely new investment. These negotiations usually entail an application for permission to invest. This application generally asks for a variety of data on how the investment will bring benefits or reduce costs to a country. Some of these information requirements can be seen in Figure 4–2.

These items are illustrative and not all countries are concerned with each and every one. Yet in many countries these are subjects for negotiation between the government and the enterprise. For example, the country may be more generous in its allotment of foreign exchange if the firm agrees to increase the number of jobs created by the investment. Some authors who have examined the investment regulations and investment incentives offered by countries have concluded that countries do see foreign firms as having specific roles to play in the process of industrial development. Largely it is the foreign firms that are often at the forefront in their respective fields. They are a source of new technology and new managerial methods. They often complement the capabilities of locally owned firms. Of course, they also compete with some local firms at times. The consequence is that some groups may welcome them while others simultaneously see them as a serious threat. Which of these tendencies prevails depends largely upon the industry sector being entered by the firm and the capabilities the firm brings with it. Where it does not compete directly with local firms, it is more likely to be welcomed than if it is competitive. Also, the more important or valuable the technology it brings in the form of new products and processes, the more likely it is that it will be welcomed.

In conjunction with the screening and regulation of new investments, many countries also have incentive programs designed to attract firms to invest in those sectors the country deems to be of greatest value. Often these sectors could be considered "high technology" sectors. Or, in some instances, the foreign firm brings with it expertise in international marketing network and thereby increases the country's ability to develop export markets. All of these elements come into play in the negotiations process.

SUMMARY

International business requires firms to operate in complex environments. They face economic, cultural, and political systems that differ from country to country. How well they operate depends on their abilities to perceive and adapt to these differences. It also depends upon their ability to bring about changes in the host environment that make that environment more compatible to their own operating needs. Each country has a unique set of sociopolitical variables with which the firm must contend. However, there are approaches that can be used to improve the probable success in the different country environments.

DISCUSSION QUESTIONS FOR CHAPTER FOUR

1. Note the sociocultural characteristics of your classmates in this course. In how many ways do they differ? What accounts for those differences? Assuming a broad cultural representation of foreign students in your class, what are the implications of these differences for how your teacher will manage the course?

2. What is meant by describing culture as a "living, ecological, rational, integrative, and nonmonolithic pattern of living?"

3. Identify five important general U.S. cultural values. Speculate on how they became dominant value in U.S. culture.

4. Business culture is a subculture that demonstrates beliefs, attitudes, and values towards important elements of business activity. (See Table 4–1.) What would a typical U.S. business culture be like? Would foreign students agree with this assessment?

5. To be successful in another culture, businesses often have to adapt. What does this mean? What gets adapted and why?

6. "For a manager to be successful abroad she must strive to think and act like a host country national. In a sense she must 'go native!'" Do you agree? Why or why not?

7. How does the fact that a country's government has goals affect the political regulatory environment of a country?

8. Some countries have very strict controls over the sales and consumption of ethical drugs. Other countries allow over-the-counter sales of these same drugs. Still other countries prohibit their sales altogether. How can a manager of a pharmaceuticals distribution company that sells over 5,000 kinds of drugs in different forms and stages of product development realistically deal with such varying regulatory climates? Up to what point can you comply with regulations and remain competitive? At what point does ethics come into play?

9. Companies' conflicts with governments can often be traced to role problems. What are the three common role problems for firms?

10. What two aspects of a potential conflict between a firm and a host country partner and/or government does an international manager need to be especially cognizant of? Why?

11. The U.S. market is seen as one of the most open and "free" in the world. Yet doing business in the U.S. requires a clear understanding of the regulatory environment. Identify three areas of regulation that could seriously affect a foreign firm's decision to do business in the United States.

Enterprise Capabilities and Decision Making

INTRODUCTION

This chapter introduces the following five chapters which examine the degree to which firms must alter their managerial systems and strategies to accommodate a multicountry system of markets and production facilities. Each of the business functions must be adapted to a more complex set of environments and competitive undercurrents. In Chapter Three we examined the problems of resource requirements of firms and how these may conflict with the resource availabilities and constraints imposed by different economic systems. Here we wish to build on these notions at a more operational level as we look at the business functions of marketing, production, finance, human resource management, and the overall managerial systems that support these activities.

The ideal that most firms would like to see when they move abroad is a set of environments that are nearly identical to the environment in which they have been functioning. Under these circumstances the firm would be able to operate much as it does at home regardless of the country in which it locates. However, the world is not so simple and this ideal is virtually never achieved. Thus the key considerations in doing business abroad are (1) to identify those aspects of doing business at home that can be used elsewhere and (2) determine what must be done to develop substitutes for those practices at home that are not suitable in other countries. This determination requires expenditures of real resources in terms of managers' time and the time of marketing researches, financial analysts, production engineers, and other personnel who generate the information needed to make the appropriate decisions. These decisions in turn must deal with questions such as those seen in Figure 5–1.

FIGURE 5–1   Decisions in International Operations

---

1. Is the market large enough to justify the establishment of a manufacturing plant? Are there other national markets that could also be served by this same plant?

2. Can our existing product designs be used to serve this market or must there be an adaptation of the product? If adaptation is required, what should be its nature?

3. Is there an adequate distribution system for us to market our products or will we have to develop special distribution capability?

4. If we are able to install a plant, how large should it be and how should it be designed in terms of processes to be included, layout and workflow, and location?

5. Are the skills we need in plentiful supply or will we have to train for key skills? If we must create skills, what skills will these be?

6. Are the transport, communications, and other aspects of infrastructure adequate to support our needs?

7. What are the government restrictions, if any, on foreign ownership, use of expatriates, importation of machinery and components, repatriation of profits, and the like?

8. Are there government incentives available for new investments and if so, what requirements are called for to obtain these incentives?

9. Is there a well developed financial sector on which we can rely in helping us finance our operations? If not, what are the implications for obtaining financial resources from other countries or from the parent?

10. Are there media that are suitable for the promotion of our products? Can we price the product at a level high enough to cover costs?

11. How much will the investment cost in terms of buildings, equipment, customs duties, training programs, product redesigns, development of distribution systems, and market development?

12. How profitable will the operation be?

As we have already noted, most firms begin international operations simply by exporting. Exports often are looked upon as merely an extra market in which there is some demand for a product that was originally developed to serve the home market. Once demand grows, then firms do face the decision as to whether or not they should continue to serve foreign markets by exporting only or by building plants abroad to serve these markets. See News Box 5–1 for a look at how Fuji Film has answered some of these questions.

To examine the issues in such decisions, we begin with an analysis of the resource capabilities of the firm followed by the international re-

NEWS BOX 5–1
Fuji Film Continues Cautious, Step-by-Step Growth in Overseas Market
Sam Jameson

Basking in the afterglow of what he called the immense success of Fuji Film's part in the Olympic Games at Los Angeles, Minoru Onishi, Fuji's president, has set a new goal for the company.

"American consumers have embraced an image of the quality of Fuji film as having reached a top level in the world," Onishi said in a recent interview, and Fuji now hopes to destroy the "myth" that only Kodak possesses "exclusive reliability in quality."

*   *   *   *   *

He said that taking on Kodak is a difficult challenge and he made it clear that Fuji considers it a long-range undertaking.

U.S. Sales Up 30 Percent

Onishi said Fuji's sales in the United States had increased by 30 percent this year.

*   *   *   *   *

"We want to move forward step by step," he said. "Market share is not our goal. The (U.S.) market itself is moving. Planting our roots in it is most vital. Then, if the market expands, our sales will grow even if our share stays the same."

Onishi insisted that Fuji's corporate strategy does not revolve around devising methods to compete with Kodak, its chief global rival.

*   *   *   *   *

Last year, despite a 51 percent decline in profits, Kodak was still outdistancing Fuji, the world's number two film maker, with revenues of $10.2 billion compared to Fuji's $2.7 billion. Kodak's net profit of $565 million was more than double Fuji's $251 million.

This year, despite Fuji's spurt in American sales, Kodak profits are rising again and Fuji's are falling.

*   *   *   *   *

A price war for magnetic recording tape has forced the company to push back by two years, to 1989, a long-range goal of 1 trillion yen in sales ($4.2 billion). This level is considered a kind of magic plateau for Japanese firms.

Fuji's next major challenge to Kodak's dominance—Onishi said it was planned long before it won the Olympic sponsorship in Los Angeles—will come in Europe, where Fuji has 15 percent to 20 percent of the market. In October, in the Netherlands, Fuji will open its first overseas integrated production factory for photosensitized products.

*   *   *   *   *

He said he expects Fuji to move ahead in Europe on the pattern foreseen for the United States: steady but unspectacular in the short-run.

New Long-range Strategy

The European factory represents the beginning of a new long-range strategy for Fuji, he said.

"Trade friction will continue to grow stronger in the future. I think we have entered an era in which selling finished goods produced completely in Japan is becoming unreasonable. Local production where we sell is better, I believe."

He said Fuji has no plans to build a factory in the United States but added that this "must be considered in the long range." When the time comes to start planning for it, he said, one of the first questions to be examined will be whether California's unitary tax is still in effect. The unitary tax, which is based on a firm's global operations, would be a negative factor in any feasibility study, Onishi said.

He said that 33 percent of Fuji's production is exported and described this level as desirable. . . . But overseas production will rule out any similar change in the firm's export ratio in the next decade, Onishi said.

The export growth, Onishi said, came partly as a result of eating into Kodak's markets, but mainly because the global market has expanded. In Japan, where Fuji has 70 percent of the film market. Kodak ranks third with about 15 percent, behind Fuji and Sakura Film. Sakura is a product of Konishiroku, makers of Konica cameras.

Fuji's dominance here was established in a period that critics of Japan's trade policies call a "greenhouse" strategy of government protection for infant industries. Japan had a 40 percent tariff on film imports until March 1971, when it started a 12-year program of gradual reduction. Not until April of last year, however, was the tariff brought down to about the same level as the U.S. tariff on film imports. Today, Japan's tariff is 4 percent, slightly lower than the U.S. tariff of 4.5 percent.

Fuji was not complacent during the long period of protection. Onishi said it broadened its range of products and plunged into research and development to raise the technological quality of its products.

Twice, Fuji has marketed major new film products before Kodak— in 1976, when it brought out fastspeed 400-ASA color film, and this year, when it marketed 1,600-ASA color film, sensitive enough to take photographs in candlelight without a flash.

It also established a sphere of influence in Southeast Asia, where it now has 50 percent of the market.

Onishi said Fuji is putting stronger emphasis on technology by raising its research and development spending to a record 7 percent of sales this year. For many years, the company spent 4 percent to 5 percent on R&D, he said.

Fuji intends to continue to sponsor international sports events—it has already signed on as a sponsor of soccer's World Cup tournament in 1986—

but it will not be as anxious to bid for the 1988 Olympics in Seoul as it was for the 1984 games, Onishi said.

This year was the firm's 50th anniversary and the Olympics helped to commemorate it. In addition, the 1984 games were in a country that is important to Fuji's marketing strategy.

"If the 84 games had been held in Argentina or New Zealand, it is questionable that we would have been a sponsor," Onishi said. "We won't take the same approach to the Seoul games in 1988 that we took toward Los Angeles."

SOURCE: *The Los Angeles Times*, September 24, 1984, Part IV, pg. 3.

quirements in the marketing function, production systems, organizational structure, human resources, and financial resources.

RESOURCES AND CAPABILITIES OF THE FIRM

One of the first steps in strategy formulation is the internal analysis of a company's strengths and weaknesses. This usually involves an analysis of internal resources and capabilities. Successful internationalizing of a firm's operations depends upon the match of these resources and capabilities to similar strength/weakness profiles of a target country and its markets. Firm's resources generally can be classified as:

- Marketing resources.
- Production and technological resources.
- Financial resources.
- Personnel resources.
- Design and administrative system resources.

Marketing resources include the ability to assess markets, including the matching of products to market needs, the gaining of distribution channels to key market segments, and the achieving of sufficient market shares to be able to efficiently produce and sell the products. Production and technological resources include the ability to design products and the technological processes needed to produce them at cost levels that allow competitive pricing. Financial resources include the ability to generate the needed financing to undertake the operations of the firm. These activities involve the financing of production and marketing which in turn requires the financing of inventories, accounts receivable, fixed assets, and payrolls. Labor resources are comprised of the various human skills needed to produce, market, finance, and manage the entire operations of the firm. Some of these skills are brought with the firm when it moves into a country; other skills must be acquired locally. Finally, and perhaps most importantly, managerial skills include all of those systematic methods the firm uses to organize, plan, and control the firms total operations. This involves the coordination of all of the various functions to include production, marketing, financing, personnel, information systems, and public and governmental relations.

What distinguishes most multinational firms from purely national firms is their ability to identify opportunities in more than a single market. This skill relies on three precepts. First, the firm must recognize the value of its own resources and how they can be used. Secondly, the firm must be able to identify those situations in which its resources can serve new markets in alien cultures. Third, the firm must be able to assess the resources available in other countries and evaluate their suitability for use in conjunction with the firm's own resources. This simple statement makes accomplishing these three things seem easy. Nothing could be further from the truth. There is a highly complex set of relationships in each country that firms must assess. This requires the expenditure of effort and money. Firms must accumulate information and go through a learning process but as this activity is repeated, the costs of repetition go down. Stated differently, once a firm has assessed one situation and made a move into one country, the costs of assessing a similar venture in another country will be reduced since the firm has acquired a built-in expertise. There now are people who know how to undertake such market and resource assessments. These assessments require the firm to examine the various environmental constraints and opportunities which involve the economic, social/cultural, and political/legal aspects of doing business in foreign locations. It is within this context that the firm must assess its own capabilities since what may be a strength in one country situation may be a weakness or at least not represent a strength in another country situation.

Simply stated, firms must be able to define their strengths and weaknesses in relation to the resources and market opportunities available in different countries. In addition, they must be able to assess the competition they may face when they do business abroad.

MARKETING RESOURCES

The marketing resources of the firm include what has come to be known in the field of marketing as the marketing mix. The marketing mix consists of the product itself, its pricing patterns, the promotional efforts that have gone into establishing the product in the marketplace, and the distribution system that supports the product in establishing its market access. The marketing mix must be totally reevaluated once it is removed from its original home-country context. Past investments at home in the marketing mix may or may not support a firm's ability to move into international markets. For example, unless the product has been adapted it may be suitable for far fewer foreign markets. A typical example of this marketing mismatch is household appliances developed for the U.S. market where the 110 volt electrical system is the standard. In most other countries the common volt standard is 220 volts. Thus, the product must be adapted if it is to be sold in these other markets.

The Product

In marketing products the firm that is operating across national boundaries must consider whether or not a different product from that offered at home is required. Elements in this decision include the design of the product, its features, styling, quality, and function. In addition there is the question of packaging, since the package often is important in the promotion of the product. Product design must take into consideration not only the appeal of the product and its ability to perform, but also the materials and processes of production required to produce it. Multinational firms would prefer to be able to sell the same product in all countries. However, this may not be possible because consumer tastes in different countries can and do differ significantly. Even within countries, different ethnic groups may desire special versions of products. Markets may also be segmented by age group or income classes so that several different versions of products may be needed if a firm is to be successful even within individual national markets. These tendencies for differentiation become magnified when doing business internationally.

Pricing

It usually is not possible to price products uniformly across several national markets. Countries differ in terms of income levels and the amount of income typically allocated to the consumption of various types of goods. The degree to which firms have freedom to adjust prices depends on their ability to differentiate their products and distinguish them from those of their competitors in various national markets. This depends partly on the product itself, but much also depends on advertising and other forms of promotion used as well as the firm's ability to obtain distribution outlets for the product. In some countries there are relatively fewer available methods that can be used to advertise products. For example, in some countries it is not permissible to use television advertising for certain products, and in many instances where it is permissible, the breadth of advertising messages allowed is much narrower than it is in the United States. Some governments, like France, insist on very strict rules. When this is the case, then product differentiation becomes more difficult and hence the pricing decision and the ability to apply marketing resources of the firm is restricted. What may be a strength in one country is negated in another. Prices will differ across countries for other reasons too. For example, costs of production, distribution, and promotion vary due to different abundances of resources or inflation rates. These costs ultimately must be covered by the price of the product if the firm is to succeed.

There are limits on how much prices can differ across countries. For example, suppose there are protective tariffs that make it profitable to manufacture the product inside a country (rather than exporting it from the home country). The firm producing there can charge a price premium above the price in countries where there are no protective tariffs. However, the limit as to how high this premium can be is set by the amount of the tariff. If the firm attempts to charge a price greater than the cost of importing the product including the cost of the tariff, then importers will take advantage by bringing in a larger volume of the product and drive the price back down. Even where the product is unique and has no competition, a similar limit across countries is set by market forces. So long as a product can be purchased in one country and shipped to another, the price premium cannot exceed the amount it costs to buy the product in the low priced country and ship it to the high priced country. The cost of doing this sets the limit on the price differential attainable.

Promotion and Distribution

Students of marketing recognize that the pricing of a product and its ultimate profitability depend very heavily on the way the product is promoted and distributed. Promotion includes personal selling, advertising, packaging, and point of sale display. Firms differ in the resources they can bring to bear in pursuit of these activities. The accumulated knowledge of markets acquired through experience and marketing research is important to (1) the process of selecting distribution channels and outlets and (2) the choice of promotional methods that can be used to enhance the possibilities of the product's being seen by various groups of potential users. Again, countries differ vastly in terms of the distribution methods and channels available to the firm. The key is to match the resources of the firm to the country's available system. Of course the firm sometimes can alter the distribution system within the country to be more in keeping with its own needs, however, this may be a costly and time consuming effort. Largely firms try to use available systems initially on entry, but for some products it may be necessary to make the investment in distribution to gain market position.

PRODUCTION AND TECHNOLOGY

Firms differ in their production and technological capabilities. This in turn affects the strategies and management methods that each firm will adopt. In each firm there is a mixture of proprietary and nonproprietary technology. Proprietary technology is either secret and not available to other firms or protected by law through patent rights. Firms can choose to sell these rights or rent access to the rights or they can choose to exploit the technology themselves. Most multinational firms choose to do the latter.

Generally, nonproprietary technology is available to everyone, but not all firms are equally adept at applying this knowledge. Thus, it is the combination of proprietary and nonproprietary technology that is important. For example, any firm can buy machines and buildings and hire workers to run the machines, but this is not the key to success. It is the ability to combine the capabilities of the machines and workers to produce a product of consistently high quality relative to its cost and deliver it to the marketplace that is important. Repeatedly we read accounts of modern equipment sitting unused, even still in its packaging, because local employees have received rudimentary or no training and simply do not trust the new equipment. Also as we have noted under marketing capabilities, the product must be conceived in such a way that it attracts a large enough group of users that it can be produced economically and sold at an acceptable price.

Ultimately then, it is the combination of human skills and plant facilities that constitutes the production and technology resource. This includes management, research personnel, technicians, production workers, marketing personnel, and administrative personnel all working together to tie together a system of physical facilities with suppliers and customers to produce and market a product or service. Strategies of doing this will depend on the nature of the resources available, the nature of the product, and the type of market being served. This can be a complex system—particularly for a multinational firm which attempts to coordinate multiple plants across several countries.

In the automobile industry, Ford Motor Co. has plants in over 20 countries. Some of these plants are specialized, i.e., one plant will produce engines while another makes axles and transmissions while still others make body components and do final assembly. Usually there are more assembly plants than there are axle and engine-making plants. Thus, the engines and axles must be shipped to several assembly plants—these plants often are not in the same country. For example, Ford has an engine plant in Germany and an assembly plant in Belgium. Engines are shipped from Germany to the Belgian plant where they are installed in the final automobile. The automobiles are then marketed throughout much of Europe. The issues facing firms with this production spread are: (1) To what degree can products be standardized across various national markets? (2) To what extent is it necessary to produce abroad rather than at home in order to serve these markets? (3) To what extent can the processes used to produce the product at home be used abroad? (4) Is it better to have specialized plants or more general purpose plants to produce the product? The firm's marketing strategy and the resources available largely dictate the answers to these questions.

Market size and the interrelationships among markets is a key element in the decision as to what type of production system will be suitable. If markets are small and isolated either by distance or by government policies, plants will then be designed to serve individual national markets and will be less specialized. Of course this depends upon whether the firm has a full line of products or only produces a narrow product line. Firms with a full product line, under most circumstances, would prefer to produce a few different products in each plant and then ship these to several markets. But when added up, with each plant producing different products the combination of plants is able to produce a full line of products. These more specialized plants are able to have longer production runs and gain from economies of scale by serving several markets rather than only one market.

Market size also figures prominently into the decision of whether to exploit one's own proprietary technology or to license it to others. If markets are small and the technological capabilities of the country low, the firm is more likely to license its technology. Where the opposite situation prevails, the firm is more likely to invest abroad and exploit the technology on its own rather than to license it. Much therefore depends on the value of the technology. As we saw in Chapter Two, under these circumstances firms prefer to either export from the home country or if they do produce the product abroad, they do so in wholly owned facilities.

FINANCIAL RESOURCES

Financial resources represent the capital resources a firm is able to get access to and use to finance both its operations and investments. The sources of capital in international business are expanded because of access to more country capital markets, governmental sources not usually available to domestic firms and expanded parent firm sources. However, international financing requires capabilities of working in multiple national currencies whose value change with market conditions. Multiple currencies complicate the financing of business activities such as inventories, payrolls and fixed capital. They also make the measurement of financial performance a complex task. Thus a firm's financial capability is measured in two ways—its access to international sources of capital and its ability to develop an effective financial management system capable of working under complex, changing conditions.

The strength of financial resources also depends on the currencies a company is able to work or borrow in. The value of currencies differs greatly. The so-called "hard currencies" such as the yen, pound, dollar, or deutsche mark, tend to hold their value longer than "softer" currencies. They are thus more in demand as the key currencies in contracts to sell or invest. Since multinational firms must manage multiple currencies regularly, they have better expertise than national firms in dealing with multiple currencies. They also have extensive linkages with banks that assist them in managing their foreign exchange risk. Thus a part of a multinational's financial strengths derives from its experience in managing multiple currency transactions and its knowledge of foreign exchange markets. The multinational firm can take advantage of its "hard" currency position more often than national firms.

Multinational firms, because they operate in several national jurisdictions, often have greater borrowing capacity than would other firms. They can borrow in one country and move funds to another. Or they may take the profits of one subsidiary and move these funds to another subsidiary in another country. While national firms might be able to do this also, generally they are both less aware of the opportunities to do so and have few if any overseas assets that can be used as collateral in countries where they reside. Moreover, multinational firms have well-developed financial connections with multinational banking concerns not only in various national financial markets but also in the Eurocurrency markets as well.

Finally, multinational firms are usually large and well diversified in terms of their product lines, industries of participation, and geographic spread across several countries. For example, Nestle Foods Corporation, headquartered in Switzerland, has more than 200 overseas operations and, although heavily committed to food products, also produces a wide diversity of products in the pharmaceutical and cosmetic fields. In addition, it is in the restaurant, hotel, vending machine, and food retailing businesses. In 1981 it had 95 administrative centers, 302 factories, and 751 sales branches and depots. Its sales were over $15 billion and total assets were almost $10 billion. With a total debt to total asset ratio of only 0.48 Nestle probably had an additional borrowing capacity of about $1 billion. Thus, whenever Nestle wishes to increase the financial resources available to any of its foreign subsidiaries, it has ample unused leverage capacity because banks would be willing to lend to Nestle because it has the capacity to service considerably more debt.

To summarize, the financial resources multinational firms bring with them are not so much different in kind when compared with other firms. However, they do have superior knowledge about financial markets and sources of finance. Also, they are usually large and well diversified in ways that allow them to take greater advantage of leverage. The parent firm is in a position to guarantee the financing of its overseas subsidiaries because of these characteristics.

HUMAN RESOURCES

Perhaps the most difficult aspect of managing international operations is that of managing human resources. While it is true that certain key positions can be staffed by people from the parent firm, the large majority of positions will be staffed with nationals from within the host country. Because of this the systems used at home must be adapted to the needs of these nationals. Language, culture, and the country's political/legal system all dictate the degree to which the home country's (parent firm's) methods must be changed. The broader the scope of the firm's activities within each foreign location and the greater the number of countries involved, the greater will be the need for adaptation.

Firms do try to reduce the need for adaptation by training nationals. In other words, the multinational firm tries to alter foreign environments to be more like the firm's home environment by training the workforce to use the methods established at home. Many firms do have considerable success in doing so. For example, in making a product certain types of equipment must be used. The multinational firm attempts to use similar methods and similar types of equipment in most of its plants. There are efficiencies in doing so and one of those efficiencies is that of training equipment operators. Moreover, there are limits on how far any firm can move in making adaptations to its production processes. Thus, in many instances it is essential to train people rather than adapting every production process to the people and their culture.

Just as there are limits on how much the production process can be adapted, there also are limits on how far the local environment can be adapted. There are cultural norms and there are limits to the availability of skills. The firm usually must fit in with such cultural norms as the work ethic, the concept of time, attention to detail and quality, response to discipline and rewards, accepted length of work day, religious holidays, the concept of nationalism, and the role that enterprises are expected to play in society.

In terms of skills the firm often must adapt its methods to accommodate the existing skills. For example, where the level of literacy is low training will have to be done using pictures and color codes rather than written training manuals. Even where literacy rates are high if the language differs from that of the home country, manuals will have to be translated into the native language. In some countries the bulk of new entrants to the labor force comes from rural areas. Village life often does not prepare young people to understand the demands of an industrial environment. Even a notion as supposedly simple as punctuality may not have been part of village life. Tardiness and absenteeism are high in some cultures because the culture is deficit in this training or perceives the nature of production work quite differently. The manager's job is thus complicated due to the shortage of people who are appropriately trained. Selection and training become both more important and more difficult.

To avoid such misunderstandings, many multinational firms staff positions that are culturally sensitive with nationals. Such positions include production management, industrial relations, public relations, and sales management. These are positions in which the manager's actions directly affect workers, customers, and the larger public and government agencies. Those positions that tend to be staffed by expatriate (nonnational) personnel include the chief executive officer, financial officer, accounting and control officer, and chief technical officer. Also expatriates tend to advise on quality control and the application of technology, but usually from positions as staff rather than line personnel.

The world's industrial environments are becoming more and more similar. As this happens there are growing opportunities to move key people from one country to another as organizational needs change. This broadens personnel choices and it also blurs distinctions of nationalism. Loyalty to one's enterprise substitutes for loyalty to one's nation. Who is a national and who is an expatriate is becoming a question of diminishing significance. Moreover, as firms develop a cadre of managers with multinational experience, many of the difficulties of selecting managers for foreign assignments will diminish as well.

Many of the issues in the management of human resources will be discussed further in Chapter Eight.

ORGANIZATIONAL DESIGN AND ADMINISTRATION OF OPERATIONS

In the sections above we have been concerned primarily with the so-called "business functions" of production, marketing, finance, and human resources or personnel management. Now we examine the broader role of general management to include organizing, planning, and control. These aspects of organizational management are intimately related and, properly executed, they represent a major resource. The choice of organization structure does much to establish responsibility and decision-making relationships. Structure aims to provide for an efficient flow of information and decisions. It also aims to identify who has the authority to make what type of decision and places limits or boundaries around the scope that decisions can take at different levels within the structure.

Organizational structure should enhance the ability to plan and coordinate across the business functions to balance production against market needs and to arrange for needed financial and human resources in support of this process. Structure can either enhance or impede efficiency and the ability of the enterprise to respond to change. Stated differently, an appropriate structure can make the enterprise effective whereas an inappropriate structure can get in the way and unnecessarily complicate decision making and taking action.

Structure

Firms can choose five different methods of structuring themselves. They can organize around (1) *business functions* such as marketing, production, and finance; (2) *processes* such as exploration and development, production, transportation, refining, and marketing in the petroleum industry; (3) *products* such as steering gears, suspension systems, axles, braking systems; (4) *geographic areas* such as North America, Northern Europe, Southern Europe, South America, Asia, and Africa. A fifth way of organizing is called matrix structure in which special projects or products coordinate directly with functional areas.

When we classify firms in terms of organizational structure we are referring to the first or highest level in that structure. Stated differently, we are broadly identifying the responsibilities of those managers who report directly to the chief executive. In actuality within virtually every large firm the four structures will appear at some level in the organization. The functional form seldom appears at the first level in large firms—especially those that produce a variety of products. Most large firms do produce numerous products and most have adopted the product division structure in their domestic operations.

A large number of multinational firms separate their international operations from their domestic operations by establishing an international division or group. This division is responsible for export sales and has control over plants operating abroad. The most common structure within this division is the area or country structure.

Some firms have established worldwide product groups at the top level of the organization. These groups then tend to adopt an area structure at the next level.

The choice of structure is largely a matter of interdependence among operating units in terms of communication, decision making, and taking action. If units are highly interdependent (where the actions of one unit significantly affect another unit) they should be grouped together. Structure also depends on strategy and performance goals. Given a set of goals for international markets, a strategy is chosen to achieve them. If vertical integration in an industry or conglomeration is the strategy, then the structure should reflect the design most appropriate for strategy implementation. Thus, structure is a dynamic characteristic that changes.

Managerial Control Systems

Structure is important for purposes of planning and controlling the firm's total operations. An inappropriate structure complicates rather than clarifies the planning and controlling process. Planning has the purpose of establishing the goals the enterprise is attempting to achieve. It also provides a map of the ways to be taken in achieving the goals. Control is the process of monitoring progress in terms of the plan, but since structure is a system of responsibility and authority assignments, planning and control cannot be effective if these assignments are not consistent with the tasks involved in pursuing and meeting goals.

While these generalities apply to any firm, their importance is magnified for firms operating internationally because of the problem of integrating activities of extended time and geographic zones. Planning and control along with structure are the glue that holds organizations together and provides direction to the firm's activities. This triumvirate largely defines what the organization is and is expected to become. It also establishes information flows and provides guidelines based on this information on what actions should be taken and by whom. It constitutes the intelligence-gathering antennae of the organization so that testing, sensing, monitoring, and reaction can take place.

As countries differ so too will the information available differ. Also the variables that can be controlled by the firm will differ across countries. The balancing act for multinational firms is to design these systems so that they are responsive to intercountry differences but still provide the information needed for the firm to make decisions intelligently. This usually means that the international operations of the firm must be more flexible in terms of the design of the organization and its planning and control systems.

SUMMARY

In this chapter we looked at the firms capabilities of engaging in international business. Five resources were defined in terms of traditional management functions of marketing, production-technology, finance, labor management personnel and organizational design. For the firm to be effective abroad it needs to be able to answer the operational questions in Figure 5-1 in terms of the resources and capabilities it both has and is capable of developing in each of these areas.

Perhaps the most important resource that distinguishes highly successful firms is that of management skills. It is out of these management skills that superior knowledge and its applications will flow. For the multinational firm, as we have noted, it is essential to be able to perform at a higher level than the local competition simply because, as foreign entities, multinational firms operate at a disadvantage in terms of being residents in an alien culture. There is a learning cost in doing business outside one's home base. Communication is more complex and costly. Business practice, language, distribution systems, and so on are different. The foreign firm must incur the costs involved in acquiring an understanding of these differences so that the firm can operate effectively in the host culture. To offset these extra costs of doing business the multinational firm must be in a position to reduce costs elsewhere in its system if it is to compete effectively. This cost reduction can only come from superior management and other skills in technology, marketing, finance, and operations.

DISCUSSION QUESTIONS FOR CHAPTER FIVE

1. The resources a firm possesses indicate its relative strengths and weaknesses. Cite at least one strength and weakness a firm might have in each of its functional areas.

2. In your opinion, what strengths in marketing would a foreign manufacturer of low-cost kitchen ware (e.g. potato peelers, aluminum cake pans) need to sell in the housewares section of major U.S. food chains?

3. "Since nonproprietary technology is freely available to everyone, all it takes to be successful in international business is capital to buy machines, a place to put them in, and labor to work them. With the general low costs of both fixed and variable costs abroad, a business can't fail to do well in a market like the United States." Do you agree? Why or why not?

4. Compare the historical production of Henry Ford's Model "T" on the first assembly line with Ford's modern day international production of cars. In what ways do they differ? Why has the production of cars changed so?

5. What problems of coordination among the various functional strategies might a manager have to deal with when locating a subsidiary business abroad?

6. Doing business in one foreign country is complex enough. How is the strategic management task complicated by locating various business activities in many countries? In what ways do you think decision making in a global oriented firm differs from a firm that is domestic oriented?

7. How many ways can you structure a firm internationally? If you say "five ways," does this mean there are also only five strategies? What is the relationship between strategy and structure?

Decisions in Marketing Management

INTRODUCTION

Marketing may be the most important aspect of an international strategy for any firm. Until the firm has a grasp of its marketing opportunities and constraints it cannot really address the issues of plant design and location, staffing and organizational structure, or financial requirements. Everything begins with the market. Does the market exist? What is its nature in terms of consumers' tastes, size, and potential competition? Does our product meet market needs or will we have to adapt or replace the product? Which situation affects the costs of market entry?

To understand international marketing we must analyze how domestic marketing differs from international marketing. Understanding these differences aids in making key decisions that constitute international marketing strategy. This chapter focuses on the diversity between domestic and international marketing, key strategic considerations, operational decisions required to make international marketing effective, and some major current issues in international marketing.

KEY DIFFERENCES

Marketing Control

The first major difference occurs in what has been identified as the *"controllable"* and the *"noncontrollable"* variables noted in Figure 6–1. Controllables are those factors and decisions that generally can be controlled by the firm. Within the marketing function these are usually identified as the marketing mix of product, price, promotion, and channels of distribution. Given the special nature of many contemporary

---

FIGURE 6–1   Marketing Control Continuum

Controllables	*Influenceables*	*Noncontrollables*
Product	Through contacts with country	Geography
Price	elites, modern information tech-	Demography
Promotion	nology, and "new ideas" in products,	Culture and core
Distribution	firms can exert limited influence	values
Packaging	over regulatory policy, monetary	Structural character-
Servicing	controls, business practices, and	istics of society
Payment/Credit	social preferences.	Infrastructure
		Development

---

products (e.g., electronic based, specialized use, miniaturized) further decisions regarding packaging, postpurchase servicing and adaptation, and payment in the international system tend to become important controllable variables. In contrast to these are a series of variables that are considered *"noncontrollables"* because they are, by nature, under the control of other organizations or institutional arrangements, like governments.

There is always a range over which these variables move. While the structure of a political system may be noncontrollable, the direction of political regulatory policy can be influenced. Again, Koreagate, a case of Korean companies' attempts to use illegal payments to some U.S. congressmen, exemplifies an attempt to influence policy to favor these companies' interests. There are situations in which seemingly controllable factors may not be so. For example, a subsidiary's product offering may be controlled by a home office, by a joint venture partner's performance requirements, or by a government's policy. Thus, the terms "controllable" and "noncontrollable" are in reality relative concepts.

Consumption Function Differences

Marketing focuses on consumption habits and patterns. The marketer aims to influence consumer habits and patterns to favor a particular company's products. For this reason a country's consumption function is of crucial importance. Two factors that appear to influence it most are the level of economic development and the level of marketing development.

Level of Economic Development.   One author states, "The economic level of the country is the single most important environmental element to which the foreign marketer must adjust the marketing task in a developing market. The stage of economic growth within a country affects attitudes toward foreign business activity, the demand for goods, distribution systems found within a country, and, indeed, the entire marketing process.[1]

The level of economic development affects the capacity to consume in two ways. First, there is the ability to use a product or service as intended, consistent with the consumer's needs. Sometimes inappropriate use results from consumers' lack of skills and product knowledge. Inappropriate use of baby food formulas and misuse of farm equipment in Third World countries are often the result of low levels of knowledge and literacy. Poor marketing contributes to misuse of products. Inappropriate use of products and services is a problem because it can lead to dissatisfaction that can affect future purchases of a company's products. In certain cases misuse can also lead to liability for damages if the product causes personal harm.

The level of economic development also establishes the ability of customers to purchase various products. High levels of economic development and high levels of per capita income go together. In advanced countries the consumers' discretionary income is higher because the basics of housing, food, and clothing take a relatively lower percentage of income. Consumers are thus more likely to consume a wider variety of goods of higher quality, including foreign goods. In countries at lower levels of development, discretionary income is a smaller proportion of total income and accordingly purchases of luxury goods is less evident. To meet this income restriction domestic producers may develop lower quality and lower-priced products that are similar in other respects to products produced by firms in advanced countries.

The influence of level of economic development on consumption can be seen by looking at recent experiences in China. Foreign marketers became excited by the prospect of a "billion person" market. Obtaining only one tenth of one percent of such a potential market would seem to make the marketing effort easily worthwhile. However, initial enthusiasm was dampened by two factors. The very low per capita income in China meant that many products simply would be inappropriate for the Chinese market for reasons of cost. Second, while the Chinese may be very willing to consume foreign products, the ability to pay for them was constricted by credit constraints and China's foreign exchange policy. Thus, while a market of one billion people may seem an easy market, the reality is that the level of economic development constrains the ability to consume.

---

[1] Philip Cateora, *International Marketing*, 4th ed. (Homewood, Ill.: Richard D. Irwin, 1984), p. 135.

Level of Marketing Development.   A second major determinant of the consumption function is the level of marketing development. By this is meant the relative level of development of institutions, business practices, distribution channels, and selling methods that facilitate and support marketing activity. The extent to which these supporting conditions exist and are similar to those in the home country, the easier the marketing effort should be. However, marketers cannot expect to transplant well-developed domestic marketing programs to a different country and expect similar results. If key elements of marketing development are missing (lack of mass market retail stores or low per capita ownership of television), the program may fail. Thus, level of marketing development is a key determinant of marketing.

THE STRATEGIC CHALLENGE OF INTERNATIONAL MARKETING

The challenge of international marketing to the domestic business can be seen in Figure 6–2. The goals of the marketer are to search for market opportunity, gain access to a country's market, and develop that market. However, there are barriers to market entry coming from both the firm's internal weaknesses and external environmental forces. The challenge is to overcome those barriers. Not all firms are successful at this. Long-term presence in a market depends on the choice of competitive strategy that is responsive to the country's economic and market development. Market presence also depends on the firm's ability to gain a market share in competition with domestic and foreign-based competitors.

A firm's international marketing strategy involves several key considerations. Experience and research have identified these as being: (1) the nature and extent of a firm's commitment to international business activities; (2) the marketing research capabilities which provide an analysis of market opportunities; (3) the degree of adaptation in the marketing mix to meet foreign markets needs; and (4) market management design and control.

Commitment to International Markets

The first major consideration is the evaluation of the firm's international marketing objectives and resources. These derive from management's commitment and philosophical orientation towards international business. Commitment reflects the importance with which a goal is held. The commitment to international marketing depends on how top managements perceive international markets as a means to achieve enterprise goals. Some firms seem to see foreign markets as

FIGURE 6–2 International Marketing Challenge

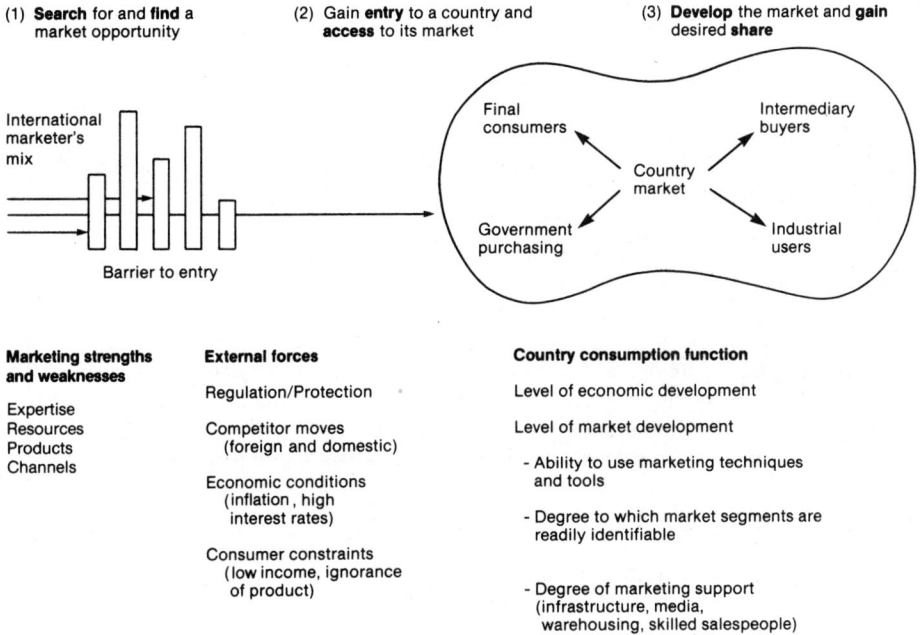

(1) **Search** for and **find** a market opportunity

(2) Gain **entry** to a country and **access** to its market

(3) **Develop** the market and **gain** desired **share**

International marketer's mix

Barrier to entry

Final consumers

Intermediary buyers

Country market

Government purchasing

Industrial users

Marketing strengths and weaknesses

Expertise
Resources
Products
Channels

External forces

Regulation/Protection

Competitor moves
  (foreign and domestic)

Economic conditions
  (inflation, high
  interest rates)

Consumer constraints
  (low income, ignorance
  of product)

Country consumption function

Level of economic development

Level of market development

  – Ability to use marketing techniques
    and tools

  – Degree to which market segments are
    readily identifiable

  – Degree of marketing support
    (infrastructure, media,
    warehousing, skilled salespeople)

"sinks" in which to "dump" excess production or as a means of providing temporary markets to offset domestic downturns. For example, the highly cyclical Pacific Northwest fishing industry has tended to look at the Japanese market as an outlet for excess production. When the cycle is normal firms tend to serve only traditional domestic markets and forgo foreign opportunities. There is a lack of commitment to international business. For a look at how U.S. software firms are viewing Japan as a market, see News Box 6–1.

Analysis of Foreign Market Opportunities

A second major consideration in marketing strategy is an analysis of foreign market opportunities. Successful marketing depends on objective information. The nature of the international marketing research problem is depicted in Figure 6–3. The objective is to improve on present knowledge and to reduce uncertainty with respect to real market conditions.

Marketing research methods used in domestic markets may not be applicable in foreign markets. Collecting primary data may be too

---

NEWS BOX 6–1
U.S. Software Firms Set Sights on Japan
Stephen Kreider Yoder

It's hard to imagine a high-tech market here that the Japanese can't dominate. But Jim Manzi, president of Lotus Development Corporation, thinks he sees an opening. The U.S. software company set up shop in Tokyo last month to sell the business program that has made Lotus a household word among Western companies.

Japan's market is "on the brink of explosive growth," Manzi says. "We have a very, very good chance of achieving the kind of dominance here that we have everywhere else in the world."

Lotus isn't alone in setting its sights on Japan. With high-technology markets in the West crowded and hotly competitive, Japan's market for microcomputers and software looks like a gold mine to companies such as Lotus. Japanese consumers are just starting to buy the kinds of business programs Westerners have used for years. Japanese companies have barely tapped the market, and the Americans see a prime chance to get a foothold.

Not Newcomers

Americans aren't newcomers to Japan's microcomputer market. Apple Computer Inc. and a few others have been selling personal computers here since the 1970s. U.S. software houses also have made inroads in Japan. Microsoft Corp., for example, started selling Basic computer language programs to local computer makers in 1978.

But until recently most companies did business through Japanese sales representatives, without setting up local offices. Some, like Lotus, didn't even try to sell to the Japanese market. Others, such as Apple, set up subsidiaries several years ago but put little effort into marketing. Their international marketing departments back home focused on Western consumers, because language and cultural barriers weren't as formidable. "We paid very little attention to markets in the Far East," says Alexander van Eyck, president of Apple's Japan subsidiary.

That's all changing. Foreign software and microcomputer companies are setting up subsidiaries and forming partnerships with Japanese distributors. Apple revamped its management here early this year to step up its sales effort. Lotus opened a Tokyo office and plans to sell a Japanese version of its main business program, Lotus 1-2-3. (The program combines accounting and data-base functions, and has led best-seller lists in the United States for years.)

Ashton-Tate, another U.S. concern, set up a joint venture last year with its Japanese distributor. Autodesk Inc., a software house specializing in computer-aided design programs, opened a Tokyo office last year.

Microsoft caused a minor stir in March by cutting off relations with its Japanese distributor and setting up a wholly owned Tokyo subsidiary.

"Microsoft has a very strong commitment to the Japanese market," says chairman William Gates. Japan is the company's largest market after the United States.

Many others are eager to get in. JI Consulting Inc., a Tokyo company that helps foreign software houses set up here, has been swamped by inquiries from U.S., Australian and European companies. "A few years ago we had to go out and contact companies to get their products over here," says William Smale, JI's president. "Now they're banging on our doors."

Foreign software houses view Japan as a potentially huge market, Smale says. The Japanese have about four million personal computers in use, or one machine for every 30 people. In the United States, there are about 21.5 million machines, or about one for every 11 people, according to InfoCorp., a Cupertino, California, market-research concern. Marketers expect that gap to narrow quickly, Smale says, translating into a Japanese boom in demand for machines and programs.

Japanese businesses haven't taken to business software as quickly as those in the West, partly because few good Japanese-language programs are available. Japanese consumers are just beginning to use the kinds of business programs Americans and Europeans have had for more than three years.

Local computer experts say that, although Japanese computers are often faster and cheaper than foreign machines, business software lags several years behind the United States. "There's really no competition," says Yuichi Murano, a researcher at Dataquest Japan Ltd., a consulting concern.

Foreign software companies think that could give them a big edge in Japan. Apple, for instance, believes that the sophisticated software in its Macintosh personal computer will capture Japanese users. Apple introduced a Japanese-language version of the machine last week.

'Can't Ignore' Japan

Apple has less than 1 percent of Japan's microcomputer market. But the company is pinning its hopes on Japanese and other Asian markets to help it increase international revenues to 35 percent of sales by 1989 from 22 percent last year. Says Apple's van Eyck, "You can't ignore the second-largest market in the world."

Tapping that market will be tough. Foreign high-tech companies say tailoring software for Japan involves more than just translating English programs into Japanese. One company, for example, found that Japanese users prefer having numbers on balance sheets appear in a grid of boxes, rather than standing alone as in Western programs. Japanese users also require clearer graphics and better color than Westerners, who mostly use monochrome screens.

To make matters tougher, many Japanese suffer from self-diagnosed "keyboard allergy." Unaccustomed to typewriters, many of the middle-aged managers who would be most likely to use foreign programs dislike keyboards. To cure the allergy, Lotus plans to include a hand-operated "mouse," a device that moves the cursor around on the computer screen, in the Japanese version of its 1-2-3 program, a feature the original doesn't have.

The technolgical hurdles in adapting software to Japan are so great that some companies have formed special engineering teams to tackle them. Microsoft's Tokyo operation for example, is its only subsidiary worldwide that has research-and-development capabilities. Lotus hired a Japanese software company and spent 18 months rewriting its program and adding scores of modifications.

SOURCE: *The Wall Street Journal* May 30, 1986, p. 22.

costly for many firms. Thus, they depend on secondary sources of information published by governments or private sources. While some data are competently collected, other data may not meet strict requirements and hence lack validity, reliability, relevance, or practicality. Even data gathered by the firm may not inspire confidence since the methods used in collecting the data often cannot be standardized or controlled.

There are a number of sources that can be used to pursue international marketing data. Business International Corporation, for example, is a private source of regularly updated international market information. Similarly, most major consulting firms also provide international market research services.

Most governments use their central banks, statistical bureaus, and specialized agencies to develop and publish data on the local economy's

FIGURE 6–3 The International Market Research Problem: Fit Facts to Fiction

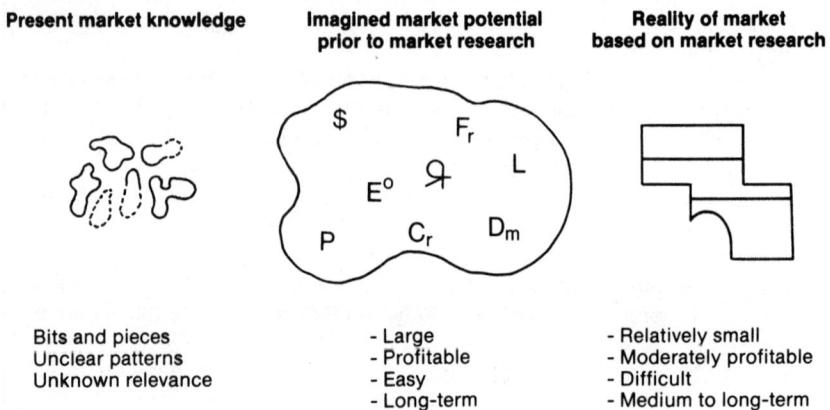

Present market knowledge	Imagined market potential prior to market research	Reality of market based on market research
Bits and pieces	- Large	- Relatively small
Unclear patterns	- Profitable	- Moderately profitable
Unknown relevance	- Easy	- Difficult
	- Long-term	- Medium to long-term

FIGURE 6–4 General Issues in International Marketing Research

---

Nature Of International Market Information—Broad in scope, uneven in coverage, differs in depth of coverage, differs in definitions from country to country.

Each Country Is A New Market—Low transferability and application of data from home to new situations.

Market Research Key Question Follows Goals And Strategy—Research depends on questions to be answered; data should address the needs of strategic and operational questions.

Identification Of User And Probable Utilization Of The Data—Motivations and expected use by different decision makers. Who are the decision makers? What are their legitimate information needs?

Need for Creative Talent In Adapting Research Methods To Situation—Ingenuity and resourcefulness (e.g., use of indirect indicators or estimation by analogy). Patience and persistence. Healthy skepticism that does not accept data at face value, cross-check information.

Integrity Of Market Research—Must resist pressure to adapt and interpret data in line with popular notions and favored solutions. Clarity of research goals, assumptions, methods, and potential weaknesses of studies undertaken.

Market Research Is NOT Equal To Management Decisions—Research provides data. Decisions require judgements based on reasonable interpretations of the data.

Research Is Not a Perfect Substitute For Personal Experience, Including Travel and Contacts Abroad.

---

performance. For example, in the United States the Federal Reserve Banks, the Census Bureau, Bureau of Labor Statistics, and Bureau of Economic Research create data banks that are used by other agencies including the Departments of State, Commerce, and Agriculture. There also are international organizations such as the International Monetary Fund (IMF), the Organization for Economic Cooperation and Development (OCED), and the United Nations that gather data. The challenge of international marketing research requires an intelligent sensitivity to data issues and a sensible response to its shortfalls. Figure 6–4 identifies the more general issues in doing international marketing research.

Market Mix Adjustments

The third major consideration is the degree to which the marketing mix must be adapted to meet the peculiarities of foreign markets. Adjustments may need to be made in response to barriers and opportunities presented by the country's level of economic development, cultural characteristics, and marketing practices. Figure 6–5 identifies the types of adjustments that might be required in the controllable aspects of the marketing mix. The key decision for the firm is to decide whether and how much to adapt the marketing mix for each country market. For most firms market attractiveness and competitive factors will determine the need for marketing mix adaptations.

Research on trade patterns and export behavior of companies suggests that firms first enter foreign markets that are similar to their home market. For example, empirical studies indicate that the range of a country's manufactured exports is strongly influenced by internal home country demand. This implies that a product will most likely be produced and consumed in a home market before it becomes a potential export product. Thus, a firm will export products it already knows how to make at home rather than create a new product for a foreign market. In this case, product design will not have to be extensively changed. Similarly, it has been shown that exporters, at least initially, tend to sell to markets that are most similar to home markets. This reduces the need to change market mix variables and also reduces the uncertainties of totally new market environments. Generally speaking, firms would often prefer to standardize both their marketing mix and operations rather than specialize for each separate country market because of efficiencies resulting from standardization. These include economies of scale, location benefits, low factor costs, and learning curve gains that yield lower costs and improved ability to compete.

Market Management Design and Control

The final consideration in marketing strategy is the design of the marketing system to ensure that implementation of strategy is consistent with firm goals and objectives. Design means to develop an appropriate "fit" among organization structure, human resources, and methods of control so organizational goals can be pursued effectively.

Marketing structure should include the major marketing functions of marketing research, product design and development, sales, advertising, and customer service. When an international dimension is introduced into corporate goals, adjustments often need to be made to ensure that coordination and control adjust to the increased complexity of international marketing. Organizational adjustments include the development of a separate international department or division, a project organization aimed at developing a particular product or market niche, and the creation of special functions such as custom brokerage or geographic or product line based structures. Regardless of the organizational form chosen, the major management issue is that of balanc-

FIGURE 6–5 Type of Adjustments to the Marketing Mix

Product
Product form
Product function/use
Features
Color/style

Price
Denominated currency
 of billing
Inflation factors
Wholesale/retail
 quotes practices
Transfer pricing
Export services costs

Promotion
Local advertising
 practices
Media availability
Message (form/content)
Use of sales promotion
Personal selling

Distribution
Use of traditional
 channels
Storage/warehousing
 availability
Channel incentive
 systems
Elite versus mass
 market orientation

Servicing
Warranty
Backup equipment and staff
On-site installation, adapt-
 ation, and repair
Instructions and technical
specifications translation
 to other languages

Payment
Acceptance of foreign currency
Barter and credit practices
Accounting practices
Collection practices
Countertrade requirements

Packaging
Export adapted
Form/function
Labeling
Branding and trade
 mark use

ing the need for differentiation and specialization of international functions with the need for overall integration of the marketing effort.

Complexity increases as the firm's international activities become more diverse. The marketing task for a small single product business in a single foreign market can be structured into an internal export-sales marketing department. As the volume grows and more products are added, however, the firm faces strategic commitments to the international market. Further proliferation of product offerings and expansion into new markets may require the development of an international division. Thus, what began as a relatively simple operation becomes increasingly complex to manage.

The international marketing design task also involves selecting, training, rewarding, and retraining employees. The problem for marketing design is to recruit and develop employees who can deal with the international dimensions of the marketing task.

Finally, the evaluation and control of international marketing effort involves the development of marketing performance indicators that can be used to guide decisions. Given the differences in time, location, language, culture, and attitudes towards performance evaluation, international marketing control is less easily managed.

INTERNATIONAL MARKETING OPERATIONS: MARKET MIX DECISIONS

The Product and Product Mix

Marketing has to work closely with other elements of the firm when considering the suitability of various products. There are considerations of product design, styling, cost, and so forth that must include design engineers, technical research personnel, production engineers, and country level managers. Products that meet the market needs of the home country may not be adequate for sale in other markets. It cannot always be assumed that there is little need for product modification. Suppose a product is not acceptable. Is it then fruitful to develop another product or product line to serve these markets? This can be determined only through market research including possibly the development of product prototypes that can be used to evaluate consumer preferences.

The more likely approach is to do a market research study to see what product modifications may be needed. Such studies can and do lead to new versions of a product that are better suited to foreign markets. For example, automobiles produced in the United States have generally been too large and fuel inefficient to meet the needs of most foreign markets. However, the American automakers developed entirely different versions of automobiles from those produced at home. These versions are made abroad and rely on European styling and smaller engines. These products have appeared in the U.S. market, but they were not produced in the United States. Many similar examples can be found in most industries.

Where consumer tastes abroad differ from those at home, it may be possible to alter these tastes through advertising. This has occurred in the fast-food field. It is more likely that the product will be altered to fit in with the differing needs of different markets, but it should be emphasized that there are limits to how far firms can go in doing this. As a rule of thumb, the more that cultural idiosyncracies influence national consumer tastes as they do in foods, automobiles, clothing, and household goods, the more likely it is that product modifications are needed to meet the needs of highly differentiated markets. Thus, so-called "consumers" goods are more likely to require modification than are industrial goods such as machinery.

Product modifications are often made in order to use locally supplied materials. Indeed, many countries, especially developing ones, are quite sensitive to the use of imported materials because such materials require payment in foreign exchange. Issues of national pride in local products may also be involved. As a consequence, firms are forced by the "local content" laws to modify the product and sometimes the manufacturing process to accommodate to local materials and other factor inputs that may be different from those used at home. This is quite often the case in developing countries where the technological capacity at times does not permit the manufacture of materials commonly used in many products made in the advanced countries. For example, silicon steel is used in the production of small electric motors in Europe, the United States, and Japan, but for cost and technology reasons this type of steel cannot yet be produced in a large number of developing countries. Older versions of electric motors, however, that were based on the use of cast iron can be constructed in most developing countries. These older versions are less efficient in their use of energy, but in the interests of local content and use of local materials, the older product versions are produced. This is not so much a matter of product modification as it is one of using an old design to meet a market constraint imposed by government policy.

To summarize, multinational firms do make adaptations to their products when they go abroad. These adaptations usually involve changes in styling and features rather than changes in function. There may be modifications in quality, but more likely these firms will adhere to the same quality standards abroad that they follow at home. Since reputation is an important element of strategy, quality is seldom sacrificed.

Promoting the Product

Perhaps the most important aspect of marketing strategy to be altered when going abroad is that of product promotion. Countries differ widely in the diversity and availability of communications media that can be used to bring products and services to the attention of potential consumers. As one moves up the scale of development, the mix of available advertising media changes from heavy reliance on word of mouth, newspapers, and radio to greater reliance on specialty magazines and television. However, there are exceptions. Some advanced countries have placed limits on the use of television as an advertising medium. France is but one example of a country that imposes such limits. Thus, a sound understanding of the availability and restrictions on use of the media is fundamental to the design of promotional strategies.

The choice of promotional techniques depends on the strategy chosen. There are two common strategies: a product push strategy and product pull strategy. A push strategy involves personal selling and price incentives to gain support of the retail and wholesale levels of trade to push the product. A pull strategy relies more upon advertising, in-store displays, and price promotions to "pull in" the consumer. Which of these strategies is used depends upon the available channels of distribution and the types and quality of promotional media. Generally, in developing countries the use of a push strategy rather than a pull strategy is more prominent. The opposite tends to be true in more advanced countries because the level of marketing development differs.

Firms cannot expect to pursue the same strategy abroad that they use at home—particularly if the home country is the United States where there is great freedom in the use of various communications media. For example, when Polaroid Corporation introduced its instant photography products into the French market it attempted to use much the same advertising methods it had used in the United States. The problem was that television advertising was not available as an advertising medium. It was important that potential customers see the product demonstrated. In the United States this could be accomplished by demonstrations made in television ads. In France the closest one could come to this type of advertising was in the movie theaters using similar ads, however, this constrained the audience that could actually see the product demonstrated to movie-goers. Even so, Polaroid spent only about 10 percent of its advertising budget on cinematic ads. It relied instead on magazine and newspaper ads that were less effective in demonstrating how the product operated. In addition, the incentives to dealers were not adequate to encourage them to demonstrate the product. There were other deficiencies in the promotional program, but the key point, and one learned the hard way, was that one should not blindly attempt to use a promotional program that is successful in one country in other countries as well. While it may work, it is more likely that a better program can be designed—one that more nearly matches the available media and distribution system to the needs of the product and its characteristics.

Advertising is not the only form of promotion of the product. In addition there are personal selling, publicity, and sales promotion. Personal selling consists of the use of sales persons and sales representatives. Publicity involves such things as news releases and product announcements, public relations such as plant tours and distribution of product samples, and general public relations of the firm such as community support activities like donations by the firm to worthy causes. Sales promotion includes in-store displays of the product, price reductions or other special offers, and cooperative advertising campaigns with retailers or wholesalers. The degree to which these types of promotion can be used, just as we noted with advertising, depends on local business ability and willingness to use them.

For example, U.S. exporters need to be aware that traditional modes of distribution in a foreign country market can inhibit the promotional strategy. Many country retailers have been accustomed to serving their elite home markets and are not mass retail oriented. They often have near monopoly distribution of certain products and can sell all their products relatively easily because they effectively control the supply. They therefore are not accustomed to competitive promotional strategies and may actively oppose or hinder them.

The promotional mix a firm can use will also be affected by physical factors. For example, in-store displays are difficult to use effectively where most of the stores are small because the number of people who actually see a display will be small also. In addition, small stores have little room for special displays. In countries where the retail distribution network has not evolved toward the large supermarket or discount house, in-store displays will not be an effective promotional device. The marketer must then rely upon personal selling to wholesalers and retailers to gain most of the in-store recognition for the product.

To illustrate the practical problem more clearly, take the case of an Italian firm attempting to sell kitchenware products through U.S. mass retail outlets such as Thrifty, K Mart Corp. or Uncle John's. These stores offer a large selection of products and compete mainly on price. Their products generally must sell themselves since there are few clerks to assist customers. Under these conditions the Italian firm should not attempt to sell through such stores any kitchenware products whose proper use must be demonstrated to potential customers.

Finally we must recognize that consumers need to learn what a promotion means. All consumers are not automatically receptive to promotions. They may not understand its purpose or assume the promotion is deceitful by nature. For example, free samples may be interpreted literally, that is, that the store is giving away the whole product free. They may assume the product's form in the package is the same as the sample, without understanding the preparation involved. Thus, promotion can be a misunderstood marketing tool if not used in a culturally sensitive way. Awareness of country limitations, in terms of what is possible and allowed, is necessary in analyzing the probable success of promotional strategies.

Channels of Distribution

Products are made available for purchase to a consumer by means of the channels of distribution. Channel structures, the relationships between the various kinds of firms that play a role in moving goods and services, differ because of the nature of the market structure and the level of socioeconomic development. In other words, different goods get to different consumers based on the ability to reach a defined market segment (e.g. middle class urban manufacturing workers) using defined channel means (e.g. neighborhood stores).

Figure 6–6 shows how a foreign market channel might look to a U.S. exporter. The choice of a channel is dictated by cost. This in turn is determined by the length of the channel and the numbers and kinds of services needed. If a firm cannot perform its own channel functions at lower cost, it should use outside agents. The best route to a market depends on the firms' knowledge of channel practices and its ability to use alternative methods. The more traditional and fragmented channels are, the more difficult it is to manage channel relationships. In developing countries there are often dual systems of distribution. One is traditional and often publicly managed. It meets the basic needs of the low income consumers. The other is often a modern retail system patterned after advanced countries and serves middle-class urban consumers.

One of the more notable aspects of the United States, when compared with any other country, is the enormous emphasis on mass marketing through chain store outlets or discount hardware stores. For a number of reasons most countries cannot begin to approach the United States in the proportion of total sales that go through multiple outlet enterprises. U.S. firms operating abroad cannot expect to find distribution systems that are as diverse or as fully developed within large multiple outlet retailing and wholesaling enterprises as those in the United States.

FIGURE 6-6   Channel Alternatives In International Marketing

Export Side		*Import Side*

◄───►

U.S. Producer	Export merchant	**Intermediary Services**	Import agent	
		Shipping lines		Foreign Consumer
	Export agent	Freight/Forwarder Customs house	Local wholesaler	
			Factory representative	
	Export marketing company	Port authorities		
		Banks	Retailer	

Factors In Channel Effectiveness And Cost

Technology development such as container shipping

Number and types of services provided (i.e. insurance, credit, packing, freight, storage, etc.

Channel Relations—linkages affected by ownership, contractual relations, traditional loyalties and practices

Government Regulation—competition policies, consumer protection, national security restrictions, protectionist policies

Transportation interface-development as in ships to rail to truck to plane

---

In most other countries the channels of distribution require greater direct effort by the producers of the product. This means that manufacturing firms must rely to a greater extent on personal selling that in turn calls for a larger sales force. The larger number of independently owned outlets results in smaller orders and thus requires more sales calls. Also, because of smaller and weaker wholesalers, the manufacturer often must take a larger role in warehousing the product and financing of wholesalers through which the product must flow. Because of the greater fragmentation some firms are forced to establish their own distribution systems. But this, too, may be difficult because of traditional ways of doing things. If there are long-standing business relationships within various trade groups, as there are in Japan, it may not be possible to gain acceptance for a new distribution channel.

Channel structure abroad often depends on how the retail trade level of distribution is organized; this largely depends on how the larger urban society is organized and how people shop for their goods. For example, in Japan, much of Europe, and many other locations, retailing is oriented to neighborhoods. There are many small stores. The people shop in their neighborhoods to a very large extent as pedestrians, that is, they walk to the neighborhood store. Items such as bread, fresh vegetables, meat, and dairy products are purchased almost on a daily basis. Large combination freezer/refrigerator units are not common in the home and storage space is at a premium because the people live mostly in apartments with small kitchens. Shopping patterns then are dictated by living arrangements and these call for neighborhood shops. Thus, it is difficult for firms to establish a system of large volume outlets that depend heavily on a broad base of customers from more than a single neighborhood. In the United States the urban society reflects the dominant emphasis on consumer mobility, large storage capacity, and the automobile.

Marketing regulations often perpetuate channels of distribution. Retailers and wholesalers are highly protected in many countries. Specialty shops are protected by regulations that preclude distribution of a particular product except through these specialty shops. For example, in the United States a wide variety of patent medicines can be sold through virtually any retail outlet; in many other countries these medicines can be sold only through drug stores. Much the same could be said of products such as liquor, electrical appliances, and hardware. Only recently have large discount stores emerged outside the United States and then only on a limited scale. The norm continues to be the small specialized retailer and wholesaler.

Channels of distribution affect other aspects of the marketing mix. They impinge on promotion in particular. For example, as we have noted, if most of the retail outlets are small the rate of sale per store will also be small. Consequently, for reason of cost relative to benefits, use of large, elaborate in-store displays is ruled out as a means of building consumer interest in a product. In fact, it may even be difficult to obtain shelf space for a product. The result of this type of distribution system is that firms must rely more heavily on a skilled sales force to conceive retailers to stock a product. The key for international marketers is to identify the nature of the distribution channels and the degree to which they can be used as a means to implement existing marketing strategies.

Product Pricing

At first glance it would seem that pricing of a product or service would be quite simple. All one need do is figure out the cost of producing and distributing the product and then price it accordingly. If the cost is greater in one country than in another then the price would differ between the two countries. While there is a nugget of truth in this view, there is more than this to the pricing decision. A simple cost approach to pricing looks only at the supply side of the supply and demand relationship.

In countries where there is little competition the price can usually be higher than where there is strong competition from other similar products. This depends, however, on other things like the level of income, consumer tastes, and availability of distribution channels. In many low income countries there is little competition, but the price that covers costs may not attract many customers because the income base is not adequate.

Furthermore, culture can be a constraint that causes consumers to resist. What may be considered a bargain in one culture may be considered exorbitant in another. Consumer priorities can also differ for reasons other than relative income levels. For example, at the same relative income level the average German consumer might be more willing to buy an expensive automobile than would the average American.

There are other elements to pricing. Prices cannot differ too much across countries in relation to cost otherwise smart traders could buy the product in the country with the lowest price and sell the product in countries with higher prices. Thus, a large multinational firm cannot charge whatever it pleases. If it does, independent traders will fulfill the arbitrage role of buying in low-price countries and selling in higher-price countries. The limit on price differentials is the cost of transporting the product between countries plus any added costs due to customs duties, distribution, and marketing within the country having the higher price. It should be noted that firms often engage in price discrimination whereby the price in the home country is higher than in the foreign country. This occurs in situations where the good is being exported from the home country but requires that the demand characteristics of foreign countries differ from those of the home country. Under these circumstances the firm can maximize its profits by pricing the good differently across countries. Whether the price in the foreign country is higher or lower than in the home country depends on the elasticities of demand and the marginal costs of serving each market. For example, even though Japanese auto manufacturers must incur transport costs to the United States, the price of an identical automobile may be lower in the United States than in Japan because the U.S. market is large and marketing costs are much lower than in Japan.

Governments figure into the pricing decision in many ways. Some countries use various schemes of prices control including outright specification of what prices are to be and the degree to which prices can be raised or lowered from some base price. Retail price maintenance is quite common in many countries. Under retail price maintenance it may be illegal to engage in discount pricing, for example. Usually though, governments are more concerned with the amounts by which firms can raise prices from year to year. This is especially true in countries that are undergoing rapid rates of price inflation. Price control is used as a tool to compensate for economic mismanagement and too rapid expansion of the money supply that causes inflation, but this type of control often results in so-called "black markets" in which illegal transactions take place. Generally, large firms are more tightly policed to guard against such transactions. Consequently, multinational firms may be at a disadvantage in countries that use price controls simply because they are quite visible and are more easily policed than are small local entrepreneurs.

To summarize this section on marketing mix decisions, firms operating abroad face many problems in the development of marketing strategy that calls for close examination of the need for product modification, alteration of promotion programs, development of distribution channels, and special treatment of product pricing. Making the needed adjustments requires more than simple solutions. Firms must evaluate each aspect of the marketing mix to determine the combination best suited to each market. Usually the solution will differ from that considered appropriate for the home country.

CONTEMPORARY INTERNATIONAL MARKETING ISSUES

The growth and success of international marketing has contributed to the internationalization of domestic economies. This has been a long-term process but demonstrates that marketing efforts can be successful despite the difficulties of dealing with rapidly changing country environments. However, the future success of international marketing depends on a number of issues.

Four particular issues provide important challenges: the role of marketing in economic development, the rise of a world customer, the effect of marketing on culture, and the increasing attraction of bilateral trade agreements. The importance of each of these issues will be briefly reviewed.

Marketing and Economic Development

The role of marketing and its contribution to economic development of all nations appears to be on the increase. The economic success of the Japanese vis-a-vis the United States can be attributed in large part to their success as marketers.[2] Perhaps the comparative weakness of the U.S. economy vis-a-vis Japan may result from a lack of strong marketing efforts by U.S. firms in competition with Japan.

The U.S. government has explicitly recognized this problem in re-

---

[2] P. Kotler, Liam Fahey, and S. Jatusripitals, *The New Competition* (Englewood Cliffs, N.J.: Prentice-Hall, 1985).

cent legislation and programs designed to increase U.S. exports. For example, the creation of Foreign Sales Corporations gives tax benefits for exports while the Export Trading Company Act gives firms protection against antitrust liability if their joint efforts lead to the development of export markets.

Developing nations are diversifying their economies away from production of basic commodities to higher-valued industrial and consumer products. This shift requires more attention to customer needs. Many of these products are more sophisticated and involve specialized use. Thus, they tend to require higher quality control standards and postpurchase product support. For example, Brazil's entrance into the U.S. light aircraft industry not only requires meeting customer standards but also requires constant attention to government regulations. Moreover Brazil faces stiffer competition in the United States than at home. As compared with the product orientation of yesteryear, today more attention must be paid to contemporary marketing and its sophisticated consumer orientation.

One aspect of marketing poses a dilemma because of its influence on developing countries' consumption patterns. Two problems are of concern. The consumption of foreign goods requires the use of foreign exchange. Since foreign exchange is needed to buy capital goods for investment in new industries, its use for consumer goods is seen as wasteful of a scarce factor of production. Secondly, increased consumption reduces the savings rate which in turn reduces capital formation. Therefore, since marketing encourages increased consumption, it is often seen as a threat to industrialization strategies. To counter this, some countries institute strong savings oriented programs, as in Japan, to reduce consumption and dependence on foreign markets. Yet an increased ability to consume foreign products is an important indicator of an improved personal and national standard of living, the goal of all governments. Some governments realize that to make modernization pay for itself an increase in international marketing effort will improve the flow of exports to pay for the increased demand for imports. The logic of economic development requires this. Thus, the marketing function is likely to play a growing role even in developing nations.

A World Customer

The rise of the "world customer" is related to the marketing function.[3] A number of writers have argued that tastes for many products will become universal and national tastes will converge. Hence there will be

---

[3] R.Z. Sorenson and U.E. Wiechmann, "How Multinationals View Marketing Standardization," *Harvard Business Review*, May-June 1975, pp. 72–80.

a worldwide market for many products. Developing as well as developed nations' consumers are seen as wanting the same basic attributes in a wide variety of products including automobiles, consumer appliances, and fast foods, for example. Methods of marketing also seem to reflect this convergence. Since each country has significant segments of consumers that can purchase such goods, it is possible for the marketer to think in terms of a global market and not just a large number of differentiated national markets. This allows standardized market mix strategies and yields benefits of economics of scale. This reduces the number of separate marketing programs needed.

The existence of a true world customer is both fact and fiction. For some products like blue jeans, the portable calculator, or certain footwear, there are worldwide markets, so a wide variety of nations do not require much differentiation in marketing effort.

Increased communications of lifestyles and greater exposure to material goods as a basis of the "good life" has led to a slow but perceptible emphasis on commonalities among peoples. National differences as a way of establishing product differentiation may disappear.

Marketing Influence on Culture

Research demonstrates that marketing activities can influence national culture. It appears that as an economy develops, consumers' desires for foreign products increase. This happens because of increased income and increased awareness arising from travel and improved communications. Foreign products are often seen as superior in quality and/or are more fashionable. Whatever the motive some consumers, when possible, will choose foreign products that are seen to have desirable attributes not available in domestically supplied products. The problem of culture arises when the demand for foreign products reaches such a level that national products and consumer customs that are seen as basic to national identity are threatened. For example, the American fast-food business has been criticized in France as threatening to French cuisine, family eating habits, and even the French language as "le hamburger" or "le Colonel's chicken" become popularized words. Furthermore, heavily emphasized materialist and capitalist values are often seen as inherent in the production and consumption of foreign products. To national elites with "cultured" values and nonmaterialist pretensions, foreign materialism is often anathema. Underlying these fears is an imagined homogenization and standardization of consumer habits into a worldwide consumer ethos that threatens national identities. Thus, the fear that we will all become "mindless consumers with vulgar tastes" in part drives the desire to protect national identity, values, and customs.

Beyond the threat of standardization of consumer tastes, however, the concern is also aimed at *controlling the means* of cultural expression. For example, the fact that U.S. companies produce a majority of the magazines and literature that Canadians read has sparked controversy about the "Americanization" of Canadian national values. Control over the media and telecommunications thus becomes a focus for dispute.

Trade Bilateralism

The fourth issue is a very complex one. World trade relations appear to be moving towards a reduced use of multinational trade agreements, such as the General Agreements on Tariffs and Trade (GATT). Indeed, a number of countries are turning to bilateral (two-country) agreements.

The implications for marketing of protectionism and bilateralism are direct. Protectionism makes domestic goods less competitive in international markets and closes off some foreign markets. Bilateralism means that two countries can make special agreements between themselves the benefits of which need not apply to third country transactions. This can take the form of special prices, orderly marketing agreements or tied marketing arrangements. The resulting differential treatments of country markets goes against the multilaterism of international trade agreements and threatens to increase trade friction. If this trend continues and a new round of GATT talks fails, the implications for marketers is a world of increasing fragmented and isolated markets. It also means markets will be less open and require more negotiated agreements on access and share of markets. Under these circumstances the marketing task becomes increasingly complex.

SUMMARY

In summary, this chapter shows how the marketing function differs when a marketer moves from serving a domestic market to serving the international market. By recognizing the key differences that exist, the marketers face a number of major decisions concerning where, when, and how to serve foreign markets. This requires the firm to make an assessment of its own capabilities in relation to the foreign market's potential. It must also assess the need for adaptation in the marketing mix required to serve that market. Once the commitment to international marketing is made, the entry strategy and experience leads to a continual assessment on how the foreign market can be more effectively exploited and how benefits can be shared across marketing efforts in different countries.

DISCUSSION QUESTIONS FOR CHAPTER SIX

1. Of all the business functions, marketing is often the most internationalized. Why would marketing be different from accounting or finance in this respect?

2. Distinguish between marketing factors that are "controllable" versus "noncontrollable." In what ways do they differ?

3. If a country's offering of products on the world market represents the outcome of its production capabilities (function), what does a country's consumption function represent? What factors affect the consumption function?

4. How would you explain the international marketing challenge as seen in Figure 6–2? What are the key goals? Major tasks? Problems to be overcome?

5. The international marketing strategy involves a number of key strategic considerations. What are they?

6. Market research abroad is a significantly more difficult task than in the domestic market. What factors do you think would contribute to this difficulty?

7. Suppose your company sells a top line of beauty/skin care products in U.S. markets that you are considering moving to markets in Japan, Brazil and Australia. What kind of product, packaging, and promotion adjustments might need to be made for each of these country markets?

8. We have all learned about the "4 P's" of marketing. Yet when you go abroad there is an important "5th P"—payment. How does payment affect the market mix?

9. Given the channels relations in Figure 6–6, what are the key strategic decisions in the use of channel intermediaries? (Hint: decisions affect price and customer.)

10. What factors directly affect the price one can charge on U.S. goods sold abroad? Which factors does a manager control?

11. "Marketing is the most damaging capitalist invention from a developing nations perspective. It drains savings potential for development through its encouragement of consumption of luxury and useless products; it introduces false materialistic values that corrupt a nation's culture and it reduces us all to a single mindless world customer where variety and differentness give way to humdrum sameness." Do you agree?

_____

CHAPTER SEVEN

Decisions in Production Management

INTRODUCTION

In this chapter we discuss the problems firms encounter when they decide to install or expand production facilities in countries other than their own home country. From what has been said in previous chapters it should be obvious that the decision to invest abroad involves a somewhat different set of decisions than investing at home.

As we have noted, firms have various reasons for deciding to develop international operations and they have several institutional devices with which they can do so. What is key here is the extent to which the firm has special resources it can exploit. If it has not been able to differentiate itself significantly from other firms through some kind of competitive advantage such as technology, it is not likely that the firm will have much to offer that cannot be offered by others. Hence, the level of competition will be high. Accordingly, it has little basis for investing abroad since local firms and other international competitors can offer the same goods or services. The more we move from a competitive business environment to one of imperfect competition where individual firms have differentiated themselves through ownership of unique or specialized assets, the more likely the firm will have a basis for engaging in international production. The more valuable that set of assets is, the more likely the firm will choose to invest abroad to exploit this special distinctiveness.

TAKING ADVANTAGE OF UNIQUE PRODUCTION CAPABILITIES

There are various ways in which firms can exploit their unique capabilities, particularly the manufacturing enterprises. However, the concepts need not be confined to the production of physical goods. Firms in the service fields of finance, insurance, transportation, travel and lodging, engineering/construction, management consulting, mining, and other fields also have specialized knowledge and techniques in the services that they provide for international markets. To simplify the analysis we concentrate on large manufacturing enterprises that produce products at home and abroad. These firms have several choices regarding how best to apply their technology and know-how. As we noted in Chapters Two and Five, it is largely special knowledge that allows these firms to compete in markets outside the borders of their home country. Two key questions, regardless of the nature of the business, are: What are the various ways in which special enterprise capabilities can be exploited? How much control and ownership is necessary?

Firms have many options and do any one or all of the following:

1. They can produce products at home and export these to be marketed in other countries.
2. They can export the know-how required to produce the products through licensing agreements with other firms operating abroad. These firms can be owned by local interests in the host country or owned by other foreign firms. In this case the licensor usually does not take possession of the final outputs.
3. They can contract with firms abroad to produce the product on contract in which case they do take possession of the goods that may be sold in markets other than that of the host country. For example, U.S. Beatrice Foods Company may contract with Scholhammer International in Germany to produce milled grain products for sale in southern European markets.
4. They can install manufacturing plants abroad to produce the products for the host country market only or additional markets outside of the host country including the home country market.
5. They can establish joint ventures in which they supply most of the know-how but do not take full ownership of the production facilities.

The issue of ownership strategies was taken up in Chapter Two. The firm's ownership strategy depends on several variables. The more important and valuable the assets or specialized knowledge are to a firm, the greater is the incentive to keep ownership to itself. An asset's uniqueness, relative to demand for it, puts the firm in a strong position to exploit market conditions of low or no competition. Thus, if the sharing of information could be damaging to long-run profitability, it is likely that a firm would not become involved in licensing agreements, supply contracts, or joint ownership ventures where the sharing of know-how is essential. For example, the production of microwave ovens was licensed in Japan over 10 years ago. Since then the

Japanese have become major competitors to the original U.S. manufacturers. Where the know-how is valuable, it will be kept within the firm to the greatest extent possible. This means that the two methods of doing business abroad will tend to be manufacturing of the final product at home with exportation of the product to foreign markets or, if there is to be manufacturing abroad, it will take place only in wholly owned subsidiaries.

There are some modifying conditions to the strategy of keeping ownership internal to the firm. If the firm's investment involves high risk, it may seek risk-sharing partners. In that case most partners will probably demand some ownership control as a condition for entering the venture. Secondly, a firm may need the specialized assets of another company to get the value out of its own asset or the rate of return it requires for an investment. In that case both firms are risking some loss of proprietary advantage because they must share know-how. The General Motors-Toyota joint venture in car production in California may be such a case. Thus, there are some circumstances that will require a firm to modify its ownership and control goals. However, in most cases, firms still prefer to maintain control and autonomy.

Market Entry Decisions

The decision to enter the market comes once the market has been assessed in terms of size, location of major centers of concentration, and accessibility. Assuming that there are adequate elements of marketing infrastructure like distribution channels and promotional media, the next decision is that of determining the method of entry. Some firms prefer to export from the home country for as long as possible before deciding to establish production facilities abroad. Exporting is a low-risk strategy since firms may use agents to perform all export work. However, wisdom would suggest that firms should constantly monitor the situation and have a prepared strategy of international production. Too often economic and political conditions change in disadvantageous ways. For example, a market can be closed off by prohibitive tariffs that preclude the servicing of that market by exports from a multinational firm's home country. If the firm has not developed a plan for domestic production in the country, then a market developed through exports may be threatened or even taken away by competitive firms. When such political developments occur, being first with a new production facility in the country is important.

It is not only the current costs of production that firms must concern themselves with. They must also be concerned with the cost of having markets denied to them because of government threat and tariff and quota actions. Some of the recent moves by Japanese and European automobile manufacturers to establish production facilities in the United States are probably in response to the possibility of a "tariff wall" which would keep exports down. One result was a voluntary export quota negotiated between the United States and Japan. By having facilities in the United States, these manufacturers have a strategic option of production in a host market that can be expanded should the political situation change to reduce access to the U.S. market via exports. Throughout the remainder of this section we will be dealing with the situation in which the firm has already decided to install a plant to serve an existing export market.

Logistics of Plant Design and Location

What are the elements of the decision to install a plant? And what are the strategies open to firms in designing a multicountry production system? At a more specific level the questions in Figure 7–1 are pertinent to these broader questions.

As seen in News Box 7–1, the logistics problems of producing vehicles in China continues to plague foreign producers.

These questions can be addressed under four categories of decisions: (1) plant design, (2) selection of production processes, (3) plant location, and (4) production control. A fifth heading which usually is included is that of product design was discussed in Chapter Six. Here

---

FIGURE 7–1 Production Logistics Decisions

---

1. Which product or products should we produce?
2. How many units of each product should we produce?
3. Should we install a single plant or should be have multiple plants?
4. Where should the plant(s) be located? Which countries or regions?
5. What production methods should be used in each?
6. How should the plant be designed and configured?
7. Should the plant be a general purpose plant or should it be specialized?
8. How should this plant fit into the larger production system of the firm, that is, should it be a stand-alone plant or should it interact with other plants by using inputs from other plants or providing inputs to other plants?
9. How highly integrated should the plant be in terms of the processes included? Should we make our own parts and components or buy them from someone else?
10. What constraints do we face in terms of raw materials, financing components, labor skills, and access to technology?
11. Given consumers' tastes and buying patterns, what is required in terms of product quality, size and frequency of production runs, and inventories?

NEWS BOX 7-1
Jeep Production Is Resumed in Peking
James R. Schiffman, Vigor Fung, and Julia Leung

Assembly of jeeps resumed at American Motors Corporation's troubled joint venture in Peking after company and Chinese officials negotiated a compromise that provides for injections of fresh foreign exchange.

Work at the Beijing Jeep Corporation plant had stopped for two months when the venture ran out of hard currency to purchase jeep parts from A.M.C. in the United States. China agreed to loosen its currency controls to make more foreign exchange available after A.M.C. agreed to scale down production of jeeps made from imported parts, a move that also allowed the joint venture to invest in facilities to make parts in China.

The A.M.C. venture has taken on an importance to other foreign investors in China far beyond its size. As one of the earliest Sino-foreign experiments in heavy manufacturing, the joint venture had been touted as a flagship of China's open-door policy. But when problems developed, the company's difficulties began to epitomize problems faced by many, if not most, joint ventures in China.

SOURCE: *The Wall Street Journal*, Thursday, August 28, 1986, p. 20.

---

we assume the decision on product design and adaptation has been made.

Plant Design

Plant design and layout depends on the product or products to be produced in the plant and the degree to which different processes are to be included. The products to be produced in a plant is a question of both marketing and production economics as well. Marketing research can be used to assess market size and consumers' tastes and thereby help in identifying how much of what products will probably be marketed. Once these are known, the decision about whether or not the product should be made rests on the economics of the manufacturing process. Goods differ in terms of the technologies used in their production. Some products may use the same equipment in their assembly and hence are complementary. Often it makes economic sense to produce such goods together in the same plant. However, if products require distinctly different processes, there may be little or no reason to make them under the same roof. It may make economic sense to have more than a single plant, so here the economics of location come into play. For example, a firm that is manufacturing dairy products and vegeta-

ble oil products may use two plants instead of one. It is more economical to transport raw milk in bulk than to transport the final products.
Thus, milk processing plants are usually located near centers of consumption near large cities. Also, the shelf life of many dairy products
is short so that once the milk is processed it should be moved to market
as quickly as possible. Thus, the distance from the processing plant to
centers of consumption should be relatively short. Vegetable oil products, on the other hand, usually have longer shelf lives and do not have
to be moved to market quickly. Thus, it is less important to be near
centers of consumption and hence there is more latitude in the choice
of plant location. Moreover, dairy products and vegetable oil products
involve different processing methods and little money will be saved by
making the two types of products in the same plant.

One of the important criteria in plant design is that of economies of
scale. Generally, final assembly stages of manufacturing can be undertaken economically in smaller volumes than can the production of
parts and components. Thus, the size of a fully integrated plant, which
includes all of the manufacturing processes, depends on the economic
volume required to gain the economies of scale of the highest volume
process. For example, suppose the assembly stage of production requires only 50,000 units per year to achieve the lowest production cost
but the parts making stages requires 100,000 units per year; the
smallest integrated plant would be one with a capacity of 100,000
units per year. If the market size is only 50,000 units per year, then
only the final assembly stage of production would be included in the
plant and the parts and components needed in manufacturing probably would be imported from abroad.

Depending on conditions, there may be several competing sources
of supply of parts and components as is outlined in Figure 7–2.

There are various options open to multinational firms serving
markets using combinations of local production and sources of supply
from the parent firm or other sister subsidiaries located in other countries. Also, a plant may rely on independent vendors either located in
the host country or abroad—these may be locally owned or foreign-
owned vendors. For example, General Motors Corp. and Ford Motor
Co. in their automobile plants in Brazil purchase some of their needed
parts and components from locally owned firms and other parts from
foreign-owned firms; they produce some of their own parts and components; some components are imported from the parent firms in the
United States as well as some from subsidiaries in Europe. This gives
firms many options in its supply logistics. This is also why some firms
are truly global in their strategies.

Plant design depends on a variety of factors including the degree to
which there are reliable vendors of quality products already available

FIGURE 7–2   Degree of System Integration

	Company Sources of Supply	*Independent Sources of Supply*
Imported parts and Components	Parent Overseas sister subsidiary	Independent vendor
Locally Produced Parts and Components	Own production Production from local sister subsidiary	Locally owned vendor Local subsidiary of other foreign-owned firm

in the country. Also important here is the degree to which the country allows importation of components and parts. The larger the local market, the greater the constraints on importing parts and components will probably be. This happens because the greater the importation of component parts, the more foreign exchange will be used up paying for them. Also, a larger local market suggests that local manufacturing could reach an economy of scale, making those parts competitive with imports. This, of course, assumes that the quality of domestic-made parts is comparable to that of imports. The less reliable are outside sources of supply of parts and components, the more highly integrated will the plant be in terms of the number of components produced and the processes included in the plant. Under these circumstances it is better to invest in a whole plant than to risk uncertain supplies of key parts and components.

Plants can vary in design from being simply an assembly operation with nearly complete reliance on local country vendors for parts and components to increasingly higher levels of manufacturing of one's own parts and components up to the point where virtually everything used in final assembly is produced in the plant itself. Stated differently, plants can vary from having a very low level of integration to being nearly fully integrated. The decision regarding the degree of integration is very important to firms that have multiple operations abroad. Essentially the firm needs to decide where the greatest efficiencies are to be gained: Should it integrate production in-house? Should it contract with outside vendors? Should it import parts and components from another branch plant?

In a multiple plant system one must decide whether to have plants that are independent of one another or to have an integrated system of interdependent plants. A major problem with a system in which the plants are highly interdependent is the danger of having supplies coming from another country cut off by import controls, labor strikes, transportation difficulties, or curtailed sources of foreign exchange. At the same time, an interdependent system allows for greater exploitation of economies of scale. In many instances an efficient size of plant may exceed the amount of production needed for a single market. By serving several markets in more than a single country, economies of scale can be achieved when this type of condition exists. However, it should be recognized that such a system is potentially more risky than a system of less-efficient, stand-alone plants. The riskiness usually emanates from government intervention or from changes in exchange rate values.

To summarize, plant design depends on the goods to be produced, the size of market, and the degree of plant integration. In addition, the degree of integration depends on government policy and the reliability of local and overseas sources of supply of raw materials, parts, components, and the like. Also of importance is the extent to which the firm is attempting to establish an internationally integrated system of interdependent plants. Where risks are high in serving a country market from abroad, the greater will be the incentive to establish a plant within the country and the higher will be the level of plant integration.

Selection of Production Processes

Once a firm has decided to establish a plant, it must select the processes to use in each aspect of production. The process to be used usually depends on the nature of product complexity, the volume of production, and the cost of equipment, the need for special conditions as power supplies or material quality, and labor. It also depends on competitor technology and government incentives for modernizing technology. There usually are several options from which to choose at each level of production. Sometimes we refer to this as the "choice of technology." The degree to which a plant installed abroad will differ from one at home in terms of its production processes depends on the size of the market to be served and the expected cost of using different manufacturing processes. Where market size is great enough to accommodate an efficient size of plant and where the costs of labor and equipment do not differ much from costs in the home country, there is likely to be little difference between plants at home and those installed abroad. Where we see major differences is in situations where the market is small and/or the wage rate is substantially different from the wage rate at home. Of course it should be recognized that the availability of skills is also important. If a particular process requires special skills that cannot be found in the host country, that process may have to be left out of the plant's design; whether it is or not depends on whether or not the skills can be acquired or developed. Sometimes, because skills are lacking, it simply is not economical to try to use technologically difficult processes. This is particularly true in many of the developing countries. Not only may the operating skills be lacking, but also, and perhaps more important, the skills needed to maintain complex equipment are lacking. Where this is the case, it may be possible to substitute a simple technology to accomplish the same purpose.

In the developing countries multinational firms often use older plant designs that were originally used in the already advanced countries. In fact there are times when an existing plant in the United States or another advanced country is dismantled, shipped abroad, and reassembed in another country. For example, in the semiconductor industry firms headquartered in the United States and Japan have taken older plants to Malaysia to produce standardized semiconductors. The production process tends to be labor intensive and it is accordingly more economical to produce these products in countries where the wage rate is much lower than in the United States or Japan.

The quality and availability of raw materials was mentioned as a factor in the selection of technology. Material inputs are not necessarily uniform throughout the world. For example, wood fiber from the exact same species of tree may vary because of different growing conditions in different countries. This may require adaptation of equipment. Furthermore the availability of an input is important. Possibilities of longer-term access to high quality supplies may lead to decisions to install larger and more modern equipment in a plant. In cases where supplies of traditional inputs are cut off, the adaptability of a technology to substitute materials may be an important criteria in production process choice.

To deal with situations where markets are small, as they are in many developing countries, firms in some industries have developed special plant designs. For example, in the automobile industry firms have developed special assembly plant designs for low-volume operations. In some of these small plants perhaps no more than 10 units per day are assembled. The process uses mainly small power tools and the assembly line may not even include a conveyor system. The process is very labor intensive since there is little investment in automatic machines.

To summarize, selection of processes depends on a known set of factors, which include the size of market, the availability of resources, and the cost of labor. Where the market is large and wage rates high, plants installed abroad tend to be very similar to those installed at home. In countries where the wage rate is low, there is an effort to include more labor in the process, which means that much of the automatic equipment seen in plants in the United States is excluded. Where markets are small, plants require special designs for the low volume of operation. Processes that require large volumes of output in order to be economical are not found in these small plants. Most of the small volume plants are found in the developing countries where wage rates are also low. Thus, emphasis is placed on the use of labor-intensive processes where possible.

Location of Production Plants

There are several considerations in the location of plants abroad. Much depends on whether the plant is to be a stand-alone plant or is to be a part of an integrated complex in which one plant depends on another. Also, if there is to be an integrated system, the system can reside in a single country or it can be a complex of plants which crosses national boundaries. In Europe GM and Ford have specialized plants that make engines and transmissions to serve several assembly plants located in other countries. Ultimately the objective is to locate plants in such a way that the total costs of serving markets can be minimized. Thus, markets again enter the equation. Production should take place in locations that achieve lowest total costs but not necessarily the lowest cost of production in terms of raw materials, labor, or transportation. For example, it may be possible to achieve the lowest cost of producing the product by locating the plant in a developing country that has very low wage costs. However, these low wage costs may be more than offset by the cost of transporting the product to the key markets where the product is to be consumed. There is some optimum that should be struck so that the combination of costs is at its lowest for a given product of a given quality. But as we have noted above, this also has to be tempered by the degree to which products may be complementary. To achieve least costs it may be necessary to produce several products in a single plant. Taking all of these elements into consideration makes the decision on plant location a very complex one.

Another element in deciding on the country of location has to do with the policies of various countries. Many countries offer investment incentives to firms to invest within their borders. Within countries certain areas are often designated as being "preferred areas." If firms are willing to locate in these areas the incentives may be quite attractive. For example, in Great Britan if a firm is willing to locate an investment in Liverpool, the British Government will provide cash grants equal to 22 percent of the investment. In addition, the firm can take accelerated depreciation on its plant. Most countries have similar programs that they use to entice investment into economically depressed areas. Also, there may be a desire in these types of programs to encourage firms to invest outside of highly congested urban areas. These types of incentives affect not only the location decision between countries but also the location within a country.

If the plant is to serve as a supply source to other plants in a multiplant system, or if it is to serve more than a single country market, or if it is to do both, then the decision is much different than one in which the plant is independent of such influences. Whether the plant is to be a single stand-alone plant or is to be part of a larger, more complex system depends on: (1) the industry the firm is in, (2) the complexity of the firm itself, and (3) the country environment being served. Where the country's market is small and the plant's presence is induced by tariff protection, the plant is likely to be a stand-alone plant. Where the decision is not influenced by such considerations, the decision will depend on the complexity of the firm's product line and the degree to which it already has plants operating abroad. It is under these latter circumstances that the location decision becomes extremely important to the overall success of the firm's international operations.

To summarize, the decision regarding which country is best and which site within a country is best depends on a balanced trade-off of choices among factor costs, the economics of the market, and government incentives. News Box 7–2 highlights some of these criteria in GM's intention to set up a joint production venture with Egypt in car manufacturing.

Production Control

Once a plant is operational it must be monitored. Doing this has come to be known as production control. Production control includes planning and scheduling of inputs and outputs, quality control, inventory control, and plant maintenance. There may be little differences in an international context than in the home country setting, but there usually are differences. For one thing, communication may take longer and yet it may be more critical because the plants may serve multiple markets and rely on one another. Thus, assessing the amounts of outputs required from each plant can be a complex problem. Also, because individual country markets may differ, there can be a need for a wider variety of product versions. This complicates not only the scheduling of production, but also requires greater attention to inventories of final products as well as raw materials and components. The cost of financing and housing inventories increases as the number of product versions increases and as the number of markets to be served increases.

NEWS BOX 7–2
GM–Egyptian Joint Production Venture

General Motors Corp. appears to be edging ahead of the Italians, the French, and the Japanese in the competition to build cars here in a joint venture with the government.

GM's plan calls for a joint venture with Egypt's state-owned Nasr Car Co. to assemble two lines of GM's Opel cars to sell in Egypt. The component makers manufacture parts for GM's Opel Anscona and Corsa four-door passenger cars that would be made in Egypt, and they also would export parts.

Firms that already have signed up to start operations in Egypt if GM's offer is accepted include TRW, to make steering components; Kelsey-Hayes, wheels and brakes; Pittsburgh Plate Glass, paints and coatings; Inland, a GM subsidiary making seats and headliners; and DI Avia of Italy, air-conditioners.

GM is luring component manufacturers with a promise that its Opel subsidiary, which makes the medium-sized Ascona in West Germany and the small Corsa in Spain, will buy a portion of its annual component requirements from Egypt. A GM official estimates the new component industries would export at least 60 percent of their Egyptian production.

While GM initially only intends to make cars for sale in Egypt, the move would position the company near what many consider to be a growth market in the rest of Africa. In the initial stage, the $700 million investment project wouldn't earn Egypt much-needed hard currency for its hard-pressed economy because the joint venture would need to import components not manufactured in Egypt. By one conservative estimate, half the foreign exchange needed to buy those imported components would be met by the project's exports over five years.

GM's guarantee provides a ready market for its plants exports, which is crucial because local demand—an estimated 50,000 to 60,000 cars per year—wouldn't provide an economy of scale.

SOURCE: Excerpted and adapted from an article by Barbara Rosewicz, "GM Is Leading Bidder for Joint Venture With Egypt's State-owned Auto Firm," in *The Wall Street Journal*, September 12, 1985, p. 34.

This is another reason why firms attempt in their marketing programs to induce consumers in different countries to consume the same products. If this can be accomplished successfully, the costs of production and inventories can be reduced and operations simplified.

In conjunction with the above, if the product line can be kept to one or a few product versions, production scheduling, plant design, technology selection, and plant location can be simplified. Production runs can be longer and hence the cost of changing over from the production of one product to another can be reduced. From this it can be seen that marketing strategy has a great deal to do with how the production system is to be designed. That in turn has a great deal to do with the costs of production. Production control then must be viewed more broadly than merely an activity that occurs after a plant is put into place. Production control should be looked upon as a key element in the overall design of the production schedule.

The role of control in product quality is of particular importance. The Japanese production processes have achieved high product quality. They use it as a strategic competitive tool because the country-of-origin effect is an important factor in purchasing decisions. People tend to buy Japanese products because of an overall reputation for quality. The key to quality is of course production control. This includes more than mechanized and computer automated inspection. It requires a labor force that is trained to care about quality and able to solve quality problems on the production line. This becomes particularly difficult at an international level where country production environments differ in their potential for achieving high quality outputs.

Plant maintenance is generally a lower level problem of importance. However, when serious accidents occur as in the Bhopal disaster in India, firms may find that the resulting liabilities make maintenance a more serious issue. Controlling maintenance quality is particularly difficult from abroad because maintenance problems often require a hands-on experience at a site. Secondly, maintenance is often postponed to make economic performance reports look better. Unless such practices are recognized by the home office, firms leave themselves open to the possibility of serious failures and liabilities.

Introduction of New Technology

The use of new technology and new methods of production increasingly has become a competitive tool in international business—just as it has in doing business at home. It is notable that the intense rivalry between firms headquartered in the United States and those headquartered in Japan and Europe is to a very major degree influenced by the introduction of new product and process technology. The battle for markets on a global scale depends on a continuing flow of new products. This in turn often depends on the application of technology—especially in such fields as computers and microelectronics. However, it is not confined to these industries. (See News Box 7–3.) To take an example from the field of semiconductor devices, firms in the United States were largely responsible for the initial revolution in memory devices and microprocessors. Firms such as Texas Instruments Incor-

Japan Tinkering with New Technology in Effort to Hold Its Shipbuilding Lead
Stephen Kreider Yoder

Setsuo Takezawa beams with pride as he holds up the model ship he keeps in his office. Turning it over, he points to two tubes that look like elongated jet engines running along the bottom.

To Mr. Takezawa, the odd-looking model represents a revolution in shipbuilding. The proposed ship is part of an ambitious Japanese effort to create boats that shim through water propelled by huge magnets built into their hulls.

"We think it's time to do away with the prop," says Mr. Takezawa, the director of the project. "Airplanes moved from propellers to jets a long time ago. But ships haven't changed a bit."

While Japan still makes about half of the world's ships, they largely have been left behind in the country's high-tech boom. Now, like many of Japan's smokestack industries, shipbuilders hope to brighten their future by adopting more technology. The innovations include magnetic propulsion, shipbuilding robots and "smart" ships piloted by computers.

These technologies, they say, will help Japan stave off fierce competition from Asian rivals such as South Korea. "We have to stay one step ahead technologically just to be competitive," says Akira Kono, a Ministry of Transport official in charge of maritime technology. Japan can't compete with conventional ships, he says. "From now on, it's a contest of technologies."

Shipbuilders also want to shed the shipyard's grimy, low-tech image, which scares off bright university graduates who might have become the young engineers shipbuilders need to help refine today's vessels and keep the industry afloat. "The biggest bottleneck in the industry," Mr. Kono says, "is getting good people."

Japan's dream boats resemble something from science fiction. Superconductive linear motor propulsion, the magnetic "engines" Mr. Takezawa's group is developing, will make ship and sea water act together like an electric motor. An American patented the idea in 1961, but no one has built a full-scale version.

The Japan Foundation for Shipbuilding Advancement hopes to build a 60-metric-ton prototype by 1989. Joining forces with Japan's big shipbuilders, the foundation is footing 80 percent of the $21.7 million bill for the project. It expects the first commercial versions to ply the seas in the early 1990s.

In working scale models, electrodes generate a current in the water. Onboard magnets then pull and push the charged water, just as a rotor pushes and pulls its way into a spin inside an electric motor. In one version, magnets pull water through a tube and jet it out at the ship's stern. In another, the bottom of a boat is lined with magnets that push against charged water, propelling the boat forward.

The linear-motor concept is also used in magnetically levitated trains being developed in Japan and West Germany. Most marine and train versions often use supercooled coils: magnets that are frozen to about minus-450 degrees Fahrenheit. At such low temperatures the coils become "superconductive," carrying current indefinitely without resistance.

Developers think magnetic ships would be able to travel at speeds above 100 miles an hour with none of the noise and vibration of craft powered by diesel engines and propellers. The ships wouldn't have moving parts, making maintenance easier.

Officials concede that the technology is still unproved and that its effects on the environment aren't clear. For example, electric current sent through sea water produces hydrogen and chlorine gases that could harm sea life. But perfecting linearmotor ships "will put Japan a stride ahead," says Yoshiro Manabe, a director of Kawasaki Heavy Industries, Ltd. "If it's cost effective, it will be a boon to business.

High costs could foil the project, Mr. Manabe cautions. The most amazing innovations won't impress shipowners if the vessels are more expensive than conventional craft, he says. The project's backers aren't saying yet how much a magnetic ship might cost.

Cutting costs is the goal of a separate development project for a "smart" conventional ship that would pilot itself and not break down. The Ministry of Transport is orchestrating a $100 million project to develop an ocean-going ship that can be run by a crew of four or five. Conventional ships require about 16 people.

An "intelligent" computer—perhaps the "fifth generation" computer Japan is developing—would lie at the heart of the craft. The computer would check the ship's position using satellite signals and analyze data on weather, geography and delivery schedules to steer the most efficient course. Sensors would help the vessel avoid obstacles.

The system also would extend the time between repairs. Sensors on machinery would check for irregularities that presage breakdowns. The computer, programmed to "think" like an experienced mechanic, would give corrective commands. The engine would be made of engineering ceramics and other new materials that make it less prone to trouble. Today's ships need repair once a week on average. The ministry wants to stretch that to six months.

Ideally, such ships could dock themselves and robots could unload them. The vessels would make it possible to control a shipping business much as a fully automated factory makes machines work together. "Our objective," says the Transport Ministry's Mr. Kono, "is a ship that can sail itself."

Planners also hope that robots can help trim shipbuilding costs. Labor makes up 35 percent of the cost of building a ship. A group of shipbuilders and electronics companies is spending about $30 million in an effort to cut that to about 10 percent. An artist's illustration shows robots picking up beams and placing them together to be joined into units. Crablike robots crawl along inside a hull to weld beams.

Intelligent ships and automated shipbuilding, says a Transport Ministry paper, "are powerful weapons we expect to uphold Japan's shipbuilding industry in 1990s."

SOURCE: *The Wall Street Journal*, Thursday, August 28, 1986, p. 19.

porated, Motorola, Inc., Fairchild Camera and Instrument Corp., and Intel Corporation developed and dominated the 8-bit, 16-bit and 32-bit microprocessor chips, but Japanese firms are increasingly dominating the field of memory chips. For the next generation of even more highly powered devices, the race is on among U.S., Japanese, European, and even Korean firms to bring these to the market. With each expansion of memory capabilities, the intensity of competition has increased. Moreover, the chips have brought rapid change to the end products, that is, the devices into which the chips go. Computers have become more and more powerful and faster and the applications of end products have become ever more complex and intelligent. Although U.S. firms continue to be dominant, this dominance is being challenged through international competition.

The microelectronics revolution has found its way into every industry in terms of production techniques involving computerization of process technology. For example, machine tools can now be fully automated to produce certain goods, parts, and components. For many goods this has reduced the importance of wage rate differences across countries because in highly automated plants using "smart" machines there is little need for unskilled labor. Another aspect to this is that flexible, highly mechanized plants can be used even for short production runs because the time required to change a machine over to produce a different part or product is virtually zero. In many production operations, the changeover can be accomplished by a few key strokes at a computer terminal. The electronically controlled machine automatically changes over to a new set of dies and tools to begin making the different part. These types of machines broaden the scope over which firms can operate in terms of the number of products in the product line. The size of production run to achieve a reasonable level of efficiency has been substantially reduced by these "flexible manufacturing systems." Accordingly, firms in international business have greater technological freedom in terms of plant designs and plant locations. As a final note it should be remembered that where long production runs can be justified because of large volume, specialized machines are still more efficient than are computer-controlled, more adaptable machines.

Management methods are critical to the success of new technology. Technology alone is useless without a managerial system to organize its effective use. We have learned much in the United States in the past few years by observing the methods used in Japanese factories. While much of the technology used by the Japanese was developed in the United States or Europe, the Japanese did much to make the managerial systems and methods more effective. However, the Japanese also have brought their own unique methods to bear including the "just-in-time" inventory system that conserves on inventories and hence on the amount of capital tied up in the production process. Just-in-time matches the production of parts and components very closely with production of the final products that use these parts and components. Instead of using large inventories of parts to buffer shifts in demand, the two production systems are balanced and react to changes in demand as a single system. This requires tighter coordination throughout the entire production system including relations with outside vendors. Another way in which the Japanese have reduced the need for inventories is by shortening the time required to accomplish changeover of machines from producing one part to the production of another. This reduces what is called "economic lot size," or stated differently, the length of production runs can be shortened and fewer units made in a single run. All of these techniques reduce the need for capital stock by improving machine utilization rates and reducing the level of required inventories.

There are numerous other technological and managerial methods that can be cited as having had a major impact on production in recent years. As noted, many of these have been developed in other countries. There is a cross-cultural nature to these developments that requires managers to have a broader appreciation of international competition. Those firms which rely heavily on efficient production as a competitive tool cannot afford to ignore such developments.

SUMMARY

In this chapter we have been concerned with the management of production—especially in terms of the design of systems of manufacturing plants in overseas locations. An international system is similar to a purely national system, but it is also different because resource availabilities differ, government rules differ, and access to markets differs. Whether or not a firm should choose to install a system of interdependent plants scattered across several countries is a complex problem. Interdependence among plants can be very risky, but it saves more money than small general-purpose plants. Government policies in most countries tend to favor the use of stand-alone plants that are less efficient. The smaller the national market and the more insistent the government is that production be on local soil, the greater will be that inefficiency. Plant design is affected by all of these considerations. However, new technology has become available and this technology tends to broaden the freedom that firms have in designing their plants for overseas locations. New management techniques also have increased the need for international awareness and have intensified international competition.

DISCUSSION QUESTIONS FOR CHAPTER SEVEN

1. Taking advantage of unique production capabilities allows a firm to compete more effectively in foreign markets. What examples of unique production capabilities can you cite?

2. We usually think of production capability as manufacturing of a physical product. However we also "produce" insurance, engineering, and hotel services. In what ways could a hotel service (e.g. Hilton, Kubai Yashi, or Curarrehue International Hotels) be considered a "unique" competitive advantage?

3. Identify at least three ways a firm's special capabilities can be exploited. What makes them different?

4. One problem of moving production abroad is the potential loss of company "secrets" to competitors. How can a company protect itself against this loss?

5. The strategic decision to move production abroad involves five major subcategories of decisions. Identify those subcategories and explain each.

6. Some people argue that it is better to move older and even outdated U.S. technology to developing nations because it is more "appropriate" for their general level of economic development. Is this a good idea from the firm's point of view? How might a developing nation's government react to that idea?

7. Mexico offers an attractive "maquilladora" program for U.S. firms that wish to locate certain manufacturing operations in Mexican border towns. What strategic issues might be raised by this opportunity? What questions should U.S. management ask itself and Mexican officials about this program?

8. One of the more important aspects of plant design is that of economies of scale. Why is an economy of scale important?

9. What critique can be used to decide which country and site is best to locate a production plant? Suppose a Finnish piano company was looking at your present city of residence as a potential site for a manufacturing plant and you were hired as a local consultant to help them make a decision. How would you apply these criteria?

10. U.S. firms move manufacturing abroad to take advantage of things like cheaper labor and low-cost materials. This often results in plant closings, unemployment, lost business, and lowered tax revenues at home. Should anything be done about so-called "runaway" plants? If so, what?

11. How might General Motors be an example of an "internationally integrated system of interdependent plants?"

12. How does the introduction of new technology make production a more strategically competitive tool for a firm? Give examples.

_____

CHAPTER EIGHT

Decisions in Managing People Abroad

INTRODUCTION

This chapter deals with one of the most important managerial tasks in international firms: human resources management.

There is a growing trend in the human resources management (HRM) field whereby employees at all levels are treated more as valued assets than as costly liabilities. People are viewed as more than simple factors of production like buildings and equipment. Research and experience demonstrate that the quality and effectiveness of personnel is improved when employees are given opportunities to more fully participate in their jobs and contribute to the well-being of the organization. The success of the Japanese management system can largely be attributed to their strong emphasis on effective human resource management.

Just as in international operations, the human resource function faces multiple and changing country environments. This chapter will focus on the ways in which human resource management differs in a multinational firm when compared with purely national firms. By focusing on the differences, the special problems and decisions posed by the international environment will be highlighted.

Before proceeding we want to emphasize that the human resources management problem is essentially a problem for all managers. The challenge of attracting, developing, and motivating quality employees in an organization is, in reality, a part of every manager's job. Even accounting and finance departments must deal with the human factor in their own personnel! Thus, unlike other specialized functional departments, the management of human resources is a broad function that crosses departmental boundaries.

THE HRM MODEL

Most management and personnel texts present a HRM model like the one in Figure 8–1. The major personnel task is one of matching individuals to job requirements to obtain desired outcomes such as good individual performance, satisfaction with the job, continued commitment to the organization, and enterprise profitability. The various personnel activities, such as job analysis, assessment, and compensation represent the means by which this matching is achieved. If successful, the fit between the individual and job is congruent and successful. Finally, the model recognizes the influence that external country environments exert on the HRM function.

There are two aspects to the HRM problem:

1. The set of formal procedures and practices established by organizational rule making and government regulations. This includes a record-keeping function.
2. The actual management of employees in terms of their motivations, personal abilities and skills, work habits, career concerns, and other interpersonal needs.

The first tends to be somewhat impersonal and objective. It includes a variety of personnel decisions such as performance evaluation and compensation. Relationships among the various HRM activities create a problem in making consistent, fair, legal, and coordinated decisions. For this reason the HRM function has developed what is considered by most managers to be a complex set of policies, procedures, and dictums. The resulting personnel/HRM system tends to be bureaucratic. But policies and regulations provide guidance and standards to managers when new decision situations arise. They also serve to restrict decision options and managerial autonomy. This in part explains the lowered esteem the personnel/HRM function has in many organizations. However, recent studies have shown that more and more of management's time is being taken up by "personnel problems," leaving less time to get the rest of the manager's work done. An effective HRM system should reduce time spent on such decisions. Furthermore, the control exerted by HRM systems is partly intended to protect the organization from legal liabilities and strong government regulation.

The second aspect of the HRM problem concerns the more personal, less-standardized interpersonal style of management. In Japan and Latin America where firms are more paternalistic in their relationships with employees, a more personal style of management is required. Interpersonal problem solving and group decision making are often more the norm. This style requires less use and dependence on rules and more use of interpersonal skills in management. A recent

---

FIGURE 8–1   The Human Resources Management Model

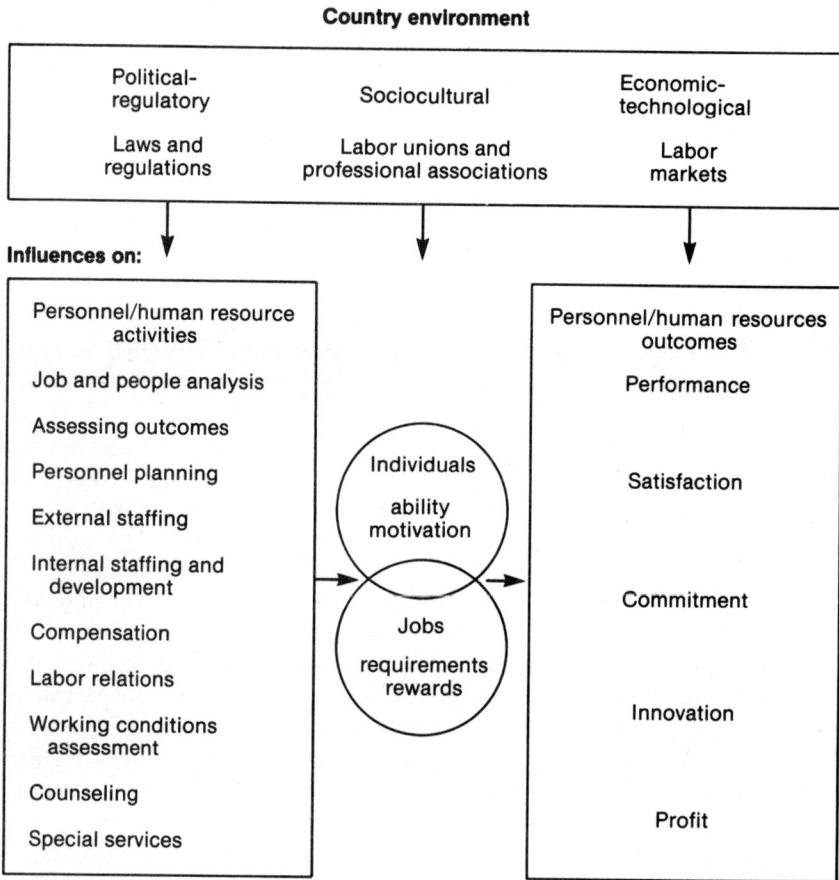

SOURCE: Adapted from Herbert G. Heneman III et al., *Managing Personnel and Human Resources* (Homewood, Ill.: Dow Jones-Irwin, 1981).

study of international managers indicates that a major cause of failure among U.S. overseas managers is an inability to develop adequate interpersonal skills. Effective managerial style, however, is not easily developed and is strongly influenced by cultural considerations.

The HRM model is internationalized in two ways. First, the external environment is a "country environment" that represents a set of interacting socio-political-economic variables. These variables in turn create conditions that require changes and adaptations to HRM practices. Thus, restricted labor markets, due either to market forces or

regulations, may require different approaches to compensation policies. Country environments also reflect how relations between countries also carry over to the workplace. For example, Argentine–British
relations, both friendly and otherwise, have implications for a U.S.
firm wishing to appoint a British manager to head an Argentine unit.
Argentine nationalism may make the British manager's job difficult to
the point of ineffectiveness. Finally, country environments are multiple. Firms are often located in more than one country at the same time.
The more countries involved, the more complex the management problem becomes.

The second way the HRM function is internationalized is via the
adjustments to standard personnel activities and the addition of special service activities. The latter suggests a need to create new functions and services to serve the personnel needs of overseas employees.
While some needs are generally shared by all employees, the nature of
a particular job tends to determine the individual's needs. For example, a British firm that sends an unmarried, female technical specialist
to the United States on a two-month assignment may only need to
make minor adjustments such as level of compensation to reflect differences in living costs. By contrast, suppose a Spanish plant manager
with a family is assigned for three years to a post in Minnesota. In this
latter instance, the hardships of weather, cultural isolation, and family create special problems. For the Spanish manager and his family
there is a further issue of eventual repatriation and resocialization
back into their own culture. Some specialized personnel services to
deal with such problems are seen below.

- *Cultural Shock*—Cross-cultural training aimed at preparing a
  manager for overseas assignment through education about
  country environment, training in language, and the handling
  of culture-based problems; heightening sensitivity to and empathy towards the foreign culture.
- *Family Problems that Affect Employee Performance*—Family
  counseling and support to make the transition to a foreign setting less traumatic and to address personal concerns regarding
  family needs in housing, schooling, travel, and health.
- *Unrealistic and Unfair Compensation Situations*—Foreign-
  based compensation adjustment to make up for hardships of
  foreign posts, currency exposure risk, keeping up with home
  country and foreign inflation rates, and tax adjustment liabilities, both foreign and domestic.
- *Repatriation and Resocialization (Reverse Culture Shock)*—Career repatriation counseling to keep the manager informed
  about inside job opportunities for changes in policy or direction

of the company; allowing for the difficult resocialization problem for a manager (and family) that come home after assignment abroad; formal recognition for service abroad.

The internationalized HRM model demonstrates the same problem of general/specific tradeoffs faced by marketing, production, and other areas. Namely, can HRM use proven standardized policies and practices on a worldwide basis or do policies and practices need to be adjusted to country or regional characteristics? The answer is of course both, depending on the circumstances. A standardized approach provides increased control and efficiencies—since common practices can be followed and changes in their practices can be communicated and implemented quickly. However, company policy must usually adjust to country conditions, not the other way around. Furthermore, firms often have operations located in more than one country, complicating the issue even further. Thus, differences between domestic and international HRM practices need to be identified.

One of the key international differences is that job requirements differ across countries as do the availability of skills and abilities. Generally, multinational firms are forced to train for a broader range of skills in their international operations than in their home country situation. This occurs because foreign educations systems often do not provide the needed training—particularly in many of the developing countries. In some countries, however, little emphasis is placed on job skills. Instead the objective is to provide a broad general education. In other countries there is a dual system of education in which young persons are tested for their intellectual skills at about 15 years of age. Those who score well are allowed to continue on toward a "college education." Those who do not score so well are directed toward "vocational education" institutions to be trained in the arts of a trade. In still other types of systems students are placed into apprenticeship programs where they learn a trade through a combination of on-the-job training and formal classwork. Multinational firms must adapt their personnel operations to each of these various systems in terms of their training, selection, and hiring methods.

INTERNATIONAL STAFFING

It is not the task of this book to catalogue how each country environment influences each HMR activity differently. Its purpose is to emphasize differences from domestic practice. To do this more effectively we focus on two of the most important HRM activities from an international perspective, staffing and labor relations.

The nature of jobs to be filled provides a variety of job classifications including managerial, technical, administrative/supervisorial, skilled, and unskilled. Any of these can be either permanent or temporary workers. The complex set of job requirements may mean that it may not be possible to meet all of the staffing needs within a country's pool of talent. Thus, multinational firms must decide whether they will attempt to staff abroad in the same way they do at home or adapt their systems to accommodate to the local situation. Some of the key issues here are:

1. Whether to staff with people from home or from the host country.
2. Which job skills and attributes to seek in the labor market and which skills to acquire by use of training programs.
3. Whether to adapt production and other processes to meet the available skills or to adapt the labor force through training.
4. What mix of skills to use, i.e., the same capital/labor mix as at home or some other to be determined upon existing circumstances.

These diagnostic questions essentially ask whether changes are needed in the sources and abilities of employees or whether changes are needed in the job and work requirements.

From the firm's point of view the ideal would be to use the same staffing procedures everywhere. But this is virtually impossible, except perhaps in the simplest of business activities. Since countries' schooling and training systems differ, the availability and quality of skills also will differ. Generally, the more industrialized the country, the easier it will be to hire people with the needed skills; the less developed the country, the more it will be necessary for the firm to create the needed skills through training programs. The availability of skills or lack thereof can affect the design of production plants and determine the degree to which various production processes can be included in the plant. For example, in developing countries plants are usually less integrated than plants in industrial countries. By this we mean that there are fewer separate production processes included in the developing country plants on average. This comes about because the skills needed to produce components are not available or are in short supply. When this occurs the firm must import the components from home or from another source located where the skills are available. In this case the job needs to be adjusted to fit the people available.

When deciding on whether to use a home or host country person to staff positions, that decision usually rests on a trade-off between the availability of skills and abilities needed and the cost of training or creating a skilled person. As might be surmised, the more difficult the job and the higher the skill level involved, the more likely the position will be filled by an expatriate. An expatriate is a person resident in a country who is not a citizen and in this instance would include anyone sent in from the home country or a third country who is not already a citizen of the host country. Expatriate personnel usually fill high-level managerial and technical positions. The skills they bring cannot be easily created through training programs. These skills involve lengthy formal schooling, considerable additional training within the firm, and years of experience on the job. Thus, whether or not a position will be staffed by using expatriate personnel depends on the cost and time required to develop the skill. The lengthier and costlier that process, the greater the likelihood that an expatriate will be chosen for the job.

Two other factors influence this decision. First, the firm will choose an expatriate because that person has knowledge and experience with home office management and technical systems. Headquarters, in this case, would prefer to have a knowledgeable and trusted person in a job where the foreign office needs to be brought into line with new corporate strategy or it needs experienced people to put in a new system. Secondly, the choice of expatriate or host country personnel depends also on government policy. Some Third World countries have policies of "indigenization" of management personnel—that is, they require that a certain percentage of the management employees must be local citizens. This is thought to give the country an increased skill base and increased possibilities for government influence over company policy.

Training Abroad

In the case where the skills needed may not be readily available in the labor market, the firm will find it necessary to create skills through training programs. This is not so different from the situation at home except that the firm in the developing country may have to train for a broader range of skills in relation to the total number of employees. In this connection the firm may be forced to adapt its production processes simply because the skills needed for it to operate in its desired way are not available. It may have to simplify technical production processes so that skill requirements are reduced or it may be forced to change its product so it does not require the same level of quality. However, firms are reluctant to reduce quality; the product quality standards are usually the same. Instead, a different process may be introduced and often this is an older process that the firm used earlier in its history. When changes such as this occur, they change the mix of skills required when compared with those being used in the home country. These alterations in turn change the way in which the firm manages its overseas operations.

Hiring skilled workers away from other companies is always an option. However, this may have some negative side effects. In those countries where skilled labor is in short supply, the foreign company that hires away skilled workers essentially drives up the cost of labor for other companies and eventually for itself. Secondly, government regulation of labor practices could increase. Host governments and business communities have implicit expectations that the location of a plant in their country will bring benefits to the economy and society in general. One of those expectations is an increase in employment and an improvement of local labor skill levels via training and more challenging jobs. If a foreign firm begins hiring away local labor, they break this implicit "contract." The effects can be a decreased support from local businesses in other important areas such as importation of component parts or access to local capital. It can also lead to increased government requirements for training and restrictions on firing.

Even if there are adequate skills available, there will be need for specialized training in the methods of the firm. Each firm has its own way of doing things. While each may use the same basic skills, it nevertheless uses these skills in a somewhat different way than any other firm. As we have noted, each firm has its own culture, orientation, and set of values. These are largely established by high-level managers who tend to perpetuate the value system. New entrants to the firm, whether in a foreign country or at home, will become socialized into this culture where values are shared. A part of the training process is to develop these values and methods in the workforce. An example of this can be seen in News Box 8–1 with English workers in Japanese firms. The other aspect of training the already skilled workers has to do with the application of these skills to the peculiar needs of the firm. Even though a person might be a highly skilled machinist, the application of that skill will differ depending on the task. Tasks differ between firms and hence it is necessary for firms to train even the already skilled.

There are various ways firms go about training to develop skills. Some try to rely on outside schooling while others prefer to develop their own schooling programs. Still others use a combination of both. Managers and technical personnel are more likely than unskilled workers to receive formal training off the job through special coursework. However, there may be instances in which firms must conduct their own training programs if they are to succeed at all. For example, a major electronics firm established a plant in Surinam to manufacture wiring boards. The needed skills were not available. It was evident that the firm would have to develop its own skilled workforce.

NEWS BOX 8–1
Britons Learn How to Work the Japanese Way
Christopher J. Chipello

In this port town south of Yokohama (Oppama), Steve Milner, a 32-year-old Briton, squirts a white sealant along the edges of the doors on a Nissan automobile as it moves along the assembly line. Then he steps back to wait for the next car, but he is checked by his eagle-eyed supervisor, Fusaji Hagiyama.

The Japanese gestures toward a gascap cover that also needs sealant, and he points to excess sealant that must be wiped from the auto's body. Only then is Milner ready for the next car.

In about a year, Milner will be directing a similar operation at a Nissan factory now taking shape in Tyne and Wear County in depressed northeast England. Hagiyama's mission is to train Milner, formerly a foreman at a frozen-food plant. Although neither man speaks the other's language, Hagiyama's animated hand signals seem to get the basic message across.

Many overseas factories incorporate elements of the Japanese management system. And the success of some has lent support to the view that at least part of the Japanese system can be grafted onto Western organizations.

At the Oppama plant, admiration gushes from both sides of the culture gap. "The whole place is well laid out," says John Burton, a husky 33-year-old whom Nissan lured away from a foreman's job at BL PLC, the British auto maker.

The British trainees "are very eager to learn," says Takeo Yamazoe, general manager for production control and engineering at the sprawling Oppama plant. "We expect good results back in England."

Not a Question of Salary

Burton says he made the move from BL "because of the opportunity Nissan was offering to help build a new company on a green site." The money, he says, is "better, but not by much."

The trick for Nissan's British management will be to instill in its workers that sense of purpose, along with the attention to detail the British supervisors are being taught at Oppama. "Where I come from, you tend to forget about the little things," says Sean Brown, a 30-year-old former food-plant foreman from northeast England.

Hiring will play a big part in achieving the Japanese way of doing things. "The selection process is the tightest I have ever seen in the U.K.," says Cushnaghan, a former manufacturing manager for the Cowley plant of car maker Austin Rover Group, Ltd.

"We are looking for people with the right attitude—people who will pitch in," says Geoff Baxter, who will be a quality-control supervisor for Nissan.

SOURCE: Excerpted from *The Wall Street Journal*, June 28, 1985, p. 31.

Thus, while the plant was being constructed, the firm set up a "tent city" using a small version of the assembly line to be installed in the plant. Using this production line, the firm trained the workforce prior to completion of the actual plant. By the time the plant was completed there was a well-trained workforce ready to begin production of the wiring boards. The task of assembly required mainly manual dexterity and an ability to produce to a predetermined standard. Those who could not achieve that standard were dropped from the training program and new recruits were added until enough people had been trained to meet the needs of the plant. Much on-the-job training is of this type.

One of the great strengths of many multinational firms is the ability to take human raw material that has not had adequate schooling or training and develop a productive workforce. This ability has proven particularly useful in the developing countries. Foreign firms often train for virtually every skill they need in these countries from managers to relatively unskilled maintenance personnel. Even very basic skills are often included, such as reading and writing. However, most training is designed to provide the particular skills needed in the operations of the firm. Only under extreme circumstances, where it is necessary to the development of firm-specific skills, is training in basic literacy offered by the firms, and then it is usually in conjunction with programs supported by governments.

Much of the training provided is done by specialized training personnel who are borrowed either from the parent or from a third country subsidiary. For example, a well-known U.S. multinational firm was establishing a new foundry in Brazil. This foundry was to be similar to one which the firm had already established in Mexico. To train the Brazilian workforce the firm brought key technicians, foremen, and skilled workers to Brazil for a few weeks to assist with plant start-up and to train Brazilian employees in the foundry's operating methods. There is much trading of personnel on a temporary basis to aid in training. In addition, key personnel from a subsidiary are usually sent to the parent's operations for special training—especially in the fields of technology and management.

To summarize, staffing can be either by the use of nationals or by the use of expatriates. Most positions are staffed using nationals. However, if skills are not available locally and it is difficult to create the skills, expatriate personnel will be used. Firms train for a wide variety of skills—even basic ones. The higher the level of skill, the more likely it is that personnel will be sent to off-site locations to receive formal training. The lower the level of the skill, the more likely it is that training will take place on the job. News Box 8–1 again shows how the Japanese have attempted to deal with the problem.

LABOR RELATIONS

Labor relations is not a neutral concept. It tends to be a product of culture and country history. For example, in some countries physical manual labor has a low status. To dirty one's hands at work is to demonstrate a lower social status. In others, such as the United States, the values of action (e.g., getting things done), pragmatism, and efficiency dictate that when the situation requires, everybody is expected to roll up shirtsleeves and get physically involved in the work at hand. Thus, attitudes towards manual labor, the working environment, and social status have an impact on how labor relations are treated in different countries.

Secondly, the institutional relations that historically have evolved between labor, management, and government continue to exert a controlling influence on the practice of labor relations. Generally, the history of labor relations in most countries can be characterized by struggle, adversarial relations, and outright animosity between labor and management. This can be expected because of values and beliefs with respect to the right to employment, autonomy of management decision making, safe working conditions, property rights of owners, equity in pay, and so on. When differences occur between management and labor they both may turn to coercive means (e.g., strikes, employer lockouts), structured conflict resolution (e.g., negotiations, mediation), and political/administrative means (e.g., legislation, government bureaus) of resolving differences. In those societies characterized by strong capitalistic, free-market traditions, the relationship has continued to be an adversarial one. In countries characterized by strong Christian, democratic, and socialist traditions, labor unions through political activity have successfully moved governments to accept strong social controls that often favor labor's concerns.

Unionization of the workforce in the United States often has led to industry-wide unions—especially among industries such as steel, mining, and automobile manufacturing. In some countries free labor unions are actively repressed and considered illegal, as in Chile or Poland. In others if free unions exist at all they are very weak. Sometimes unions are sponsored by companies themselves, as in Japan. This variation in union form tends to reduce outside political and interest group influence on union employees and therefore tends to allow more company control over labor. In fact, in Japan company unions often go through a yearly ritualistic and symbolic strike. These "strikes" are intended to remind workers of their status in the company rather than to seriously change company policies. In contrast to the relatively docile Japanese, labor unions in the United Kingdom have their own political party and accordingly have more political strength. Given these wide differences, the methods used in U.S. labor relations may not be appropriate to other countries.

Because of those country peculiarities, multinational firms try to tailor the labor relations function to the local situation and, in so doing, they usually appoint a local national to be in charge of labor relations. Even if there are no unions, there still are local customs and work rules that have become established either by government regulation or past practice. These rules require a knowledge of the local situation. In some instances it may not be possible to use an outsider to deal with the workforce. Suspicion of adverse political influence of unions is widespread in Latin America. Tribal animosities in Africa and caste system restraints in India also influence the effectiveness of union. Communist government policy in most of the socialist bloc outlaws separate unions. The point is that, like virtually every aspect of doing business abroad, the approach to labor relations must be adapted to the specific country circumstances in which the firm is doing business. Some multinationals, to their disappointment, have tried to transfer their labor relations practices abroad with little success.

GOVERNMENT VIEW OF HUMAN RESOURCES

As stated in our opening theme of this chapter, the human factor in work is increasingly being considered an asset and not a cost. Most government policy towards economic development implicitly, if not openly, treats the improvement of its labor force as an investment in future development of the country. To this end, most foreign investment activities are viewed not only for their direct contribution to output, but also for their contributions to labor force development. This takes many forms. On the start-up side of a foreign investment project there is the basic issue of jobs—how many new jobs will be created, what kind of jobs will they be, how long will they last. Third World governments are particularly sensitive to the capital-labor mix of an investment. While wanting modern equipment, these governments are aware of the tradeoffs—more capital generally means less labor input. Jobs may therefore be a politically sensitive issue.

Once a project is developed, country concerns may turn to the provision of health care and general education for employees. There also are concerns about the amount of management and technical training and increased local participation in managerial work. This may include further developments of local technology to provide high skill jobs and prevent the loss of talented people to the better opportunities offered by more developed economies.

Lastly, government's concern over unemployment has led to restrictions in two important areas: (1) the layoff and firing of employees and (2) required advance notification and compensation for the social costs of plant closings. In the former, some governments put restrictions on firing in terms of requiring a firm to pay costs of unemployment, retraining, temporary health benefits, and the like. The effect is to make layoff and firing a more costly decision. In the latter case, firms are required to give advance notice of intentions to close a plant and may be further required to incur costs of the social dislocation caused by such decisions. Such plant closing legislation is common in Europe and has recently become part of some state-level legislation in the United States, as in Massachusetts. Thus, the treatment of the human factor as an input like land or capital is largely inappropriate in most countries today. An increase in government sensitivity to workers' needs suggests need for an effective HRM strategy.

Work Culture

Despite appearances, a country's work culture is not fixed. Fluctuations in economic growth, foreign investment in high-technology industries, severe foreign competition in basic industries, and political influence on economic decisions can cause significant changes in the work culture. For example, economic success in Germany has led to claims of a weakening of the work ethic. As seen in News Box 8–2, people increasingly choose to consume and enjoy the fruits of their labor.

Interestingly, the work culture has partially contributed to the present difficulties Japan is experiencing with its Western allies in trade relations. Japan is seen by some observers as a country of workaholics—they work six days a week, spend much of their after-work hours with their work colleagues, often do not take vacation time, are fanatic in their dedication to work discipline and quality of output, and save a whopping 17 percent of their income. In short, the Japanese are seen as international rate busters!

The Europeans in particular have reacted to this Japanese work ethic that they see as an "unnatural" and perhaps unhealthy dedication to work. In fact the EEC recently has sought to get the Japanese Planning Ministry to include a deemphasis on work in its future plans for the economy. Suggestions included a reduction of the work week to five days and a requirement that vacation time be taken. The underlying notion is to motivate Japanese to consume more relative to their production. The recent high-level Maekawa report in fact makes many such recommendations for restructuring Japanese work and consumption habits.

The U.S. response, in contrast to Europe, has been dedicated less to getting the Japanese to work differently and more to getting them to

---

NEWS BOX 8-2
Germans Become Less Obsessed With Work

Fifteen years ago, Mercedes cars were rolling smoothly from assembly line to autobahn, Arno Geier was working 48 hours a week, and a clear majority of hausfraus surveyed declared it unthinkable to let dirty dishes stack up in the sink.

Today, Daimler-Benz and other West German auto makers are idled by strikes, Geier and his co-workers are walking picket lines in the rain, demanding a 35-hour work week. And the hausfraus are telling the pollsters they're letting the dishes sit in the sink awhile.

Sociologists deliver a grave diagnosis, and wage-earners nod in reluctant agreement. The famed German work ethic—that near-obsessive pride in work that produced some of the world's fastest cars, finest clocks, and favorite beer—is dying.

"A sizable part of our work force is no longer ashamed to say 'I don't like to work,'" said Cologne University sociologist Erwin Scheuch.

It isn't that the Germans have become lazy, the researchers say, just somewhat weary and anxious to enjoy the fruits of their labor.

One social scientist borrows a colleague's pun to sum up the situation:

"We are not living through a postindustrial, but a postindustrious phase," she said.

SOURCE: Excerpted from *The Los Angeles Times*, June 4, 1984, Part IV, p. 2.

---

consume more foreign goods, particularly U.S. goods. Through nontariff barriers and threats of further restrictions on imports, the United States hopes to get the Japanese to make their own markets more accessible to foreign sellers. Exhortations by the Japanese Prime Minister to get the Japanese consumer and industrial buyers to buy more foreign goods may reflect a beginning of change towards more consumption relative to production. The United States's self-serving interest is, therefore, to create in Japan a consumer society patterned after its own.

The lesson in this is that seemingly successful human resource management systems can also create international problems. In terms of outputs, the Japanese system has been most successful. From a management perspective, Japan represents a near ideal situation— relatively docile, dedicated, and disciplined workers. There is, however, a cost to the Japanese of this strong work ethic that is generally not recognized by Western observers.

In the United States research has recognized that the overemphasis on work among U.S. managers has been identified as a source of personal stress, ill-health, drug abuse, dysfunction in family life, and other social costs. Personal accounts of Japanese life suggest that despite their phenomenal economic success, the personal life of the Japanese worker is not without its problems. Again, workpace stress, pressures for conformity, constant self-discipline, and postponed gratification suggest that all work and no play can make Yoshio a duller worker. Somehow, the golden rule of moderation may be coming into play because Japanese businessmen have begun complaining that the younger generation is showing signs of being less work-oriented. Furthermore Japanese executives seem to be more open to looking at the cost of their work habits even to the extent of using therapy. The well-being of the individual Japanese is tied up in an intricate way to the workplace and the fate of the nation. Thus, the issue of work culture, productivity, and economic well-being are interdependent in ways most Westerners do not readily understand. Competition with Japan has made the Japanese work culture more understandable but no less disconcerting.

MOTIVATING EMPLOYEES ABROAD

In many cases experience with foreign workers in one's own country leads one to conclude that "they are like us and therefore have similar motivations." However, the international manager faces two often overlooked questions: (1) Are people in work settings in foreign countries motivated by the same things as people at home? (2) Can a manager use the same leadership style and management practices abroad to motivate employees as at home? Both questions are asking whether motivation is a universal phenomenon or a product of a particular country's setting. The answers to these questions are both yes and no. The answer is yes insofar as all managers face the same basic motivational issues on the job. All people share basic personal aspirations and needs that a job helps them meet. The answer is no insofar as the relative conditions under which people can be motivated differ because of country. Thus, a contingency approach is appropriate in dealing with questions of management practice and motivation. Such an approach recognizes that seemingly universal phenomena are altered by the environmental setting.

The HRM model recognizes that motivation and ability are basic to individual performance. People with deficiencies in either will not perform as well as others. A highly motivated rural laborer in Peru with little industrial experience or an experienced Ecuadorian welder with low motivation will probably have poor productivity records. While HRM attempts to discover and match abilities to jobs, motivation of the employee is less open to testing and control. An understanding of working conditions, compensation, and employee personnel problems can contribute to better maintenance of employee well-being and therefore retention of the better workers.

Are People Abroad Motivated Differently?

Motivation is concerned with the factors that arouse, give direction to, and sustain people's behavior on the job. Do people in France find the same satisfactions or dissatisfactions at work as do people in the United States? Why are Germans often seen as "a hard working people?" Are some workers really lazy and respond only to a tough management style?

Effective work motivation requires understanding of those factors that create in people the potential to respond to incentives and deterrents in pursuit of organizational goals. All organizations have three behavioral requirements. The relationships between these requirements and the management tasks are seen in Figure 8–2. All three are directly linked to individual motivation. Recruitment is successful to the extent it arouses individual interest to join a firm. Satisfactory task performance results from continued management direction toward productive job behaviors. Creative output establishes a basis on which people can sustain a given level of effort over a longer period of time. For the international manager finding the right people for the right job is complicated further by the influence of three environmental factors. These are the culture of the country, the level and rate of economic and technological development, and the the role of government.

In the first part of this text we already described how culture influences the management process. The second variable of economic-technological development influences HRM because it determines the basic "rules of the game" under which a manager can motivate people. For example, low levels of economic development suggest the following as probable general country conditions a manager will face:

1. Predominance of traditional management approaches that are characterized by paternalistic attitudes toward employees and a more authoritarian style of decision making.
2. Simpler job tasks because of simpler and possibly older technology.
3. Higher labor-based production systems because labor is cheaper than capital.
4. More people per work unit leading to crowded work conditions and underutilization of employees.
5. A displacement of economic efficiency as a criterion for success because of unemployment and other social concerns.

FIGURE 8–2   Organization Behavior Requirements and the Universal
Management Task

Organization Behavioral Requirements	*Management Task*
Join and become a member	Create within the organization conditions that make it attractive to potential workers; create conditons which will cause valued employees not to look at alternatives outside of the organization while encouraging less valued employees to leave the organization.
Satisfactory Task Performance	Create and maintain conditions that allow employees to perform the tasks for which they were hired in a satisfactory manner
Innovative and Creative Output	Set up conditions that encourage employees to go beyond average performance and engage in creative and innovative work thus giving the organization a competitive edge, avoiding organization stagnation while extending organizational life.

SOURCE: This is based on work by D. Katz and R. K. Kahn, *The Social Psychology of Organization,* 2nd ed. (New York: John Wiley & Sons, 1978).

6. An emphasis on monetary rewards as the sole basis for compensation.
7. Low-level employee skills due to weak schooling and generally weak technical infrastructure that does not allow employees to learn via job experience.
8. Higher health and safety risks in the workplace.

This list of potential conditions suggests that an industrialized country manager would probably find the basic work environment in many countries to be "restrictive." That is, the conditions do not allow them to make easy transfers of industrialized country techniques and practices of motivating people. Generally, higher levels of economic development lead to more sophisticated work settings. The higher education of employees, more complex technology, and larger organizational systems contribute to this increased sophistication.

This does not mean workers in a relatively poor country are more difficult to motivate. If there is any lesson in the present explosive growth of the Asian–Pacific region, it shows that people can be highly motivated when the economic gains are direct and visible. What it does imply, however, is that adjustments in compensation and training-development programs, for example, should tend toward simpler, not more complex, programs. By comparison, where a manager moves from a less to a more sophisticated work environment, adjustment in the opposite direction should be expected.

An application of this thinking can be seen in the needs theories of motivation as developed by Maslow and McClellan. These theories contribute directly to our understanding of how the level of economic/social development influences the motivation process. Three points are of importance. First, low levels of economic development suggest that deficiency needs (psychological, safety, group membership) may be more important to larger segments of the workforce than personal growth needs such as self-actualization. This suggests that bringing sophisticated reward systems from the home office in Los Angeles may not be all that appropriate for the workforce in Nigeria. As economic development progresses, however, the desire to meet higher level needs should grow accordingly. Secondly, cultural differences likely will result in different needs. Japanese managers have found that American workers appear to have a lower need for group affiliation and a higher need for autonomy than Japanese workers. Similarly, American managers are sometimes confused by the apparent "groupiness" of other cultures where people often choose to work with other people rather than alone. Lastly, McClellan has argued that economic development and prosperity can be influenced by relative levels of achievement behavior demonstrated by a country's population. His work showed that a fairly consistent correlation exists between the mean levels of what he calls "n Achievement" and a country's current state of economic development. Furthermore, historical country studies seem to indicate that increases in the achievement motive tend to precede economic development.

The role of government influence on management practices is a third constant theme in contemporary international business literature. A variety of factors contribute to this—political goals for economic development, vestiges of historic colonial practices, lack of an entrepreneurial business community, public demands for immediate action, rise of authoritarian governments. In response to foreign competition, more governments are setting national policies that provide both incentives and restrictions to management action. Furthermore, governments take the position that maintenance of the economic system is their responsibility. Government activity often tends to establish the rules of the game. These usually involve more than just a passive "referee" function. Increasingly, governments are setting national industrial policies that can intrude on the traditional prerogatives of managers. For example, demands for an increased percentage of management positions to be filled by host country nationals, requirements for reduced pay differentials, or stringent antilayoff policies all tend to restrict management staffing practices. Thus, the factor of government policy has an explicit impact on management's ability to motivate its employees.

SUMMARY

All people can be motivated. The effectiveness of the rewards and deterrents used can be influenced by the level of economic, technical, and social development. And, in a variation of Lincoln's admonition, "you can motivate all of the people some of the time and some of the people all the time. But you try always to motivate all of the people all of the time!" Development of an intelligent HRM strategy that treats people as assets and investments will probably yield better long-term results and motivated employees. However, the temptation to treat employees as basic labor will continue to persist, especially in those environments where the skill base is low and it makes economic sense to substitute cheap labor for capital.

DISCUSSION QUESTIONS FOR CHAPTER EIGHT

1. "The success of the Japanese management system can, in part, be attributed to their emphasis on treating employees as valued assets as opposed to expendable labor." What are the implications for these different emphases in the treatment of human resources?

2. In what ways does the human resources management function become "internationalized?" Cite two examples.

3. Why can or cannot proven standardized HRM practices and policies (e.g. salary schedule, health benefits) be used on a worldwide basis? Give specific examples of either case.

4. What are some key issues that need to be considered in international staffing?

5. What is an "expatriate?" What factors influence the decision to choose an expatriate person to fill a position?

6. Training plays an important role in allowing a firm to locate various functional activities abroad. Suppose you were planning to locate a small market survey research department in Central America. What jobs/tasks need to be done? Which would you assign to a skilled expatriate, if any? Which would you train for?

7. "Some people argue that if labor unions were able to move abroad as easily as company capital is, world standards of living would be more in balance and U.S. companies would not be so readily willing and able to move operations abroad." Do you agree? What factors prevent labor unions from moving abroad so easily?

8. An enlightened government view of human resources would be characterized how? What concerns do governments have regarding the employment of their citizens by foreign firms?

9. Are foreign workers motivated by the same things and in the same ways as workers at home?

10. In what ways might low levels of economic development affect a manager's ability to direct and motivate people?

CHAPTER NINE

Decisions in Financial Management

INTRODUCTION

In this chapter we discuss the financial function and how it is altered when international operations are taken into consideration. First we examine the effects of exchange rates on the operational aspects of finance. Included here are the subjects of consolidation of financial statements, movement of financial assets, and methods of hedging against changes in exchange rates. We then take up the methods multinational firms have available to them in mobilizing capital. Also we shall briefly review the notion of portfolio effects of investing in more than a single country. Finally we look at the requirements involved in undertaking financial analysis in an international context.

FINANCIAL OPERATIONS

The financial function must be altered in numerous ways when firms venture abroad. First of all, there is need to deal in two or more currencies. When goods are shipped abroad, for example, they are initially priced in the money units of the home country. To illustrate, suppose a new automobile is shipped from a Japanese factory to the United States. It is priced in Japan in Japanese yen, but to be sold in the United States it must be priced in U.S. dollars. Thus, there must be some method of converting the yen price to the dollar price. To do this, an exchange rate is used. In 1985 at one point in time one U.S. dollar was worth 243 Japanese yen on the foreign exchange market. In other words, with one Japanese yen .00412 of a U.S. dollar can be purchased. Thus, an automobile which costs 1,458,000 yen in Japan would bring $6,000, plus transportation costs, in the United States. However, exchange rates can and do fluctuate. In 1986 the value of a U.S. dollar dropped to around 150 yen, a 38 percent drop in value. As a result, the same car now costs $8300. We see then that there is risk involved in international transactions that do not occur in purely national transactions.

CONVERSION OF FINANCIAL STATEMENTS

A second aspect of finance that is different in international business is the need to convert accounting statements from one currency to another. When firms have operating divisions or subsidiaries in overseas locations they keep their records in the monetary units of the host country. When operating in Great Britain the books are kept in British pounds; if operating in France the values would be in French francs. When the parent company in the United States wishes to determine for its stockholders and creditors how much was earned by the total corporation, the books of the various overseas subsidiaries must be brought together or consolidated into a set of statements for the entire corporation. To accomplish this, each of the individual country subsidiaries' statements must be converted from the host country currency values to the currency values of the home country. This is done using exchange rates. However, this also results in what have become known as translation gains or losses depending on what happens to the exchange rates between the currencies of the home and host countries. If the home country currency increases in value relative to the host country currency, there are translation losses because the accounts in the foreign subsidiary are now less valuable when converted into the home currency than they were before. Just the opposite occurs when the foreign currency increases in value in relation to the home currency. Where the host country is undergoing inflation and the currency is being devalued, there will be a translation loss because book values are not usually adjusted to reflect the inflation. This is demonstrated in Table 9–1 with the Brazilian cruzeiro.

But suppose the firm decided to sell the asset in early 1987. It might receive 1,300,000 Cr or $10,000 based on market value and if it subsequently repatriated this amount it would have to report a capital gain of $2,308 in the home country. All of this is simply an accounting profit (or loss) that occurs because of the translation of financial reports from one currency to another. For the multinational firm that has most of its fixed assets in countries undergoing rapid inflation, translation losses will be the norm and the firm can be made to look like a poor credit risk. Just the opposite occurs for the firm that has most of its fixed assets located in countries where the inflation rate is lower than that of the home country.

Many countries still use this method of valuation. However, the United States has moved to correct this problem through Statement

TABLE 9–1   Year-to-Year Translation Losses on Balance Sheet

	Book Value in Host Country Currency	Exchange Rate	Book Value in U.S. Dollars
1985 Cr	1,000,000	$100	$10,000
1986 Cr	1,000,000	$130	−$7,692
			$(2,308)

No. 52 of the Financial Accounting Standards Board. Under this rule current assets and current liabilities are converted using the current exchange rate while long-lived assets and long-term liabilities are converted at the exchange rate in effect at the time the assets were purchased or the long-term liabilities incurred. This does not totally eliminate translation gains and losses but goes far toward minimizing the large swings that could occur if only current exchange rates are used to translate or convert the financial statements of foreign subsidiaries. This rule will remain in force until conditions require its modification.

The more liquid the asset, the greater the risk that its value will be changed by a change in exchange rates. For example, working capital in the form of cash or short-term securities has its value changed immediately when the local currency is losing value because of inflation. Cash, when then changed into another currency, will buy less of that currency than it would have in an earlier time period. When this is occurring, firms attempt to reduce working balances held in the host country currency to the minimum necessary to conduct day-to-day transactions. They do this by moving balances to a more stable "hard" currency that is holding its value in terms of real goods and services. Thus, we see currency exchanges such as these taking place across national boundaries as multinational firms move liquid balances from subsidiaries located in countries with depreciating currencies to the parent or other subsidiaries located in countries with strong currencies. Considering the above, it can be seen that management of the financial function in multinational firms is an extremely important and complex activity. The value of the firm's earnings and short-term assets can either be preserved, enhanced, or reduced depending upon the skill with which the financial function is managed. For an example of these problems see News Box 9–1.

MOVEMENT OF FINANCIAL ASSETS

A third aspect of the currency problem has to do with the movement of accumulated earnings from the foreign subsidiaries. Not only must the

---

NEWS BOX 9-1
Translations Risks are Real

Multinationals doing business here have a different set of problems. The president of one says he got a slap in the face two weeks ago, when the government expanded the "super-free" exchange markets, killing off the old "free" rate, which was really a special controlled rate, and setting last week's devaluation in motion.

"I was in the United States, reviewing our budget," he reminisces. He says he was feeling like "a star" because the company's Mexican operations were doing so well. They had been booming along for the last three quarters, racking up a $1 million profit for the quarter just ended.

Then came news of a devaluation. Because of the accounting rules governing foreign exchange gyrations, the $1 million profit turned into a $1 million loss.

"Overnight, I went from a hero to a villain with my boss in the United States," the executive sighs.

His isn't the only U.S.-owned company in this fix. Multinationals here are scrambling to cut expenses and raise prices. But the ones that sell basic products like household goods can't do that. Their prices are controlled by the government.

"This makes things very unattractive for multinationals to operate in Mexico," says the executive, a Mexican himself.

SOURCE: *The Wall Street Journal*, July 22, 1985, p. 20.

---

firm be concerned about changing currency values and the timing of making financial movements, but also there are various taxes that may be incurred on the income generated by subsidiaries. Different countries have different tax rates and therefore it is important to determine how and in which countries earnings are to be declared. Firms attempt to take advantage of the lower tax rates levied by certain countries so that the total taxes incurred can be minimized. They do this by reporting low earnings in high tax-rate countries and report high earnings in low tax-rate countries. This often is accomplished through transfer pricing. For example, suppose the parent firm exports some parts to its German subsidiary via another subsidiary located in Panama. Panama does not levy a corporate income tax. The parts are priced to the Panamanian subsidiary at 50 cents per unit. The Panamanian subsidiary reprices the parts to $1 per unit to the German subsidiary, the subsidiary that will actually use the parts. The profits remain with the Panamanian subsidiary but they are accrued because of price manipulation on paper rather than any additional value through work contributed by the Panamanian subsidiary. This is an example of how firms can use transfer pricing between subsidiaries to reduce total taxes paid. Since most countries are interested in collecting their share of tax on the real value added, they take considerable care to see that transfer prices are reasonable. But for the firm, transfer pricing is a matter of trying to conduct as many international transactions as possible through countries that have the lowest tax rates.

All of the above have a bearing on the behavior of multinational firms in terms of where and when they locate inventories, working capital, and various liquid assets around the world. It also affects the timing and nature of the declaration of earnings. There are limits on how much freedom firms have in conducting business transactions such as those described here. For example, the Internal Revenue Service of the United States is quite active in policing the activities of U.S.-based multinational firms to see that they do report at least a portion of their current earnings for tax purposes rather than as they are declared at some future time or from some low tax-rate country. This prevents firms from never declaring their overseas earnings for tax purposes in the United States. This shows that firms with overseas operations do have advantages that purely national firms do not. However, they also bear risks, such as foreign exchange risks, that national firms ordinarily do not.

FOREIGN EXCHANGE RISKS AND HEDGING

While we have mentioned foreign exchange risks above, there is more to the story. Exchange risks occur in importing, exporting, and the ownership of assets abroad. We have mentioned only a few of the complexities involved. All of the instances mentioned have to do with the movement of goods, services, and financial assets through international markets where these items begin by being valued in one currency and end up being valued in another. Since currencies can change in value relative to one another, there are threats of loss and opportunities for gain in value. Most firms choose to forego gains in order to avoid the risk of loss. When they do we say that they have hedged their transactions. One way of doing this is to engage in what are known as forward transactions that offset or complement a current transaction. Thus, there are two types of markets. Current transactions take place in what are called "spot markets" and future transactions take place in what are called "forward markets." For example, suppose a firm in the United States is selling some machinery to a British firm but will not be paid until 90 days from now. It can sell British pounds that it will receive as payment in the forward market in the amount of the value of the machinery. All this says is that the firm will be receiving an agreed upon amount of British pounds in 90 days in payment for the machinery sold. But to assure that this will equal today's dollar value of the machinery being shipped, the firm sells the pounds for an agreed dollar value today even though it will not receive the pounds until 90 days from today. This is called hedging. See News Box 9–2 on modern problems with hedging.

Not all transactions can be hedged through forward markets however. For example, the value of long-term contracts and ownership of long-lived assets cannot be hedged in the forward market. This is not to say that firms have no measures that they can take to reduce risks —they do. If the assets are fixed in place—assets such as plant and equipment—the value of these tends to be hedged by their very nature. For example, let us suppose that the host country where the plant is located is undergoing inflation and its currency's value is falling against the U.S. dollar. Generally, because of the inflation, the market value of the plant when valued in local currency will increase. Thus, if the plant were sold, it would have a value in local currency higher than its initial cost. Now, if the foreign exchange markets are working efficiently, the value of the plant when expressed in U.S. dollars should remain nearly unchanged simply because the change in the exchange rate would just offset the inflation rate of the host country. Thus, fixed assets are in themselves a hedge against changes in exchange rates resulting from differences in the rate of inflation across countries. This tends to be true as well for inventories that can be repriced if the general price of goods is constantly increasing because of too rapid augmentation of the money supply in the host country. The fact that physical assets hold their value partially explains why common citizens in high-inflation economies tend to turn all their savings and cash into material assets. They would rather have things rather than paper money under the circumstances. It is a hedge against losses.

GOVERNMENT INTERVENTION

So long as markets are allowed to function freely, firms can largely neutralize fluctuations in exchange rates. However, governments intervene for public policy reasons in the functioning of the market and accordingly frustrate the ability of firms to manage their assets to their own best advantage. For example, many countries impose price controls on goods and services. These do not allow firms to reprice their inventories when there is inflation. Thus, some of the value of assets and earnings is lost because firms cannot price goods at their real cost. Also, when countries are attempting to maintain some fixed relation between their own currency and those of other countries they may engage in foreign exchange control. Under these circumstances firms may be disallowed from moving cash out of the country into another

---

NEWS BOX 9–2
Many Multinationals Face Major Risks in Currencies,
Try to Limit the Damage

When the Australian dollar recently plunged 9 percent against the dollar in just two days, Mack Trucks Inc.'s Australian subsidiary took a painful "several hundred thousand dollar hit" on trucks being sold at fixed Australian prices, says David J. Smith, Mack's treasurer, in Allentown, Pennsylvania.

Edward T. Sheehan, the foreign-finance manager at General Electric Company in Fairfield, Connecticut, says that because of volatile currency rates, GE's customers sometimes delay ordering dollar-priced equipment and also hold up paying their bills "until they have a window when the dollar is lower."

John Harvey-Jones, the chairman of Imperial Chemical Industries PLC, recently told a parliamentary commitee in London that he almost didn't care much at what level sterling traded—as long as it was stable.

Multinational companies around the world are being buffeted by volatile exchange rates. Although more companies are trying to hedge their exchange risks, the problems of protecting the value of exports, covering the costs of imports, and preserving the value of foreign earnings are as great as ever.

Trying Their Luck

No hedge is perfect, and no corporate treasurer can anticipate all the market swings. But they are trying. Five years ago, Mack Trucks didn't have a foreign-exchange department, and Westinghouse Electric Corporation is devoting six times the work-hours it did in 1981.

Until recently, U.S. companies have mainly complained that the government should act to bring down the dollar—to restore the competitiveness of America's dollar-priced exports and to help curb imports. But within the past year, more and more executives have begun to think that volatility can be as bad as or worse than a too-strong dollar.

Exchange rates that bounce wildly up and down can be "much more damaging than periodic currency misalignments, and prolonged volatility may be a greater threat to American companies internationally than a strong dollar," says Richard Karl Goeltz, the treasurer for Seagram Co. "Planning, controlling, and monitoring international operations becomes more difficult and expensive."

Economists disagree about whether volatility—as opposed to extreme strength or weakness in particular currencies—significantly affects international trade. Although a study by the International Monetary Fund last year cast doubt on such links, one by the Federal Reserve Bank of New York found significant effects. The Fed study contended that exchange-rate volatility can cause importers and exporters to be so uncertain about the direction and the level of currencies that they cut back on buying and selling goods overseas.

"Fast changes in a market are always counter to sensible, orderly, and profitable business," says Sheldon Weinig, the chief executive of Materials Research Corp. in Orangeburg, New York. Volatility, he adds, can "put your whole cost structure in a fluid state." He also complains: "You're making territorial manufacturing decisions: It may have been better to manufacture in France last week, the United States this week, and Japan next."

Change at Westinghouse

Partly because of volatility as well as lower labor costs, Westinghouse is studying a plan to manufacture all of a new but as yet undisclosed product line in Brazil, Germany, or Taiwan; the initial investment would total $30 million. "That is a real cultural change in Westinghouse," says Warren H. Hollinshead, the international treasurer. In the past, the Pittsburgh-based company wouldn't have even considered looking outside the United States.

"No one can predict currency values," Hollinshead explains. "The name of the game is gyrations, and when you think it will continue, you don't put all your eggs in one basket. You spread production out."

GE's Sheehan warns that foreign affiliates selling in local currencies "can be taken to the cleaners" because of sharp movements in currencies from the time of sale to payment. The same problem also exists on the buying side.

"If you order widgets at one price and find at delivery two weeks later that the price had gone up 10 percent to 15 percent, that might wipe out profits on a sale," Sheehan says. Mack Trucks' Smith adds: "The greater the number of days you're exposed, the greater your risk. All you need is the wrong 48 hours, and a sudden devaluation or depreciation" can cause severe losses.

Hedging Difficult

Conservative companies such as GE and Westinghouse routinely hedge currency risks in the forward foreign-exchange market, where currencies are bought and sold for future delivery at preset prices. But hedging can be difficult, particularly if the sale is to be completed quickly. So Hollinshead says that as soon as a Westinghouse unit indicates that it has a prospective sale to a customer in a foreign currency, the unit is told to be sure that the selling price is high enough to cover the hedging costs.

Weinig of Materials Research predicts that the dollar's recent plunge is going to prompt currency speculation by corporations. "This is a time when people are going to get cute, because they're all convinced the dollar is going on a linear line down against other currencies; they think they're going to get rich," he says. Instead, he believes, "a lot of companies are going to get suckered into losing a lot of money. Give us enough turbulence, and we'll manage to shoot ourselves in the foot."

SOURCE: *The Wall Street Journal*, July 30, 1985, p. 18.

currency. When such actions are taken by governments, firms have no freedom to reduce the risk of losing part of their assets. To reduce these risks, firms take certain actions. For example, the pricing of goods may be altered so that goods being shipped into the country with controls will be priced higher than they normally would be. By doing this, the firm takes its profits in the country of origin rather than the country experiencing inflation and imposing exchange controls. As we noted above, transfer pricing can be used to relocate where the profits will be taken for accounting and perhaps tax purposes. Other measures firms can take to reduce their exposure in the host country currency include accelerating payments, that is, paying ahead of time for imported raw materials, delaying payments on accounts payable, accelerating payments to local vendors before prices rise, and reducing extension of credit to distributors. All of these actions either reduce the amount of local currency on hand or accelerate payments to take advantage of the higher value of the local currency before it depreciates further. Of course, when all firms are attempting to do this, their transactions tend to cancel each other and these measures lose their effectiveness.

MOBILIZATION OF CAPITAL

To finance their international operations, firms have several sources, but basically these sources can be categorized as internal or external. Internal sources include retained earnings plus depreciation allowances after taxes and dividends. For the multinational firm as a whole, sources include the earnings of the parent and all of its overseas subsidiaries. These earnings can be made available to the parent or to any specific subsidiary or subsidiaries. The external sources of capital include debt and equity markets wherever these exist. A subsidiary of a multinational firm can finance itself in its host country or from sources outside of the country. Generally, each subsidiary must compete with all other subsidiaries for capital. However, most multinationals attempt to arrange lines of credit for each subsidiary in the country where it is located. These lines of credit tend to be specific to that subsidiary. But this does not mean that there are not opportunities to move funds out of the subsidiary if it has earnings. If the country or the bank extending credit does not monitor the movement of funds, it is possible for the subsidiary to borrow in its host country and transfer funds to either the parent or to a sister subsidiary located in another country.

Another aspect of multinational firm financing, which usually does not apply to purely national firms, is the ability to organize investor groups and consortia to engage in international ventures. The greater flexibility of the multinational firm stems from its knowledge of and contacts in international financial markets through its dealings with multinational banks headquartered in several different countries. Access to the Eurocurrency market is also important to these firms in these respects. It is an unregulated market that serves the needs of large banks and large multinational firms. It takes demand deposits only from such entities and converts these to short-term and medium-term loans to this same clientele. Thus, MNCs do not have to rely simply on the financial markets and banking systems in their home countries. They have access to all of the above-mentioned sources. It should be remembered though that multinationals must still evaluate investment projects in much the same way that any other firm would. The main point is that the multinationals have greater flexibility in terms of how they obtain funds and in the variety of opportunities for allocating funds. Because of this, the financing decisions become more complex. They are more complex in terms of having to deal in more national jurisdictions and having to move funds through more than a single currency.

Multinational firms can also take advantage of the risk-reducing nature of international geographic diversification in product and raw materials markets. By being geographically diversified, the multinational firm reduces the overall variability of its earnings stream. In so doing, the entire firm becomes less risky and hence more attractive to potential providers of debt and equity capital. This has come to be known as the *portfolio effect* in the field of finance. And just as some firms achieve portfolio effects by diversifying across product groups, multinational firms achieve these effects primarily through geographic diversification of assets across national boundaries. By so doing, the cost of capital from external sources is reduced and borrowing capacity increased. Thus, the multinational firm can use leverage to a greater extent than can most firms that do not have multinational characteristics.

FINANCIAL ANALYSIS

As can be seen from the above, the multinational firm is a financially complex creature and hence must have the ability to engage in advanced methods of international financial analysis. This includes risk analysis of foreign investments and foreign exchange, methods of undertaking foreign exchange dealings, and the location of working capital including cash balances and inventories. In doing capital budgeting for example, the firm must make comparisons of projects in perhaps several countries. Each project may have a different expected life. Each subsidiary may have a different cost of capital, line of credit, foreign exchange exposure, and level of economic and political risk. All of these things must be considered when making comparisons among subsidiaries regarding which ones should receive infusions of capital and which should not.

There are four major considerations for the multinational firm's financial analysis. First, it must decide how funds are to be used, i.e., which projects and subsidiaries should receive support and how great that support should be? Second, it must decide on how the desired projects should be financed, i.e., what proportion should come from internal sources and what proportion from external sources? Third, it must decide on the structure of financing. What proportion should be acquired as debt and what proportion as equity? Fourth, it must decide on country sources. Which financial markets should be used to acquire external financing? These are interdependent questions. They largely have to be answered simultaneously. Moreover, the answers are not independent of the firm's current and historical financial condition. A soundly conceived project may not obtain needed financing if the firm has not demonstrated solid management performance in the past.

The location of projects is also an important consideration in financing. Projects located in countries that have relatively unstable political and economic systems may be rejected regardless of how good they look based on anticipated cash flows. Political risk certainly has an effect on financial risk. Thus, the analysis of financial requirements has to consider the potential impact of political events. Countries do intervene in financial markets. Foreign exchange may become rationed so that the firms are unable to meet their obligations to foreign creditors and to repatriate dividends to stockholders. Deciding how and where to finance international operations calls for detailed knowledge not only of financial institutions but also the characteristics of countries' economic and legal systems.

In financial analysis, projects cannot be analyzed independent of one another because they affect the firm's cost-of-capital, capital structure, and product/market/country portfolio and hence the level of risk. Thus, financial analysis is not just a matter of examining financial ratios and immediate financial performance. It must take into account a broad range of variables that emanate from all of the sources described in preceding chapters. It is through the financial function that these variables must ultimately be synthesized into measures of expected performance that can be weighed against expected risks.

SUMMARY

Ultimately the multinational firm has the objective of optimizing its operations, as nearly as possible, across countries in such a way that long-run profitability is maximized. It should attempt to minimize the legitimate tax burden it must incur by locating assets and moving goods and financial balances in such a way that operations are adequately supported while still preserving the asset base against unnecessary taxation. This requires expert analysis of the rules of taxation across many national and regional jurisdictions. Thus, financial strategy has to be predicated upon skillful financial analysis. This skill is ever more important to multinational firms that deal in the complex environments described here.

DISCUSSION QUESTIONS FOR CHAPTER NINE

1. What is the role of money in an economy? Speculate on its functions and uses.

2. What is an exchange rate and how is it determined?

3. What causes exchange rates to change? Can managers control exchange rate changes?

4. What financial risks are involved in international transactions that do not occur in a purely national transaction? Give an example.

5. When do companies experience translation gains or losses?

6. What concerns does a manager have in moving the accumulated earnings from a foreign subsidiary?

7. What is the difference between a "spot" and a "future" market? How can a manager use these currency markets to protect against the various forms of financial risk?

8. Why do governments intervene in foreign exchange markets? Is having a stable currency important? Why or why not?

9. How does government regulatory and policy actions affect the options available to management to protect itself against exchange risk?

10. What advantages does a firm gain in mobilizing capital when it does business internationally?

11. Identify four major considerations for a multinational firm's financial analysis. Why would international finance be a more complex task?

CHAPTER TEN

Design and Administration of International Operations

INTRODUCTION

In this chapter we return to some of the concepts introduced in Chapters Two and Five. Here we deal with some additional issues where the focus is on the management of overseas subsidiaries and their relationship to the parent firm. We further are concerned with subsidiaries over which the parent has operating control. Largely what we have to say here applies to the majority-controlled subsidiary in which more than 50 percent of the ownership equity is in the hands of the parent firm. Thus, for the most part, we are also referring to firms that have financial control through voting rights. However, it is not necessary to have majority control to have operating control if the majority of the shares are widely scattered among many small owners. Owning 20 percent of a firm when all other owners have less than 1 percent gives this share percentage fairly strong control. This usually is not the case among the subsidiaries of most multinational firms. Most are either wholly owned or at least majority-owned by their parents.

Having ownership control usually provides operating control as well. By this we mean that the firm is free to make its own decisions within the constraints of the national environments within which it operates. If the firm does not have this freedom, it cannot always choose its preferred methods in terms of organizational structure, development of plans, and implementation of controls. If it is necessary to take on partners, as is true in some countries, the partners may heavily influence the decision making process. Under these circumstances it may not be possible to integrate the overseas unit into the total corporation. Where this is the case, the parent may be reluctant to continue to invest and may refuse to provide access to new technology.

While joint ventures are discussed briefly we choose to focus on the management of the total firm and its overseas subsidiaries where the firm has operating control. In the next section we discuss briefly the notion of ownership strategy. In subsequent sections we shall focus on the integration of foreign subsidiaries into a managerial system through the design of organizational structures, development of plans, and evaluating and controlling of organizational performance.

OWNERSHIP STRATEGIES

While the predominant mode of ownership by multinational firms is that of majority control, there are many instances where the preferred mode is that of taking a minority ownership position. This often is true even where the host country does not insist on majority control by nationals. Why would a multinational firm prefer to take a minority position when it could take majority control if it chose? There are several types of situations that tend to favor minority positions in joint ventures or consortium aggreements. They usually involve one or more of the following conditions.

1. The host country is politically unstable and may expropriate foreign properties.
2. The market is difficult and access is easier to achieve if a host country partner undertakes the marketing aspects of the firm.
3. A local partner is needed to deal with the complexities of government regulations or similar environmental difficulties.
4. The market is small and not highly important to the multinational firm, but it wishes to develop or maintain a foothold in anticipation of market growth and hence takes on a local partner.
5. The project is too large and/or too risky even for a large multinational to undertake by itself.
6. The partner brings some unique asset otherwise unavailable to the multinational firm, such as technology, knowledge of the workforce, or ability to marshall financial resources.
7. It is not necessary to have majority control in order to have operating control.
   a. The majority of shares are widely scattered and even a large minority position provides effective operating control.
   b. Operating control can be exerted through contractual relationships, such as management contracts, technical aid agreements, licenses and franchises, and supply contracts.

It appears that most joint ventures occur either because there is a legal requirement that mandates their use or the multinational firm needs the expertise of a local firm for there to be an effective enterprise. An example of the latter is the General Motors Corp. and Toyota joint venture. General Motors, as the local firm, needed the technological expertise of Toyota to develop and produce a subcompact automobile in the United States. At the same time, while Toyota probably could have done this independently, it preferred to have the marketing and organizational strengths offered by General Motors. Together they probably have developed a more effective enterprise in Fremont, California than either could have developed alone. General Motors had already shut down the facility for various reasons, including difficulties with labor relations. Toyota was able to enter and, in part, rid itself of these same difficulties. It has also been able to retrain many of the former employees with the result that the workforce has become more effective than it had been under General Motors' management. By operating jointly, they have reduced the risks of failure because each is concentrating on those aspects of the enterprise it does best.

It is likely that joint ownership occurs most often because of government requirements for national participation; such requirements are much more prevalent in developing countries than in the advanced countries. A very substantial proportion of developing countries do exert control over the extent of foreign ownership within individual enterprises. It does appear, however, that there is recognition that the technology and other special assets that some firms bring with them deserve more favorable treatment. Indeed, in the screening of investments most countries offer more favorable treatment to firms in so-called preferred industries. These firms usually are in high-technology fields.

Even where there is a stipulation that firms divest themselves of majority control, there often is a backing away from this. For example, in Mexico there are regulations that mandate "Mexicanization" of industry. Presumably this stipulation applies to the automobile industry. Despite this, however, the large multinational automobile companies continue to have majority control and even 100 percent ownership of their subsidiaries in Mexico. This may result partly from the problem of finding local partners that could marshall the resources required to buy majority control in these very large subsidiaries. A more likely reason for the Mexican government not to press the issue is that the level of efficiency of these firms would be considered reduced were ownership control to rest in the hands of local interests. Certainly the incentive for GM and Ford to continuously infuse new and improved methods would be less than it is at present if GM and Ford were forced to accept minority positions. Moreover, the automobile companies have well-developed international marketing channels that have made possible Mexico's substantial exportation of automobile parts and components. Also, the firms have a demonstrated expertise in increasing the local content of automobiles manufactured for Mexico's internal market.

The issues regarding ownership structure become largely moot where countries insist that foreign firms hold less than 50 percent of the equity. However, it is interesting that most multinational firms bargain vigorously to overcome such a constraint on ownership structure. With exception to the types of situations listed earlier in this section, most multinational firms simply prefer to have financial control even to complete ownership of the equity. Even the Japanese, who are noted for their greater willingness to engage in joint ventures, tend to prefer majority control. For example, in South Korea, a country that prefers joint ventures and has considerable cultural affinity with Japan, 85 percent of the Japanese firms operating there chose to have majority control over their Korean investments.

It is often suggested that joint ventures reduce political and financial risks. They can and they do under the appropriate circumstances. As we have noted, however, multinational firms do have specialized assets that are valuable. Joint venturing may cause a sharing of these valuable assets in such a way that the joint venture partner can pirate away some of that value. Also, where there is not financial control, there is likely not to be operating control. This, in turn, can reduce efficiency because without control, the multinational firm cannot utilize its best options. The result is not a reduction of risk, but rather an elevation of risk under these circumstances. Thus, joint ventures do not always reduce risk; they may indeed do just the opposite.

The strategy of what ownership structure to follow, as can be seen, is not a simple choice. Just because countries can legally control the extent of foreign ownership does not mean that foreign firms will acquiesce. The ownership of valuable assets tends to give the firm additional bargaining power in this respect. They may simply refuse to invest in countries that adamantly pursue joint ownership between foreign investors and nationals. There is considerable evidence that multinational firms choose not to invest as actively in such countries as they do in countries that take a more open and flexible approach to the issue of ownership.

Ownership control is most important at crucial times in which decisions of strategic importance need to be made. If control is shared with a partner, differences of opinion may arise. If these differences are significant and cannot be favorably settled, then overall strategy of the total enterprise may be compromised in undesirable ways. For example, the parent firm may wish to transfer assets between subsidiaries or expand or contract the asset base in the partnership. The local partner may see this as not being in its best interests. Strategic decisions where conflicts can arise include application and acquisition of technology, development of markets, replacement or movement of key personnel, changing the composition of the board of directors, relocation of production facilities, and reequipping of plants. Most firms prefer to avoid such conflicts by maintaining ownership control. As firms need to integrate their operations on a more global scale, the desire for control has become additionally important because of the need to move rapidly to counter moves of the competition in different markets. This need has increasingly affected the way in which multinational firms make their decisions and organize their overseas activities. Even the Japanese multinationals, which have relied heavily on consensus decision making, are moving toward greater centralization of organization structures and decision making. This is occurring because of the need for greater responsiveness. Having ownership control supports the firm in meeting this need.

ORGANIZING OVERSEAS OPERATIONS

Ownership control can be important to the decision regarding choice of organization structure. The concepts we consider here apply to firms that actually produce and market goods and services in several foreign locations.

There are various ways in which multinational firms can organize their international activities: These include:

- The international division.
- Functional structure.
- Product groups.
- Regional or country divisions.
- Matrix organization.

Which of these is best depends upon the size of the parent firm and the size and diversity of its international activities.

The International Division

Firms that are new to international business may begin with a simple importing and exporting activity with perhaps a few warehouses or simple assembly operations abroad. For these firms the international division is often chosen as the means of coordinating between production plants at home that produce the products and distribution points abroad which sell the products. Usually at this stage any assembly operations are simple and involve transfer of components from the home country to locations abroad. These types of transactions can easily be handled by the international division. The international division form

FIGURE 10-1 The International Division Structure

of organization is largely a sales organization, but its use may extend to coordinating substantial investments in overseas manufacturing plants. So long as these plants do not produce a wide array of products and are small in size and not very complex, this form of organization may be quite satisfactory. In Figure 10–1 an example of the international division is presented.

The international division simply separates international operations from domestic operations. The idea is largely that of concentrating specialized effort on international transactions. Specialized effort allows for reduced costs due to increased expertise and economies of scale. Even if the domestic operations are organized around product divisions, it is still necessary to have special attention placed on the firm's international efforts. Unless each product division has a large presence in international markets, it is usually more efficient to have a specialized organization unit to represent all of the domestic divisions in overseas locations. Some very large multinational firms continue to have an international division even though some of the large product groups have a worldwide product structure (to be discussed below). Most multinational firms, among their product lines, do have what we might call short product lines; that is, an offering of relatively few products in a market. Some markets may nevertheless be small even for the larger product lines. Under these circumstances it often pays to have an international division to market the short product lines

FIGURE 10–2   Functional Structure

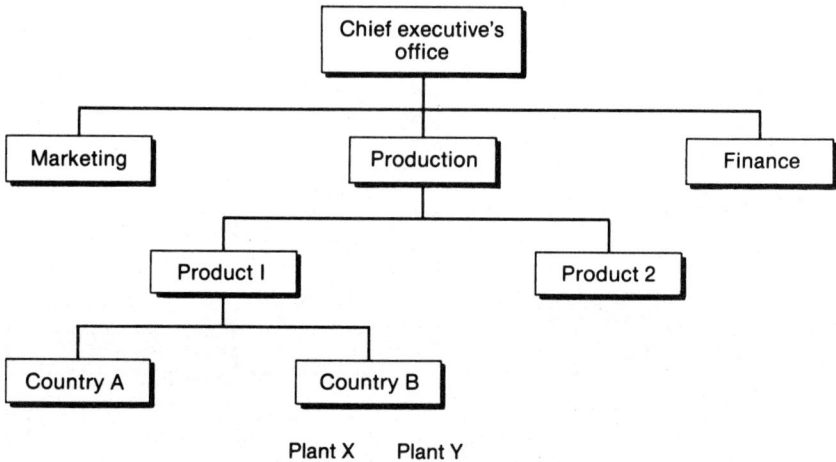

Plant X   Plant Y

abroad and to serve the product divisions in small markets. Thus, even in those companies that have adopted a worldwide product line organization, there may still be an international division that responds to the smaller markets or represents the smaller product lines.

Functional Structure

The functional structure depicted in Figure 10–2 is not widely used by multinational firms. This structure is used mainly by relatively small firms that have highly centralized organizational structures, however, there are some multinational firms that do follow it. These firms generally have product lines that rely on the same technology and tend to be sold to a relatively narrow spectrum of customers. Thus, the plants tend to be highly integrated across products and serve single or similar markets. The management of diversity therefore is not a major problem since the customers in each country are very similar. One example of a company that historically used the functional structure is Caterpillar Tractor Co.

As the firm's international activities grow and become more complex, there usually is a need to adopt additional means of coordinating foreign activities. When this stage of growth is reached, the firm must then decide on what form a more complex organization should take. One such more complex form is the worldwide product divisional organization.

FIGURE 10–3   Product Structure

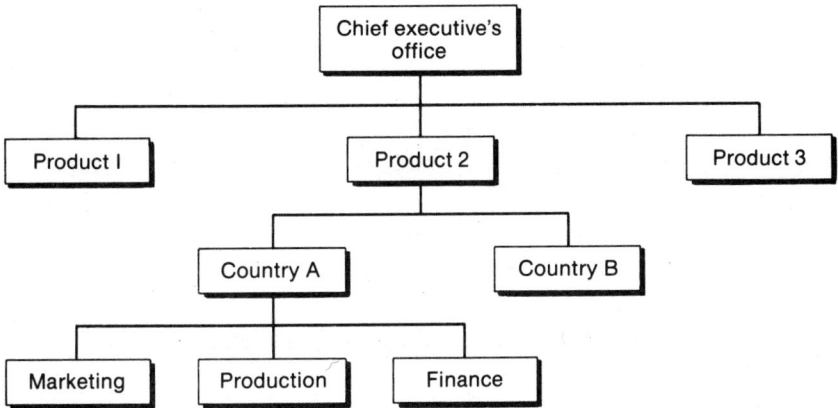

Worldwide Product Divisions

Some firms attempt to apply the same methods to their international operations that they use in their domestic operations. For example, if the firm uses product divisions at home, it may attempt to do the same thing abroad. In this scheme if the firm produces trucks, truck engines, heavy-duty axles, and construction equipment, for example, and each of these products is a division at home, the overseas operations will be organized the same way with each product division being held responsible for its own overseas operations. Thus, in each country where trucks are sold the truck division at home is responsible for the production and sales of trucks not only in the home country, but also in all other countries as well. This form of organization places the emphasis on the product but, in our example in Figure 10–3, it also means that there are four organizational groups, each with its international operations. In many instances though, such groupings are cumbersome because the four divisions may share facilities in some countries. Because a country's market may not be large enough to support four separate plants, sharing arrangements must be worked out between the four product divisions. Conflicts such as this lead many firms to adopt an area structure based on geographic regions or countries.

Geographic or Area Structure

There are good reasons why the area structure is probably the most common way of organizing foreign operations. Since countries do have

FIGURE 10–4   Area Structure

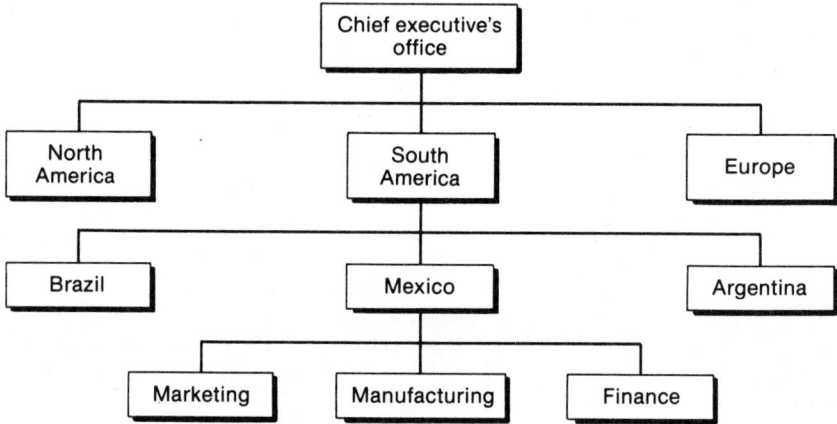

varying environments and market characteristics, it is often more convenient to organize along country lines than to organize along product lines. Furthermore, if the market is small, the sales force may have to serve more than a single product grouping. In situations where it is more important for the manager to have expertise in understanding the sociocultural and competitive situation, expertise in the products being produced is less important. The parent firm can provide the latter, but the local manager must be able to deal with the day-to-day problems in the country setting. It is unreasonable to expect that a manager who is expert in a product should also be an expert on all the markets and characteristics of several countries as well. Thus, specialization in country/market knowledge tends to dominate product knowledge. Country considerations tend to dominate over product considerations in international management, whereas it is just the opposite in a purely domestic setting. The area structure is depicted in Figure 10–4.

The Matrix Form

The matrix form of structure is used to improve coordination across complex product lines where country expertise is also important. In Figure 10–5 we have depicted an organization that follows both a product organization and an area structure. In this scheme, country managers require aid from product divisions on a continuing basis but the country managers are responsible to a broader international organization for purposes of evaluating and controlling performance within

FIGURE 10–5   Matrix Form

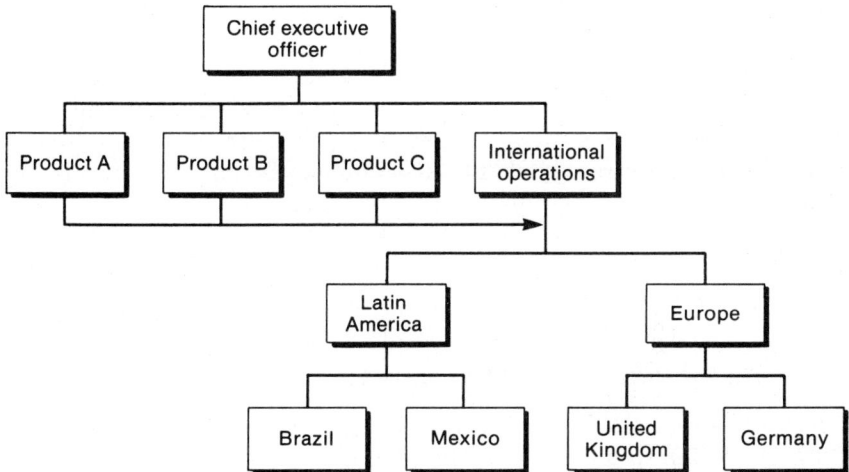

each country's market. In firms that have diverse product lines or technically difficult products, it may be necessary to wield control over the technology and production through product divisions. But, for purposes of meeting the specialized needs of country markets, there is need for special marketing knowledge. A worldwide product division structure could deal effectively with the former requirements but not do a good job of dealing with the latter requirements. Just the opposite might be true of an area or country structure. Thus, the idea of a matrix form is to combine the two in such a way that the best aspects of both systems can be brought to bear. There are difficulties in doing this since there is not always a clear notion regarding who has responsibility and authority for taking action. Largely this becomes a matter of constant communication between the product divisions at home and the country operations abroad.

The success of a particular structure depends in part on the internal organizational processes. Presumably organization structure should aid in the development of effective organization processes that include communication flows, resolving conflict, development of plans, evaluation of performance, adjustment of resource allocations, and decision making, but it is not always clear which method of structuring is best in any particular situation. Firms cannot blindly adopt one structure in preference to another, although it would often seem that they do. What works in one country or with one product may not work well for another country or product. Thus, there usually is a "trial and error" aspect to the development of structure. Regardless of which structure is chosen, there will always be some bases left uncovered. Thus, there is a need for flexibility and effective means for resolving differences on a continuing basis. This comes about through communication of various sorts, including face-to-face meetings and discussions, the planning process, formal reporting on budgets and performance, plant visits, and the like. Structure in part follows from strategy. Thus, as good changes lead to strategy adjustments, then structure as a means of implementing strategy should also change. If that structure is inflexible or does not have informal methods of ameliorating disagreements within the structure, then the structure is inappropriate and in need of change. Structure and process do make the difference in many ways in ultimate performance.

Planning for International Operations

One of the processes that is important to international success is planning. It is often said that decisions cannot be made intelligently without a plan. A plan is like a roadmap. If we want to get from point A to point B, it is necessary to make some kind of plan—especially if we place a value on resources used or time. Otherwise, any random decision is as good as any other. Of course, if there is only one way to get between two points then there is no need for a plan. But, as we are all well aware, there are few such linear decisions. Most important decisions involve numerous alternative potential courses of action. In a multicountry system of operating subsidiaries, the number of courses of action is magnified. Each subsidiary can be looked upon as an independent business or set of businesses for planning purposes. Each subsidiary manager has aspirations that can and do include the desire to introduce new products, expand plant and equipment, increase market share, and the like. But not all of these aspirations can be accommodated in most firms and certainly not all of the time. Moreover, the parent firm itself has ideas of its own regarding how various subsidiaries should fit into a larger strategy for the entire corporation. Thus, there is a need for some device that can be used to review such aspirations for all of the operating units within the corporation. Planning is such a device.

Planning involves sensing problems and opportunities, searching out alternatives, and then choosing a course of action that might be realistically open to a firm. Only by such a review can managers decide which alternatives appear to be the best given the current situation. A system of plans aids in the process of setting objectives not just for the larger corporation, but for individual operating units as well. Planning for a multinational firm is not so different from planning for any other firm. The major difference is having to evaluate more environments and market conditions abroad and from this to attempt to compare various operating subsidiaries with one another for allocating resources and anticipating profit performance.

Multinational firms, among themselves, differ in the degree to which they use formalized planning procedures. This is largely an outgrowth of management philosophy. Some senior management groups exert a great deal of control over individual subsidiaries abroad while other managements allow a great deal of autonomy to foreign subsidiaries. The degree to which planning is formalized and uses detailed written reports, specifies market and profit objectives in detail, adheres to fixed budgets, and regularly reviews formal plans can vary widely. The U.S. managerial style tends to be highly formalized when compared with Japanese or European firms. Some observers suggest that this greater formality on the part of U.S. firms also leads to a short-range view of the world and a tough adherence to the so-called "bottom line." Stated differently, the focus on short-run profits tends to overshadow longer-run concerns for effectiveness and survival. Yet, planning can be used effectively to tie together the information network and exert management control. This is important to firms which have far-flung international operations.

Control in International Operations

Control over the direction and activities of the firm is one of the more interesting and difficult aspects of managing the multinational firm. The challenge of integrating a worldwide network of subsidiaries, joint ventures, and contractual relations into a coherent corporate strategy and purpose is the essence of international management work. Control is achieved through the design of appropriate organizational structures and via management systems and processes. These include the motivation and reward systems, performance monitoring and evaluation, decision making and authority, and the more formal budgeting and planning systems.

However, we must not emphasize the restricting and constraining sides of control. Control also involves decentralization of decisions, autonomy in exploring new products—market opportunities, granting large discretionary budgets, and freedom from certain larger corporate goals. The point here is that control is a constant management activity the pursuit of which depends on unit performance and the environment with which that unit operates.

The term *control* is used here in much the same way that it is used in the field of engineering. Managers do not actually control every aspect of enterprise activity. They do require "feedback" if they are to take action to alter direction or to change the allocation of resources among various activities. In this sense, control is a device for identifying deviations from some desired norm so that action can be taken. This is much like the control we see when we set a thermostat to maintain temperature near a desired level. When the temperature falls below the desired level a signal is sent to a heating device, a furnace for example, which then comes on to heat the air and bring the temperature back up within the desired range. However, the temperature is not held at the exact desired temperature—just near that temperature. Managerial control is similar in that managers never expect that actual performance will exactly match the desired performance. Deviation from the desired performance is expected, but when the deviation exceeds some reasonable level, managers wish to be able to analyze the situation to see what caused the deviation. This is the purpose of control.

Two problems of control at the international level are particularly interesting. The first contrasts authority and responsibility with actual performance; the second involves decentralization of decision authority.

In large organizations the chief executive officer cannot possibly make all of the decisions. Thus, he or she must delegate to others the authority to make decisions, but in doing so, there must be some specification of which types of decisions can be made by whom and in what magnitude. With the delegation of authority there is also the companion notion of responsibility: did the person or group or division meet, supersede, or fail to meet the objectives it had the authority and resources to pursue? If so, was it because of events outside the control of those who had the authority and responsibility? Ultimately, in a meritocracy individuals and groups supposedly should be rewarded on the basis of good performance. However, in international operations it is not always easy to know if results were due to real contribution rather than simply on the basis of fortuitous events.

One of the problems of international control is the problem of distance and difficulty of communication. It is true that with modern air travel and electronic communication and data transmission the corporate headquarters theoretically could have quick access to each and every overseas subsidiary. Even so, there is much information that can be had only by being on the scene on a day-to-day basis. For example, managers in overseas subsidiaries must be aware of individual customers' needs and must work with local suppliers closely to balance production requirements with market requirements. This is difficult if not impossible to do from a long distance even with the most up-to-date communications system. Thus, authority to make decisions must be delegated to the local level. This is called decentralization. Decentralization becomes more important in the multinational firm simply because the local environments taken together are more complex, different, and difficult to understand and assess than the home environment. Under these conditions we can assume that the manager who is closer to the problem (e.g. the host country manager) probably has better information and perspective to solve local problems.

The ultimate objective of control is twofold. First, it is the means used by management to implement organizational strategy. And second, it is the activity that monitors and steers ongoing operations. These aspects are related, but the latter is more concerned with short-run considerations while the former is more oriented to long-run considerations. Short-run actions are merely a manifestation of incremental progress toward the longer-run objectives established by the overriding strategy of the enterprise. Operating control deals with the short-run, but it has long-run implications and hence is important to the strategy. It is the accumulation of short-run experiences that provides the basis for making adjustments to strategy. As mentioned above, strategy must be supported by organizational structure and organizational processes. It is through these two mechanisms that control is exerted.

The theme of structure has been sufficiently described earlier in this chapter. Structure generally provides a formal scheme that depicts the authority/responsibility relationships within the organization. It also is a mechanism for grouping interdependent activities together. The structure adopted in the international aspects of the enterprise may or may not follow the same principles as the structure used at home. As we noted, firms often adopt an area structure in international operations even though they may use an organizational scheme structured around products at home. Thus, key managers at home are responsible for the performance of various products or product groups. In the international arena managers in the same firm may be responsible for the performance achieved within a single country or area. Control then is exerted at the country level and each country manager is then responsible for the performance of all products in the market rather than a single product across all country markets.

Organizational processes are designed to support and reinforce the authority/responsibility relationships arising out of the organizational structure. Examining these processes and controlling for deviations from planned outcomes requires information on a large number of variables. In the final analysis, the management information is the core of control system effectiveness.

Information Needed for Control

From the above we can see that organization structure and processes provide the basic devices for control. But to utilize these there is a need for information regarding the processes being followed within the organization structure. Organization structure provides the mechanism through which decision making can be coordinated. Information is needed to see that decisions at various levels within the organization are compatible not only with one another, but also with the desired outcomes within the larger organizational strategy. With the enormous information generating capability of modern management information systems, it is important that information be timely, relevant, in a useful form, and readily available. Information is a competitive tool in two ways: (1) possessing information competitors do not have and (2) having sound internal information regarding performance. For example, the firm that can have a reasonably accurate daily report on its production and sales will be able to adjust production to market needs and avoid accumulating unneeded inventories. This makes for lower costs and greater competitiveness. With satellite communication and on-line computer systems, it is now possible for headquarters in the home country to have such information available for most of the firm's overseas subsidiaries. This is not yet a widespread phenomenon, but the potential is there and the number of such systems is growing. See News Box 10–1 for an example of how Sears is using satellite technology to get the information problem solved.

If an information system is to be used as a device to control and evaluate subsidiary operations, there needs to be some common methods of measurement and reporting the results of those measurements. A manager cannot directly compare one subsidiary with another if one subsidiary is located in Germany and the other in Australia. As we noted in Chapter Nine, there is a need for translation from one currency to another. However, there is also need for evaluation of asset values where subsidiaries are of different ages and/or where they do not produce the same products. Yet, corporate level managers, who are responsible for allocating resources among overseas subsidiaries, must make comparisons and evaluate performance across subsidiaries. Decisions do have to be made for purposes of rewarding subsidiary managers and allocating resources based on current and projected performance. Also, budgets have to be developed and performance evaluated in terms of these budgets. These activities call for reasonable commonality among the subsidiaries in terms of the information being gathered and reported to corporate headquarters.

The accounting and other management information systems should be designed to pick up data on a myriad of variables; in most multinational firms they are indeed so designed. The questions that have to be addressed in the multinational firm are different primarily because the information systems begin their collection of data starting from a different base, that is, much of the data is reported in different

---

NEWS BOX 10–1
Sears Orders Teleconference Satellite System

American Satellite Co. said Monday that it has signed a contract with Sears, Roebuck & Co. to construct and operate a private communications system for the huge retailer.

Terms of the deal were not disclosed. American Satellite described it as a multimillion-dollar contract, however, adding that it will be constructing a satellite network linking corporate offices of Sears and its subsidiaries in 26 cities across the country.

American Satellite, based in Rockville, Maryland, is a partnership owned by Fairchild Industries, Inc. and Continental Telecom Inc. The company said the Sears network, once in place, will be the largest private system ever developed in terms of offering the capability for "full-motion video teleconferencing."

Video conferencing allows individuals in different cities to conduct meetings via live, two-way television hookups.

Allstate Insurance Co., a Sears subsidiary, will be the network's initial teleconferencing user, American Satellite said. Its existing satellite network also will be used by Sears for its intracompany voice and data communications as well as to offer resale telephone services to other businesses.

"The Sears–Allstate network is further evidence that video teleconferencing is becoming a viable communications tool for corporations throughout the United States," said John N. Lemasters, president and chief executive of American Satellite. "Lower transmission costs, and increased emphasis on corporate productivity are the primary factors moving the video teleconferencing market into this long-predicted growth cycle."

---

currency units or in a different language. These must then be converted into the appropriate units or language for use by managers in the home country. But under any circumstance, data on the following variables basic to any international control system will be required.

- *Financial variables:* Sources and uses of funds, asset turnover, profitability, cost of capital, capital expenditure requirements.
- *Personnel variables:* Payroll, work patterns, seniority situation, promotions, wage scales, labor costs, training requirements, absenteeism.
- *Production variables:* Productivity of workers and machines, inventories in stock, scrappage rates, quality of output, work scheduling.
- *Marketing variables:* Productivity of sales force, salespeople's compensation, market shares, brand penetration, brand image.

The Role of Headquarters in Control

One of the key problems in the control of overseas operations is the degree to which headquarters should become directly involved in the decisions of foreign subsidiaries. Also, if headquarters is to be directly concerned, in which decision areas should it be primarily concerned? Many subsidiary managers seem to feel that there is too much interference from headquarters. Often the subsidiary sees itself as having to supply too much information to the parent—information that is often difficult to develop because the subsidiary may not have the expertise to generate all of the information on a timely basis. The subsidiaries usually are not as well endowed with equipment and staff experts as headquarters. Also, the problems with which headquarters are concerned may be of little direct importance to the individual subsidiary even though these concerns are legitimate for the corporation as a whole. For example, the parent may need information on a wide variety of variables if it is to evaluate the collective performance of all the subsidiaries. But from the individual subsidiary's viewpoint, information on all of these variables may be of little or no value in its concerns with day-to-day operations.

From the parent's standpoint then, control becomes a ticklish problem in which it must make a trade-off between forcing subsidiaries to supply all of the desired information at a cost of being seen as interfering too much, or obtaining too little information from the subsidiaries but being looked upon as being understanding. It is probable that parent firms ask for more than they really need and subsidiaries can really supply more than they would like at very little additional cost or hardship. The key is to design an information and control system that supplies and skillfully utilizes information on the variables most critical to successful operations and design of strategy. Most multinational firms attempt to use an international corporate plan supported with a system of annual financial budgets that are reviewed quarterly and even monthly in some firms. Subsidiaries tend to rebel when the review process occurs too frequently and see themselves as being too tightly controlled. These are issues that managers at the corporate level and subsidiary level must bargain about until a mutually acceptable system can be devised. This problem will be discussed from the manager's perspective in the next chapter.

The Role of Subsidiaries in Control

In a highly centralized decision-making system, control is exerted mostly from the center at headquarters. The objectives are set there and all of the decision rules are established there with the subsidiaries having little role in the process. At the other extreme, in a highly decentralized system control may be exerted largely at the subsidiary level with little role for the corporate headquarters except to assist in providing capital and the like. Most firms attempt to devise a system that utilizes the expertise of both the subsidiary and corporate headquarters. In a balanced system the subsidiaries are made responsible for those activities that are closest to the country level. This, after all, is the type of expertise in which the subsidiary is usually superior to the headquarters at home, but how much autonomy should subsidiaries have? Should they be free to raise credit any time they want to, and in so doing, should they be free to raise the credit wherever they choose, for example, in international financial markets and even in competition with the parent? How free should the subsidiary be to introduce new products on its own? Should subsidiaries be free to add plant and equipment in any amount desired without consulting with the parent firm? The answers to questions such as these generally are no. There have to be some norms established that act as control devices over the decision-making behavior of subsidiaries.

It is generally true that foreign subsidiaries do have greater autonomy than subsidiaries or other operating units in the home country. This is a matter of efficiency. In a single country where there is a common language and operating units are usually operating across no more than one or two time zones, the communications process is relatively easy and hence centralizing of decisions is possible. But where operating units may not be readily accessible because of time zone and language differences, it is necessary to give the subsidiary management greater authority and responsibility for total operation of the subsidiary. For example, if a firm headquartered in New York has a subsidiary in Tokyo, there is no time during normal working hours in either place when both units will be open simultaneously because there is an 11-hour difference in time. When New York is open, Tokyo is closed and vice versa. This does not mean that they cannot communicate. It merely means that one or the other manager must either get up early or stay late to communicate by telephone. The point of this little example is merely to illustrate that there are complications in international business that usually do not afflict domestic operations to the same degree. Time is not the only complication—there is also distance. Even in the same time zone it may still be difficult to communicate. Thus, the foreign subsidiary must be given greater latitude to make decisions.

Most firms accommodate to these needs by establishing rules regarding what types of decisions subsidiary managers can make without consultation with corporate headquarters. For example, there may be several levels of management in an international division, e.g., International Headquarters in Coral Gables, Florida; Latin American Headquarters in Mexico City; Brazilian Headquarters in Sao Paulo; and the Automobile Suspension Products Subsidiary in Bela Horizonte, Brazil. At each level the manager of that particular unit is given authority to make decisions of a certain level of magnitude. A sample set of decision rules regarding capital expenditures during any one year might appear as follows:

Organizational Level	Annual Allowable Capital Expenditure without Review
Subsidiary	$ 10,000
Brazilian Headquarters	50,000
Latin American Headquarters	100,000
International Division Headquarters	250,000

In a scheme such as this various operating units differ in terms of the amount of funds that can be expended depending upon the level occupied in the organization. But in the international operations at an equivalent level to that in domestic operations, the international unit may be given greater freedom than is the domestic unit. First, it is often more difficult logistically to review the decisions of the international units in the same detail that can be used in the domestic operations. It is more difficult in terms of data accumulation as well as in terms of the logistics of getting managers and staff people together to undertake such reviews. Yet, it may be at least if not more important to act quickly in international business as it is in domestic business. Thus, managers in the international operations are usually given greater breadth to exercise their own judgment in making decisions.

Multinational firms of different national origins appear to differ in terms of the degree of autonomy the headquarters in the home country allows its subsidiaries abroad. European firms seem to allow greater autonomy than do Japanese or American firms. Also, the nationality of the parent seems to have a bearing on the methods of control used. American firms rely on a wide variety of written reports and extensive financial budgets and written reviews, whereas European and Japanese firms seem to utilize more face-to-face consultations between headquarters and subsidiary personnel in keeping a flow of information moving back and forth between headquarters and the subsidiaries.

SUMMARY

Ownership structure is important to multinational firms for several reasons. One of the major reasons is that of avoiding serious conflicts in decision making. Majority control helps to assure that operating control also exists. However, it is not necessary to have majority control in order to have operating control. Also, there are situations in which having an active partner is beneficial, especially where risks are high and there is need for local expertise not otherwise available to the multinational firm.

Structuring the total organization is an important aspect of organization strategy. There are various ways in which firms can structure their overseas operations. The choice of structure depends on the size of the firm's overseas operations, their diversity, and their complexity in terms of products and markets.

Structure in part dictates the flow of information and influences decision-making authority and responsibility. It also influences the processes of planning and control that in turn set many of the dimensions of decision-making, resource allocation, and performance evaluation. All of these activities are more complex in multinational firms because of the variety of environments in which they operate. Even though there may be wide differences across countries, the multinational firm attempts through planning and control to bring a reasonable level of conformity among its various overseas subsidiaries.

DISCUSSION QUESTIONS FOR CHAPTER TEN

1. Why is ownership an important element in the administration of international operations?

2. Firms organize their international operations in a variety of ways. What factors determine international organizational structure?

3. Compare the functional with the international division. What are the trade-offs in using one form or the other?

4. Why would a multinational firm prefer to take a minority position even where it could take majority control if it chose?

5. "Because a multinational company has multiple operations in many countries at the same time, planning is a nearly impossible task because of the complexity involved. Therefore, the best strategy for organizing and controlling operations is developing a single 'formula that works' in the best country market and transferring that formula for operations to all other countries. That way you can control for unplanned variation in operations." Comment on the assumption and viability of the above idea.

6. Speculate on the effects that satellite communications, teleconferencing, and computer technology might have on the ability of a firm to control international operations.

7. In what ways might cultural differences influence people's perception of the value and use of information in management?

8. What are some common mechanisms or tools of control that firms use in controlling foreign operations?

9. How would you distinguish between the headquarter's versus subsidiary's view of the control problem?

10. What kind of decisions are most likely to be centralized at the home office? Which decisions would best be left to the subsidiary? Why?

CHAPTER ELEVEN

Leadership in the Successful International Manager

INTRODUCTION

In looking at general management literature in the early 1980s, there appears to be a resurgent interest in the theme of leadership. Whether it is in running a large multinational corporation, government agency, or a voluntary organization, various authors are drawing conclusions that a key to excellent performance of these organizations is leadship. With this text's emphasis on international management it is ironic to note that further impetus for the expressed interest in leadership is found in the threat that foreign economic leadership represents for the U.S. economy. Recent studies point to the need for improved "leadership for excellence" in competing against the challenge of foreign competition. In this chapter we discuss the nature of leadership, its importance to the international manager, and some of the elements that contribute to effective leadership in a foreign setting.

THE NATURE OF LEADERSHIP

Leadership is both a simple and a complex idea. Popular literature on managerial leadership tends to simplify our understanding by reducing the manager's job to a series of one-minute activities or it exaggerates the importance of leadership in the heroic and nearly mythical feats in great manager stories. However, since leadership has been one of the more researched and discussed topics in the management literature, there is a fairly good understanding of the factors and forces involved in the leadership process.

Because leadership is a dynamic phenomenon of human behavior, we can understand some aspects of leadership by looking at what people have seen and come to expect of the leadership role. Leadership role expectations are based on qualities a person is expected to demonstrate in that position and on behaviors and activities they are expected to display or perform. Because a leader's job is seen differently depending on whether you are a subordinate, peer, or superior, the expectations for leadership can be demanding. An example of ideal expectations of leadership might look like Figure 11–1.

The concept of role expectations is important because of its universal nature. This is especially relevant for the international manager who will face diverse and often contradictory job/role expectations in a foreign setting. The situation for the manager overseas is further complicated by the fact that she or he occupies several roles at the same time. As one author noted in discussing the important communicator function a manager exercises, an overseas manager may occupy the following roles: (1) representative of the parent firm, (2) manager of the local firm, (3) resident of the local community, (4) citizen of either the host state or of another, (5) member of a profession, not to mention (6) member of a family and all that it implies. To the extent that these roles conflict, communication tends to be blocked. For example, if expectations created by the manager role cannot be realized due to the restraints imposed by the representative role, the individual is in a position of role conflict. The resident and citizen roles are similarly likely to conflict. Unless the parent management is sufficiently sensitive to these possible conflicts, the overseas manager's behavior may be inexplicable and communications may become blocked.[1]

Leadership: Role Content and Context

Given the essentially dynamic nature of the leadership role, the outward expression of leadership can be seen as a result of two interacting elements: content and context. The *content* of leadership is made up of the attributes of a particular manager and the decisions to be made. The *context* of leadership refers to the nature of the situation or circumstances under which leadership is exercised. These include the attributes of the job and the basic firm/industry characteristics in a country's business environment. A listing of the factors affecting the managerial job abroad are presented in Figure 11–2.

The way these factors interact is complex and not readily understood. We do know that in some countries the effects of culture tend to dominate the way the manager needs to work. Other times complex decision situations involving governments and political-economic factors tend to have a predominate influence on the way decisions are made.

---

[1] Richard D. Robinson, *Internationalization of Business* (Hinsdale, Ill.: Dryden Press, 1984) p. 117.

FIGURE 11–1 What a Leader Is and Does

A leader demonstrates a mixed competence in technical, interpersonal, and conceptual skills. A leader understands technical matters without necessarily knowing how to do them. A leader understands that people do the work and must interact effectively if they are to work well. A leader conceptually understands the balance of interests between organizational subunits and the whole organization.

A leader gets organizational work done by motivating people, by getting commitment, by energizing behavior, by creating personal interest and excitement in the organization's goals. A leader is keenly aware of what decisions and events mean to other members of the organization.

A leader gives direction and coordinates efforts without dominating decisions; facilitates goal achievement by removing obstacles, getting resources, and clarifying paths to objectives. A leader shapes ideas in a preferred direction. Leaders know their own capabilities, but also their own limits.

A leader represents an organizational unit's interests in creating working relations and negotiating issues with other organizational units. The leader is a "link" in defining, projecting, and defending her/his organization's interests. While representing an organization purpose, the leader is at the same time flexible and adaptable.

A leader develops subordinates by sharing power and responsibility with them, by providing opportunities for individual development, by challenging people to go beyond their self-imposed limits and be creative.

A leader represents and clearly communicates real and symbolic values, goals, and a vision of organizational purposes. A leader does this by being active and not reactive, by seeing or creating opportunities, by taking intelligent risks, by being as concerned with ideas as with facts.

A leader sets performance standards. The leader does this by communicating clear standards and modelling good performance. An effective leader knows how to recognize good performance and reward it appropriately and acts decisively when poor performance threatens reaching goals.

However, in most operational decisions the characteristics of the individual manager tend to be the more important factor in leadership success abroad. This occurs because the key to successful staffing abroad involves fitting a person to a job and country setting. Since the ability to change a job's characteristics or influence a country setting is often very difficult, it is easier to seek people who are adaptable to the job and country setting. Thus we look for characteristics in people that make them adaptable.

There are a few characteristics of special importance that influence manager effectiveness abroad. Past experience and success in both a particular job and in multiple foreign settings are probably the first indicators of the probable future success of a manager abroad.

FIGURE 11–2 Factors Affecting Leadership Abroad

CONTENT

CHARACTERISTICS OF DECISIONS SITUATION

Degree of complexity, uncertainty, and risk
In-Country information needs and availability

Articulation of assumptions and expectations
Scope and potential impact on performance
Nature of business partners
Authority and autonomy required
Required level of participation and acceptance by employees,
    partners, and government
Linkage to other decisions
Past management legacy
Openness to public scrutiny and responsibility

CONTEXT

*CHARACTERISTICS OF THE FIRM
AND BUSINESS ENVIRONMENT*

Firm structure: size, location, technology, tasks, reporting and
    communication patterns
Firm process: decision making, staffing, control system,
    reward system, information system, means of coordination,
    integration and conflict resolution
Firm outputs: products, services, public image, corporate
    culture, local history and community relations
Business environment: social-cultural, political-economic, and
    technological aspects of a country/market

ATTRIBUTES OF THE PERSON

Job/position knowledge, experience, expectations
Longevity in company, country, functional area

Intelligence and cultural learning/change ability
Personality as demonstrated in values, beliefs, attitudes
    towards foreign situations
Multiple memberships in work and professional groups
Decision and personal work style

ATTRIBUTES OF THE JOB/POSITION

Longevity and past success of former role occupants in the
    position
Technical requirements of the job
Relative authority/power
Physical location (e.g. home office, field office)
Need for coordination, cooperation, and integration with other
    units
Resource availability
Foreign peer group relations

Personality is also a significant factor. It represents the relatively unchanging aspects of a person's behavior in terms of values, beliefs, attitudes, and interpersonal style. Because foreign settings often provide a very different set of conditions to respond to, a personality with a demonstrated "openness" to new situations is important. This translates into flexibility in habits and expectations about how and when work gets done. It means a higher level of tolerance for the different way things get done abroad. And it means being less judgmental without at the same time sacrificing important company and personal standards. Finally, a person's decision style and work habits need to fit both the company and country's culture. The ponderous consensus style of decision in Japan versus the creative but often chaotic style of Latins might present significant contrasts to adapt to.

In summary then we see that both the content and context of leadership describe a set of complex factors that affect the probable success of a manager as leader.

What is needed for probable success as a manager abroad? Figure 11–3 represents an educated guess of the profile of a successful manager. It lists some representative skills, experience, knowledge, and capabilities that seem consistent with the leadership conditions a manager is most likely to face abroad.

THE MANAGER'S ROLE IN HOME OFFICE-SUBSIDIARY RELATIONS

The home office–subsidiary relationship represents a common international organization design problem. This problem was described in Chapter 10. In this problem the needs of a subunit for independence and resources have to be balanced against the overall organization's need for coordination and control. The creation of a subunit, like the building of an assembly plant in a foreign country, represents a decision of the firm to specialize some activities in a particular location for competitive and efficiency reasons. This specialization often involves the granting of substantial autonomy and resources to those subunits. However, as a firm diversifies and decentralizes its activities it immediately faces the need to coordinate and control the activities of these diverse units in order to achieve overall corporate goals. Thus comes the problem of balancing the needs of subunits against corporate requirements for financial performance. To achieve an effective relationship between the home office and subsidiary, the choice of the right person for the job becomes critical. A firm's choice and placement of managers abroad then becomes the key to successful integration.

The problem of balancing these perspectives falls heavily on the shoulder's of the country manager and that manager's counterpart or

---

FIGURE 11–3   Profile of the Successful International Manager

---

Entrepreneurial drive—foreign work settings often provide unique sets of problems that require personal initiative and drive to resolve

Multicountry experience—working in a single foreign country is only a one-case experience. Broader experience increases the manager's depth in handling problems

Integrated set of functional skills—the manager abroad may find herself with no specialized staff or functional support. Being able to do more than one job is therefore often a necessity.

Cross-cultural understanding and interpersonal skills—the knowledge of a language and customs is indispensable to long-term foreign success. In the absence of personal skills in this area, access to multicultural and multilingual staff is necessary.

Knowledge of home office systems and goals—While not as obvious, managers do not always need to know home-office systems while located at the home office. However, in going abroad they may need to familiarize themselves with home-office functions, interdepartmental relations, and the status of projects that ordinarily do not concern them.

Bargaining ability—Much of what goes on abroad results from negotiations. Bargaining and mutual problem solving between governments, local parties, and the firm is a constant way of life.

Appropriate personality and behaviors—Personality represents a relatively fixed pattern of value, beliefs, attitudes, and behaviors of a person. People who dislike uncertain conditions, are highly risk averse, prefer dependence to autonomy, and easily frustrated, are insensitive, unempathetic, or xenophobic probably should not work abroad.

---

superior back at headquarters. The manager abroad plays an intermediary role in interpreting, translating, communicating, and defending both corporate and subunit goals and strategies back and forth from the home office to the subsidiary. This role further extends to representing the firm to the host country government and business community.

Studies of managerial work have generally identified a number of tasks of this manager's role:

- Coordinating and integrating foreign and domestic operations.
- Establishing appropriate control over foreign operations.
- Understanding and adapting to local conditions.
- Staffing and development of local managerial talent.
- Public relations and corporate image making.

Thus, the success of the international manager depends in part on how well he or she manages relationships with other company subunits and acts as an effective communicator and integrator of home office-subsidiary relations.

From the foreign unit's viewpoint, foreign operations should be given a fair amount of autonomy and share of corporate resources to get the job done. Since they are closer to the problems in both time and place, they have a better sense of the issues, key actions involved, and the types of timing and decisions to be made. Therefore, they would argue, they need more freedom to solve problems.

From the headquarters viewpoint, top management's need to integrate the activities of the various and diverse subunits into a corporate strategy is the paramount concern. While recognizing the need for local unit autonomy and support, headquarters argues that they need better means for coordination and integration because they have a global and total firm view of the corporation. Since the local country subunit does not share this perspective, it is headquarter's job to make these higher level decisions that may or may not be popular with subsidiary units.

From the corporate viewpoint, there is also a requirement for a balanced response by subsidiaries to headquarters control strategies. Again, two opposite foreign unit responses can be contrasted. In one case, the foreign unit manager acts more as a bureaucratic administrator of corporate policy than as a manager. Such a unit would probably be reactive (and late) to meet local competitive challenges, passive to domestic home-office attempts to deal with problems, noninnovative in decisions, and lacking a clear corporate identity in the foreign business enviornment. Such managerial behavior usually is inappropriate in rapidly changing foreign markets.

In the opposite response, the foreign unit manager exhibits a strong resistance to corporate requirements for control and integration. This might occur if foreign operations see themselves as superior to home-office operations. Foreign units can come to believe that they are the dynamic leader taking a passive domestic company into new international directions. Depending on how different a foreign unit's organizational culture has evolved from the corporate parent firm, this can lead to the foreign unit treating all home-office corporate concerns as uninformed meddling, bureaucratic interference, or purposeful sabotage. Thus the extent to which a foreign unit has created its own independent direction will in part determine the degree of challenge to integrate that unit successfully into the firm's overall direction.

The challenge to the international manager is to balance trade-offs between the legitimate concerns of home and foreign unit operations. There is no single solution to the problem of balancing. Many factors are at work. These include technological interdependence between units, nature of competition, the changing character of economic and industry conditions, and management orientation towards control. Different country conditions require different degrees of control. To enhance the foreign affiliates' position then the manager will need to develop negotiating skills and means of reducing conflict while working through the trade-offs between foreign and home units. Since neither domestic nor foreign units can be expected to readily forget present trade-offs for the next round of decisions, the international manager needs to develop clear notions of the relative costs absorbed and benefits enjoyed in the relationships between the domestic and foreign units. This should make the control and integration process easier. The difficulty of this intermediary role however cannot be underestimated because intermediaries run the risk of becoming isolated third parties—neither understood nor trusted at the home office or abroad at the affiliate.

The third task of the foreign manager, adaptation to local conditions, is a necessary task since managers most likely will be expected to spend several years in their jobs abroad.

One example of a case where the adaptation to local cultural conditions requires real changes is that of leadership style and behavior. The following exemplifies how cultural influences towards authority, power, and responsibility affect attitudes and expectations towards leadership.

Consider the implications for leadership of individual attitudes and expectations towards power. As a result of extended experiences with people who have wielded power over them when they were children, adults have expectations about how they should relate to others who have power and how they should behave in return. These attitudes are somewhat modified as a consequence of experiences and teachers, ministers, scout leaders, and other authority figures, but fundamental attitudes toward power are derived from the earliest and most intense experiences with authority figures. . . .

In spite of individual differences, however, these experiences reflect a strong common element in any given culture. As a result, there are generalized expectations about how authority is to be wielded, how the more powerful people should act toward the weaker, and what kinds of behavior the latter might expect from the former. It is expected that one will use social strength according to culturally established norms. Therefore, when acquiring control over others, one also incurs the effects of these expectations about power figures. In short, in a particular culture a person who becomes authoritative in direct relationships to others is expected to act in much the same way as a parent acts in the family. It means that as people develop their expectations of power and attitudes toward it based on their earliest experiences with it, they will tend to work from these attitudes in every encounter. A superior who fails to conform to these expectations will be seen as an inadequate, unfair, or unjust leader.[2]

Time duration on the job appears to influence success directly. A recent study has pointed out that one of the weaknesses in human resource planning in U.S. multinational firms is the relatively short duration of U.S. overseas assignments.[3] The reasons for this lie in the short-term corporate strategy perspective of many U.S. firms and in the natural reluctance of expatriate employees to be away from headquarter's activities for too long because this can affect their careers. In a sense, the old expression "out of sight, out of mind" describes this reluctance. The short duration of overseas assignments does not allow sufficient time to get a working understanding of the local environment. If such an in-depth understanding is required, the firm must do two things. It must create conditions in the overseas assignment so the manager can effectively adapt and become productive and, second, it must also make clear that the assignment abroad is an important and positive career decision for the individual. In Chapter Four we discussed some personnel practices that might help in this adjustment problem. Most firms improve manager adaptation capability by providing intense preassignment training and the development of a local host country team that can act as the "eyes and ears" of the newly arrived manager. However, if regular interaction with local business and government officials is a required part of the job, this is most often provided by managers who have considerable foreign experience. Otherwise this skill can be acquired only after considerable time in the country. Thus lengthening the assignment may be the only option.

The decision to place someone abroad involves real costs to the company and to the employee. It should be noted that the firm is paying not only out-of-pocket costs for travel, moving, special compensation for hardships, and other personnel support and maintenance, it also is risking the chance that the employee might not work out because of inability or failure to adjust. This in turn has larger ramifications for the organizational unit in terms of postponed decisions, lost opportunities, disruption of plans, and the organizational inconveniences of restaffing the position. For the employee, the risks are seen

---

[2] H. Levinson, *Executive* (Cambridge, Mass: Harvard University Press, 1984), p. 261.

[3] R. L. Tung, "Strategic Management of Human Resources in the Multinational Enterprise," *Human Resource Management* 23, no. 2 (Summer 1984) pp. 129–43.

in possible slowed career development, higher job uncertainties, increased stress to family life, and the problems of readjustment back into the domestic operations at the end of the assignment. Given these costs, it is important for the organization to make clear that the assignment abroad is an important one for the firm as well as the individual. Thus the reward system needs to adjust to this priority.

Understanding and adapting to local conditions is a self-evident condition for success, however, achieving that understanding and personally changing habits, attitudes, and behaviors is often a wrenching experience. Understanding of a culture and business environment comes through cognitive learning in formal cross-cultural training or informal personal educational effort. Changing the way one behaves, however, requires a more determined commitment to understanding how one "feels" about the requirements for adjustment. This is a part of the emotional component of learning. It begins with an attempt to develop a set of attitudes toward international work experience that reflects a sense of empathy, curiosity, and adventure; an openness to change; a flexibility in enduring personal discomfort and hardship; an increased tolerance for uncertainty, newness, and frustrations; an ability to recognize one's limits; and willingness to rely on assistance from others. A sense of humor might also help. These attitudes are not developed readily since they are not just a matter of cognitive knowledge, that is, "I understand how they work and therefore accept it!" They require a personal knowledge of basic values and assumptions regarding foreign work settings, career, and family concerns. As was discussed in the earlier chapter on culture, we readily recognize that all people can make adjustments, but that for some the cost is more than the benefits. Thus, the careful selection of personnel and their preparation for international work is a major factor in determining the international manager's success.

The fourth task of maintaining effective home-subsidiary relations is developing foreign management talent. This is done to prepare for the day when the international manager prepares for a return to domestic or other foreign assignments. Filling management jobs with talented local managers who have been trained and socialized into the corporation's culture is the mark of success for most international managers.

Management development aims to develop foreign nationals to manage overseas subsidiaries. However, management development also can have longer-term strategic aims, such as developing a pool of talented managers who can staff positions in other foreign countries as business activities abroad increase. Also, management development should aim to influence the domestic company staff to be more attuned to international affairs when they deal with foreign nationals. In the final analysis, the internationally oriented company is less concerned with the nationality of a manager than it is with talented managers who can manage foreign operations.

Developing foreign management talent, however, is a challenging task. It involves a series of trade-off decisions. A local manager has built-in local language and cultural expertise, but may not understand the home-country culture nor the subtle workings of the corporate culture that are often required to get key decisions made. A local manager fills the home country manager's position but may not carry the authority implicit in home-country manager's foreign status. Compensation differentials, reflecting relative country costs of living, often do not remain with a managerial position when the home country manager leaves. This can affect the local replacement manager's effort and commitment to the job. Yet continuing the same compensation package for the new local manager can cause other local subordinates to become less willing to accept the pay and benefit differentials they did for the foreign manager. These are but a few of the issues involved in this important task of developing local management talent. Suffice to say, as difficult as the task is, the expending nature of international business will require that it be done better as the forces of competition force more firms to go abroad.

The final major integrating task of the international manager is to provide a public affairs capability in overseas operations. Public affairs is an activity undertaken by the firm to enhance the firm's public image and to create legitimacy and acceptance by governments and the general public for the firm's activities and presence. It involves actively courting important host country elites, developing a public information function, projecting an image of company and country goals as being compatible, and responding to challenges without becoming too heavily involved in local country politics and disputes. Since the firm has private economic interests to defend, it wants to make its presence in a country as seemingly beneficial and nonthreatening as possible. The public affairs function helps accomplish this.

Increasingly, large firms, both foreign and domestic, are taking the public affairs function as a serious part of a firm's strategic planning effort. If favorable or unfavorable national reactions increasingly determine the relative autonomy and success of the company, then the firm that prepares and communicates its case well will be more effective in achieving its goals and protecting itself against government actions. Case examples demonstrate that some public affairs strategies fail. Often this function takes on a strong public relations tone when it is used as an after-the-fact defense as in the case of Union Carbide in the Bhopal accident, the baby formula problem of Nestle, or the Lockheed pay-off scandal in Japan. Overemphasis on public relations, only telling the firm's side of the story, can tend to reduce the firm's credibility with the public. For this reason, the public affairs function must be used carefully.

The role of the local country manager in this area is important even though the public affairs function is located and controlled by corporate headquarters. In foreign countries country managers are often the most visible representative of a firm or even an industry. They represent the foreign affiliates to government agencies, are the foreign representative at business meetings, head the negotiations team, and represent a "typical" businessperson and citizen of his or her own country. Thus, many local country constituencies come to expect a great deal from this manager in terms of technical expertise, breadth of understanding of world affairs, and knowledge of total company policy. The manager may or may not be able to live up to these expectations. If seen as knowledgeable and approachable, the expectations may increase. If not so perceived, then the manager may be wrongly dismissed as an incompetent representative. In any case, the manager cannot escape the role of representative. A clear understanding and development of the public affairs function should assist the manager in this important responsibility for image development and maintenance.

SUMMARY

In concluding this section, we reemphasize the linkage between leadership, motivation, and the environmental setting in which leadership is exercised. Most management texts tend to separate the topics for purposes of exposition. However, the managerial role explicitly must combine them to effectly organize, coordinate, and energize the enterprise. Contemporary management theory recognizes the need to include an understanding of contingent conditions under which leadership and motivation are successful in guiding human effort towards organizational goals. The international work setting represents an explicit set of such contingent factors and these have been described and analyzed throughout this book. In the end, the success and effectiveness of an international manager will depend on a skillful meshing of formal and informal leadership activities calling for assessment of the contingent factors specific to each country situation. These include such internal company factors as the nature of technology, the difficulty of job tasks, the quality of employees, and the general state of management-worker relations. In the international setting, however,

NEWS BOX 11–1
That 'Glamorous' Foreign Job Can Be Less than a Financial Bonanza for the Unwary
Michael R. Sesit

Ted Whitaker did all right when his company sent him to work in Tokyo in 1979.

When the dollar weakened against the Japanese yen, cutting his purchasing power, his employer, Manufacturers Hanover Trust Co., made it up to him. Yet when the strong dollar put him "ahead of the game, the bank didn't ask for money back," he says. And when Whitaker returned to the United States in 1983, the bank helped him buy a house by giving him a below-market mortgage rate and paying his closing costs.

Unfortunately, not all foreign assignments work out so well. Even with a big raise and generous benefits, what looks like a glamorous job abroad can turn out to be far from a financial bonanza.

Currency fluctuations, the vagaries of foreign tax codes, and the absence of planning can all take their toll on an employee's finances. People who don't investigate the ramifications of their companies' transfer policies, or who fail to consider the personal financial questions such policies often don't address, may be leaving themselves open for unpleasant surprises.

A 40 percent Salary Cut

Consider the experience of Guy Caruso, a former Department of Energy employee on assignment with the International Energy Agency in Paris. Caruso says his salary has fallen 40 percent in dollar terms since he moved from Washington in 1982. That's because the dollar has surged, and he's paid in francs.

Caruso has a letter from the DOE saying it will make it up to him when he returns to work there. But the executive says the letter isn't clear. "I don't know how much I'll get back," he says.

Most companies have set policies that cover cost-of-living allowances, tax reimbursements, school fees, housing, and other aspects of foreign assignments. These policies generally aren't negotiable.

At the least, accountants say, employees should try to have some of their salaries paid in dollars. After all, they say, Americans working overseas are likely to have dollar commitments, such as payments for life insurance, mortgages, alimony, and child support. And most people want to keep their savings in dollars.

Accountants also say it is essential for employees to understand how their companies' transfer policies deal with taxes. Expatriates are subject to both U.S. and foreign taxes. Although the Internal Revenue Service currently excludes $80,000 in foreign wages, plus certain housing benefits, from U.S. taxation, some foreign countries tax outside income earned in the United States.

At the same time, local tax codes often treat income categories differently than in the United States. Switzerland and Britain, for example, tax any capital gain when an incentive stock option is exercised. The United States doesn't, if the employee adheres to certain time constraints. Canada has a "departure tax" on investments for anyone who leaves after a stay of five years or more.

Most corporations calculate a "hypothetical tax," which is an estimate of what employees would pay if they stayed in the United States. In countries where employees owe more than the hypothetical tax, employers typically make up the difference. In countries where they owe less, policies differ. Some companies let employees keep the windfall; others require executives to pay the company the difference between their actual taxes and their hypothetical tax.

Employees need to know just what is included in the hypothetical tax figure, says Alan L. LeBovidge, a Boston-based partner at Coopers & Lybrand. If it doesn't take into account outside income or tax deductions, the employee can wind up losing money, he notes.

Some states also tax expatriates' income, so the hypothethical tax should include local taxes if necessary.

Hidden Tax Bite

Executives should be aware that company reimbursement plans may not cover the value-added tax incorporated in the selling price of goods in some countries. John Treanor, a vice president of Irving Trust Co., recalls that his previous employer didn't make up for the big bite that Belgium's 17 percent value-added tax took from his money.

Then there's the out-of-sight, out-of-mind problem: Some countries don't withhold taxes. In France, for instance, executives say the expatriate community is rife with stories about employees who neglected to put some cash aside and are then surprised by a colossal tax bill.

Employees also need to pay careful attention to the sorts of personal financial questions that often aren't covered in corporate plans.

How, for example, would a foreign transfer affect the cost of a child's college education? Robert Smith, a vice president at Bankers Trust Co., says Rutgers University was reluctant to consider his son a New Jersey resident while Smith was working in Paris. Rutgers eventually relented, saving the banker $1,600 in annual tuition.

One of the most common questions is whether to sell or rent one's home in the United States. Many employees rent rather than sell because the overseas assignment won't be indefinite. But they could discover, as did Malcolm Aylett, a former Avon Products, Inc. manager in Tokyo, that they will have a problem if they want to sell the house when they return.

Home-Rental Pitfall

Aylett, now a general manager with Gillette Co., was boxed into keeping his house because renting it had changed it, in the eyes of the IRS, into an "investment" property. As a result, he wasn't entitled to the tax benefits granted on the sale of a primary residence.

Company policies also aren't much help on questions like whether to buy a home overseas. F. Alan Moore, an Avon marketing manager who worked in Japan from 1978 to 1983, knows Americans who bought Japanese homes years ago and still own them, even though they have returned to the United States. "They'd lose their shirts. All the appreciation in property values has been eroded by the yen's depreciation," he says.

Of course, those executives would have done handsomely if the yen had gained, or even remained unchanged, against the dollar. But the point, Moore says, is that they didn't fully understand what they were getting into.

When it comes to foreign assignments, he adds, "People don't get enough consultation before they leave." A job overseas, he says, is "no longer a big glory spot."

SOURCE: *The Wall Street Journal*, July 15, 1985, p. 29.

culture, the level of economic development, and government policy provide a set of external contingency factors that modify the linkage between leadership and motivation. Assigning an experienced, strong, interpersonally skilled Italian manager into an auto parts plant in Argentina may be a good decision. On the surface at least the individual's background is culturally and experientially "consistent" with both the nature of the tasks he faces and the dominant values of the culture. In summary then, we have shown knowledge of motivation and leadership can be applied by international managers because the questions they seek to answer are universal. However, it was pointed out that the conditions in the work setting modify a manager's ability to apply that knowledge—it usually must be modified. Assessment of the impact those conditions have will determine the relative effectiveness of a manager in motivating people and achieving organizational goals. News Box 11–1 provides a more realistic, less romantic and distorted view of "glamorous" jobs abroad.

DISCUSSION QUESTIONS FOR CHAPTER ELEVEN

1. The U.S. management literature has a fairly complete view of the leadership function as it has developed within a U.S. business environment. In what ways might different country environments change the meaning and role of leadership? Think of the cases of Mexico, Japan, Nigeria, Germany, or Poland.

2. The Figure 11–1 suggests that leadership is a universal phenomenon. All leaders display the same behaviors. Do you agree that leadership is universal?

3. How does viewing leadership as a role help us understand its different forms of practice and beliefs?

4. Do you agree with the list of personal assets of the effective international manager? Would you add any others? (See Figure 11–3). How would you order them in terms of their contribution to effective management?

5. How would you describe the role of the manager in home office-subsidiary relations? What are the manager's most difficult challenges in this role?

6. What are the five major tasks of managerial work abroad?

7. Given incidents like the accident at Bhopal, the Nestle's breast-milk problem, and the issue of South African investment, the public relations function has become increasingly important. In these cases is it best to leave the public relations to the local country manager who is closer to the problem? Or should the issues be dealt with at headquarters? What trade-offs are involved?

8. Developing foreign management talent to fill positions and upgrade skills involves both benefits and costs. What concerns might the headquarter's office have regarding this activity? What concerns might the local government have?

9. "It's always best to place managers within the cultural context that is closer to their own. This should be the first criteria for making your manager effective. Thus a Mexican manager would do better in Argentina or Spain than in Sweden or Taiwan." Do you agree? What beliefs and assumptions seem to underlie a statement like this?

10. How might a manager's personal life (e.g. married state, children) affect their work abroad?

11. A recent study claimed that less than 5 percent of all international managers are women. Why do you think this is so? Are there situations where the sex of a manager might make them more or less effective? If so, describe one.

CHAPTER TWELVE _____

Managing Interdependence

INTRODUCTION

All social life is characterized by the simultaneous pressures of inter-dependence and autonomy. Just as families and communities experience the pulling tension of these two social forces, so do countries and business firms. Increased awareness of these forces is apparent in contemporary international business developments. Countries have become more interdependent through increased trade, investment, and concerns for national defense. Social concerns over employment opportunities for youth in Europe or migrant workers' rights in the United States require a cross-national perspective because they cannot be solved by a single country. Ecological awareness by managers and government policymakers alike can be seen in the industrially created problems of acid rain and pollution of major European rivers and U.S.–Canadian border regions.

International economic problems, such as economic growth, inflation, interest rates, or trade imbalances imply interdependence. Attempts to solve any of these problems requires cooperation among countries. Too often individual countries attempt to treat such problems as though national policies can be used without such cooperation. However, the destinies of nations and international companies are linked. Since interdependence narrows the range of options available for firms and governments alike, truly independent decisions become a will-o'-the-wisp.

In this chapter the interdependence of MNCs and the nation-states is the main topic. We begin with a short discussion of the evolving relations between the MNCs and the host countries. Government responses to interdependence as these relate to MNCs are then discussed in light of countries' desires for greater control over their economies.

Throughout this chapter the implications of an interdependent world for managers are noted.

SOME CHARACTERISTICS OF INDEPENDENCE

All social institutions, be they private companies or countries, prefer to autonomously and independently determine their own destinies. In the process of pursuing their own goals, however, they interact with other parties. Therefore, interdependence is a conditon of relationships that constrains independent choice.

The dependency that a firm experiences may be only in certain interest areas (e.g., resource, markets) and not across a whole spectrum of corporate interests and needs. Furthermore, a firm or country can be dominant in some interdependence relationships and totally subordinate in others. Thus power, which is based on command over resources, technology, or organizational capabilities, is important. Both firms and governments can create unbalanced dependencies and in achieving their own goals, force others to bear some or all of the cost. These costs of dependence usually motivate the dependent party to develop countervailing strategies to reduce the costs and level of dependence. Interdependence is thus a property of all relationships be they between countries or firms.

Interdependence translates into a complex management task for the firm. Managing a firm's operations in a world of changing market and government contrasting economic conditions and shifting interests (not to mention alliances) is a task whose inherent difficulty is hard to appreciate by the average business reader. The sheer complexity of decisions in the face of highly uncertain environments and changing dependencies makes an understanding of the structure and dynamics of international business-government relations a necessity for effective management of multinational operations. Just as the firm is seeking to make accommodations with the nation-state, so is that nation-state making adjustments to its own evolving internal economic conditions (e.g., changing comparative advantage, resource discovery or depletion, population growth) and to its external relations with other nations.

Thus two organizational systems, the country and the company, in attempting to manage the problems caused by their own interdependencies influence each other's options. The resultant relationship presents a dilemma—the country and company need each other to achieve important goals, yet the relationship often entails unwanted costs. It is the struggle over the sharing of benefits and costs to in-country economic activity of the firm that characterizes much of modern MNC-country relations.

MULTINATIONAL CORPORATION-GOVERNMENT RELATIONS: AN AMBIGUOUS INTERDEPENDENCE

The rise of the nation-state is perhaps the single most important organizational and institutional development from the 1700s to the mid-20th century. Politicians and philosophers alike have helped create and reinforce the ideal of the nation-state as an organization capable of meeting the aspirations of the citizens within its borders. A world populated by sovereign, heterogeneous, and independent nations is still the dominant pattern today in international relations.

Continued existence of countries attests to their having developed effective ways of dealing with threats to their existence. However, the rise of the multinational corporation in the last 40 years has modified nations' perceptions of and abilities to preserve national identity and sovereign interests. Some MNCs sales are larger than many small nation's GNPs and their operations are global in nature. They have flexibility and a willingness to move economic activity from one country to another. They are sometimes seen as lacking social responsibility and intentions to contribute to national social and economic development goals. And, finally, they are seen as having an ability to influence national policy. The charges against the MNC mounted as the effects of MNC operations on national economies have multiplied. As one author puts it,

> In the late 1960s and the 1970s, the issue of the multinational corporation was a critical one for host states and for the United States as the largest parent country. Trade unionists, academicians, journalists, politicians, bureaucrats, and ideologues focused their attention on the multinational corporation as a highly visible and tangible manifestation of global interdependency. Many kinds of social, political, and economic dislocations were blamed on the international firm.[1]

The charges against MNCs were both real and fanciful. They ranged from tax evasion to union-busting, from transfer of inappropriate technologies to interference in politics of the host country, and as might be expected, MNCs have both positive and negative effects on different economies. The trade-offs in terms of costs and benefits can be

---

[1] Robert Gilpin, *U.S. Power and the Multinational Corporation: The Political cal Economy of Foreign Direct Investment* (New York: Basic Books, 1975), p. 46.

FIGURE 12–1   Benefit-Cost of MNCs to Country Development

Benefits	*Cost*
	CAPITAL MARKET EFFECTS
Broader outside access to capital	Increased competition for local scare capital
Foreign exchange earnings	
Import substitution effects allow governments to save foreign exchange for priority projects	Increased interest rates as supply of local capital decreases
	Capital service effects of balance of payments
Risk sharing	
	TECHNOLOGY/PRODUCTION EFFECTS
Access to new technology and R&D developments	Technology is not always appropriate
Infrastructure development and support	Plants are often for assembly only and can be dismantled
Export diversification	Government infrastructure investment are higher than expected benefits
	EMPLOYMENT EFFECTS
Direct creation of new jobs	Limited skill development and creation
Opportunities for indigenous management development	Competition for scarce skills
Income multiplier effects on local community business	Low percentage of managerial jobs for local people
	Employment instability because of ability to move production operations freely to other countries

---

seen in Figure 12–1 where for every argument against the MNCs, whether in capital markets, technology transfer, or employment practices, a set of benefits can be identified.

The MNC however also has its champions. They forcefully argue that the MNC is the prime agent leading to a breakdown of barriers to the free flow of trade, investment, technology, and people. Because of their global reach, MNCs are seen as a basic integrating force. Through their global standardization of production and attempts to serve world customers they contribute to a convergence of national interests around the common goals of economic growth and development via capitalist market methods. And in contrast to national policies that tend to fragment issues and efforts to solve problems, the MNC can actually unify efforts and issues around the basic themes of growth and development.

In creating benefits, the MNC generates costs. This makes the MNC an ambiguous target for both praise and condemnation. This has created a dilemma for that nation-state that one expert describes as follows:

> The host government is caught in a "love-hate" syndrome. It wants the contributions to wealth and economic growth that the multinational enterprise can provide because they add to its power within the country, as well as internationally. At the same time it dislikes and fears the results: the incursions on national sovereignty and technological independence. The host government finds multinational enterprises difficult to live with, but, so long as it seeks to increase national power, equally unpleasant to live without. . . . It appears to the host government that a trade-off may be required between sovereignty and greater wealth.[2]

The MNC experiences a similar attraction-rejection syndrome. A firm may need access to certain low-cost resources, rights to market entry, or supplies of local capital. It too understands that economic activity in a market can represent contributions to its own profit picture and international growth. However, it dislikes the implications of increased governmental regulations. Thus, both parties grudgingly admit economic interdependence and the "need" for each other. This dilemma of firm-state relations is clearly demonstrated by the recent Mexican government decision to allow International Business Machines Corp. to establish the first wholly owned foreign subsidiary in Mexico's microcomputer industry. Mexico had rejected prior IBM bids for such a subsidiary. Up to mid-1985 Mexican law required subsidiaries of foreign companies to be 51 percent Mexican-owned. Both Apple Computer, Inc. and Hewlett-Packard Co. acquiesced to this rule. The reason for the more favorable treatment of IBM can be found in Mexico's faltering economy and the need for foreign exchange. In this agreement IBM plans to export most of the microcomputers it produces in Mexico. Mexico also needed to demonstrate to other potential foreign investors that it encourages foreign investment through ownership incentives. News Box 12–1 chronicles these events.

There are elements of truth in both the pro and con arguments about the MNC. A more realistic scenario and useful assessment of their role, however, recognizes other attributes. The MNC is, first of

---

[2] J. N. Behrman, *National Interests and the Multinational Enterprise* (Englewood Cliffs, N.J.: Prentice Hall, 1970), p. 31.

NEWS BOX 12–1
The ABC's of Foreign Direct Investment

A. IBM's Plan to Build Computers in Mexico was Rejected

The Mexican government has rejected a controversial plan by IBM to set up a wholly owned microcomputer subsidiary in Mexico City, according to a government report, which was disclosed to Reuters in outline form. According to Reuters, the Mexican government decided that IBM, like other foreign computer makers in Mexico, must abide by the country's investment laws that require majority local ownership of subsidiaries. The proposed plant would produce about 125,000 microcomputers a year, chiefly for export.

SOURCE: *The New York Times,* November 28, 1984, p. 39.

B. Mexico Devalues the Peso, Plans to Cut Budget in Effort to Control Economy

In an effort to get a grip on the nation's runaway economy, Mexico's government devalued the peso and announced the passage of major budget cuts and economic measures.

*   *   *   *   *

As part of its new economic program, Mexico hopes its permission to International Business Machines Corp. to open a 100 percent-owned plant will encourage more foreign investment and boost confidence in the government's economic policy.

IBM's Mexican plant, which will produce about 665,000 computers over five years, has been seen as an important test of the Mexican government's willingness to permit projects with most of the investment coming from foreign sources.

Competitors and independent analysts say the decision to approve the long-delayed, once rejected IBM plant was timed to reinforce Mexico's efforts to show it can adjust to falling oil prices and control spending.

*   *   *   *   *

The new economic program comes at a time when Mexico needs not only to straighten out its finances, but also to restore the confidence of its people. The public has begun to doubt in recent weeks whether the government is in control of the economy.

SOURCE: Mary Williams Walsh, *The Wall Street Journal,* July 23, 1985, p. 31.

C. IBM Won Approval for a Mexican Facility

The computer giant, whose IBM Mexico subsidiary has operated for more than 50 years, said it will invest $91 million in the manufacture of personal computers in Mexico, of which 92 percent will be exported. The operation will be the first wholly owned U.S. company in the microcomputer field in Mexico. It was approved under the relaxation of a law requir-

ing that subsidiaries of foreign companies be more than 51 percent Mexican owned. Richard Hojel, chairman of the 10-month-old Apple de Mexico,
an Apple Computer subsidiary that is mostly Mexican owned, charged that
approval of IBM's operation was a "complete change in the rules of the
game by which other businesses abide."

SOURCE: *The New York Times*, July 26, 1985, p. 37.

all, a private profit-seeking organization. Through their efforts to
match resource capabilities with market opportunities, the firm creates valued products and services that it exchanges for money and
other valued assets. In a world of nations the MNC is an economic
agent that must deal with the realities of country conditions. While at
times they appear to be all-powerful, the MNC can also be the pawn in
the struggle between countries over the location of a new plant, the
rights to sell a technology, or the responsibility of a debt.

While having a social responsibility, the MNC's prime loyalty and
concerns are with its own survival and growth. It is the country's responsibility to set up the rules of commerce that both creates incentives and restrictions to MNC behavior. The MNC is then left with the
problem of how to choose what countries and conditions they want or
can work under.

GOVERNMENT RESPONSE TO INTERDEPENDENCE: THE THREE "ISMS"

Despite the rising power of the MNCs, the state is not a weak giant unable to control the activities of MNC firms.

The identity and power of a country is based on the geographical
claim of territory, the ability to use military force to defend national
interests, a sovereign legitimacy recognized by domestic and international institutions, and a claim on the emotions and affections of people through nationalistic appeals. No private company, as yet, demonstrates these bases for identity and power. What role then does the
MNC play for the nation-state? The MNC is a flexible organization
able to create and readily respond to business opportunities. By its
pursuit of private goals on an international scale, the MNC contributes to the developmental goals of nations. From the nation-states'
view, therefore, the MNC becomes an important vehicle for economic
and technological development. At the same time, the international
activities of MNC's have contributed to increased interdependence
among nations. In order to control the internationalization of their

economies and preserve a reasonable level of autonomy, governments have turned to a number of strategies.

The major means for government control can be found in the three "isms" of Nationalism, Protectionism, and Governmentalism. Nationalism suggests an ability to rally loyalist sentiment in favor of national goals and against foreign influences. Protectionism represents the partial or complete closing-off of borders to threatening foreign influences. Governmentalism is an increased reliance on the use of government rather than laissez-faire market approaches to develop policies that presumably further national interests.

Nationalism

Author John Fayerweather comments on nationalism:

> Although nationalism is relatively new, its psychological roots are not. Nationalism is a manifestation of a fundamental human trait. The key motivation at work is the quest of man for security, reinforced by other social satisfactions which come from participation in a group. From earliest times these feelings have brought people together into groups with a high degree of internal cohesion and sharp separation from external elements. . . . They feel a strong identification with the group, thinking of it and acting in it on a "we" basis, and those who are not in the group are a distinctly different category. 'they,' 'outsiders,' 'foreigners'[3]

The important characteristic of nationalism is its ability to motivate people to support government-sponsored policies and programs. Governments can appeal to patriotism, national interest, and a variety of other "sacred" concepts to get people to support a policy despite the political differences that may exist and despite the possibility that long-run costs will outweigh any immediate benefits. For example, between the mid-1960s and early 1970s the progressive Chilean governments were successful by appeals to nationalistic tendencies to gain broad support for nationalization of the copper industry. This nationalization continues today, even though a fiercely procapitalist and antidemocratic military regime forcefully took power in 1973. Copper, now a symbol of national identity, has become a permanent national rallying point regardless of the political regimes in power.

While nationalism appears to be more commonly associated with developing country behavior, it is no less exhibited by the developed

---

[3] John Fayerweather, ed., *Host National Attitudes Towards Multinational Corporations* (New York: Praeger Publishers, 1982), p. 217.

world. Canada has been using nationalistic appeals to both control internal separatists movements and better define Canada's territorial and economic interests relative to those of the United States. (See News Box 12–2.) A hallmark of the Soviet regime's control over its vast territory is its relentless appeal to national identity especially with reference to the patriotic sacrifices made in World War II. Even the United States has demonstrated the use of nationalistic appeals to rally support for U.S. foreign and domestic policies as it did when it froze the use of Iranian financial assets or when it badgered Japan into accepting so-called voluntary quotas on textiles, television sets, and automobiles. In Figure 12–2 one author shows how nationalism can be expressed in a range of control policies over MNC activities.

In this figure, increased use of nationalistic appeals are associated with increasingly more punitive government actions as seen from the firm's viewpoint. The implication for MNC behavior is clear: The more the MNC pursues policies and activities that can be interpreted as threatening to the national interest, the more likely government policymakers will turn to nationalistic policies and programs to defend perceived national interests. As policies become more restrictive, they can and do threaten equity ownership interests. Developing an awareness of national interests relative to MNC activities is an important aspect of international management. Analysis of nationalistic tendencies through political risk analysis can aid in identifying emerging problem areas.

Protectionism

While nationalism provides the justification, governments readily turn to protectionism as a means of controlling the rate of flow of goods and services that cross their national boundaries. The numbers and kinds of controls available are numerous and come under two general categories: those that directly affect costs (e.g., tariffs) and those that directly affect quantity (e.g., nontariff barriers). They represent a "helping hand" for certain economic activities while penalizing others for both domestic and foreign firms. A list of the common policy instruments can be seen in Figure 12–3.

In some cases protectionism represents a way of protecting national/domestic producers of goods and services from loss of markets to foreign-produced goods. Protectionist policies are pursued to prevent economic damage to firms and their employees in particular industries by providing for both temporary and long-term relief from foreign competition.

NEWS BOX 12–2
Nationalism Is Alive and Well

Canadian Nationalist Takes on the United States, Giving Country's Pride a Shot in the Arm

The U.S. Coast Guard has been warned. If its vessels intrude into Canada's arctic waters again, they risk attack from Mel Hurtig's air force.

Hurtig, a feisty 53-year-old publisher and nationalist, masterminded the recent bombing of the Coast Guard icebreaker Polar Sea as it plowed through the Canadian arctic without having asked Canada's permission.

The bomb was a three-pound cardboard cylinder packed with stones, Canadian flags, and a testy message to the captain saying that the voyage was "insulting and demeaning to our citizens and a threat to our sovereignty."

Dropped from a small, twin-engine plane hired by Hurtig, the cylinder hit the Polar Sea's deck with a thud that sent reverberations across Canada.

Canadians swamped Hurtig's publishing office here with calls and letters praising his defense of Canadian sovereignty and deploring Prime Minister Brian Mulroney's allegedly weak-kneed stance toward the intruder.

* * * * *

A widely sought-after speaker, Hurtig combines statistics, jokes, and anecdotes to warn Canadians against getting too cozy with the United States. The idea for his encyclopedia came to him as he was preparing to make a speech at a high school in Swift Current, Saskatchewan, he says. The school library had "books about American heroes, American geography, American history, but nothing Canadian," he says.

Canada, Hurtig tells his audiences, is a "more compassionate, more sane, less violent and more sensible society" than the United States.

The Mulroney government's policies, he predicts, "will inevitably turn Canada into simply an economic and political satellite of the United States, a mendicant colony no longer able to determine its own priorities in its own national interest."

SOURCE: John Urquhart, *The Wall Street Journal*, August 1985, p. 34.

Canadian Fears Over 'Americanization' Are Reignited by Trade Talks With United States

Long-standing fears of a wholesale "Americanization" of Canada have been revived by bilateral trade talks with the United States.

The talks, which are scheduled to begin here (Ottawa) Wednesday, are aimed at a broad expansion of two-way trade, which already exceeds $120 billion a year. Canadians opposed to the talks warn that freer trade could lead to a range of evils from Detroit-style street crime to a dismantling of Canada's generous welfare system.

* * * * *

Unrestricted free trade isn't the official goal of either side, but the talks have stirred passionate debate in Canada over the prospect of "free trade" with the United States. Opponents and news reports almost always use the emotionally charged term to describe the negotiations, resulting in headlines such as: "Free trade would turn us into 'bloody Americans,' top labor official fears."

Supporters believe freer access to the U.S. market will mean more sales and jobs. Opponents dispute this. They argue, moreover, that the gains aren't worth the loss of Canadian sovereignty. "It's an issue of the heart," says Arthur Kube, president of the 250,000-member British Columbia Federation of Labor and a foe of free trade.

Free-trade opponents also say U.S. negotiators might view Canadian welfare benefits, such as inexpensive government health insurance, as export subsidies, and force Canadians to give them up.

*   *   *   *   *

Canadian publishers and broadcasters, as well as high-profile celebrities, fear the United States will demand an end to certain nontariff barriers that protect them. "The removal of restrictions would mean the final swamping and extinction of any indigenous Canadian identity," says Abraham Rotstein, an economics professor at the University of Toronto.

The key argument from opponents is over the possibility that freer trade may lead to a practical—if not official—absorption of Canada by the United States. For most Canadians, who feel friendly to the United States but who think their own country is a better society in terms of crime, corruption, and racial strife, it is a serious issue.

SOURCE: Peggy Berkowitz, *The Wall Street Journal*, September 6, 1985, p. 29.

Snag in United States–Canada Trade

A dispute over the right of an American company to own a publishing house in Canada has put a chill on talk of a free-trade pact between the two nations, the world's biggest trading partners.

The dispute, involving Gulf and Western Industries' acquisition of Prentice-Hall Inc. and its Canadian publishing unit, has become an outlet for nationalist concern over cultural domination by the United States. In turn, it has raised questions in Congress about the fairness of Canadian policies and about Prime Minister Brian Mulroney's recent proposal, warmly embraced by President Reagan, to negotiate wider bilateral trade.

At issue are Canadian rules announced last July to increase Canadian ownership of the country's book publishing industry beyond the current 20 percent level. In essence, a foreign investor acquiring the parent company of a Canadian publisher now has to divest itself of the Canadian unit within two years.

Although a final decision has been postponed until the end of January at the latest, the Canadian Government has tentatively decided to apply the new policy to the Gulf and Western acquisition, even though the purchase occurred last winter, months before the rules were issued.

An American Government official involved with Canada said the dispute might prove "very difficult to compromise," as it had become "a litmus test" for Canadian nationalists.

SOURCE: Douglas Martin, *The New York Times*, November 24, 1985, p. 32.

FIGURE 12–2 The Full Scope of Nationalism (by increasing degree)

Convertibility: Laws and regulations applying to all organizations, but recognized to affect foreign investor remittance objectives more directly. National goals override the needs of private enterprise.

Convertibility: Different exchange rates aimed at selectively affecting imports, remittances, borrowing abroad, and invisibles purchased abroad. The move is not likely to be aimed at nationalization.

Convertibility: Depreciation of after-tax flow through devaluations and inflation due to inadequate hedging mediums.

Convertibility: Restrictions on reinvestment of blocked currency resulting in depreciation or after-tax cash flow through changing of exchange rates and inflation. Could be part of a nationalization move.

Loss of Remittance Flexibility

Discrimination: Harassment without laws and other written forms of nationalism. Audits of accounts, fomenting labor unrest, bureaucratic delays, and similar tactics are examples.

Discrimination: Laws and regulations giving nationals in an industry significant advantages. Financing, labor regulations, information disclosure, and import duties are examples. Could lead to loss of assets.

Loss of Operating Profits

Nationalism: Laws and regulations requiring sale of varying degree of equity to nationals without reference to price. Often a step towards advanced nationalization, but sometimes a stimulant to trading on stock exchanges.

Nationalization: Government agency or public company takes a significant ownership position due to decree or law. Often a planned step toward industry control beginning with observation.

Nationalization: Complete takeover with remuneration reduced by fabricated devaluation of assets, inflated local currency obligations, retroactive worker obligations, and similar devices.

Loss of Assets

Expropriation: Takeover with no compensation. Subtle forms include banning sales of important products, importation of required items, and foreign funds to cover loans called with minimum notice.

Expropriation: Takeover with no compensation. Foreign personnel and their private property jeopardized. Disaster situation.

Exclusion: Investments not prevented by law, but practice eliminates foreigners generally, or specifically in certain industries.

Exclusion: Investments prevented by law generally, or specifically in certain industries.

Loss of Opportunity

SOURCE: F.T. Haner, *Global Business Strategies for the 1980s* (New York: Praeger, 1980), p. 211.

FIGURE 12–3 Some Common Protectionist Policy Actions

Government Goal	Policy Tools
	Tariffs
	Direct subsidies
	Tax relief for local home firms
Protection of domestic goods/services	Domestic threshold requirements (e.g. health, specifications in product design, local content)
	Consumer protection laws
	Administrative procedures (red tape)
Protection of nationals in employment	Legal residency requirements
	National origin restrictions
	Skill/languages requirements
	Quotas on the number of immigrants
	Minimum income/savings requirements
Protection of national financial assets	Capital market access controls
	Foreign exchange controls
	Minimum size transaction reporting requirements
	Controls on foreign travel
	Legal sanction against black-market activity

The most common justification for protectionist policies are the following:

- Local firms need a break from foreign competition in order to become more effective competitors. They need time and assistance in order to reorganize their operations, invest in new technology, or develop people skills.
- Local industry suffers from "unfair" foreign competition. Foreign firms, it is argued, have been given an unfair advantage because of their own government support in the form of tax breaks, direct subsidies, or financing support. For example, the Boeing Company in 1982 argued that the U.S. government needed to expand the U.S. Export–Import Bank's loan assistance in order to help foreign buyers purchase Boeing. Boeing attempted to show that French, German, British, and Spanish government backed financing was giving the European "Airbus" plane an unfair competitive advantage.
- Local industry is of direct national interest. Such economic sectors as telecommunications, defense production, and strategic materials are often seen as having an overriding importance to

national security. As such they are given preferential governmental treatment either by excluding any type of foreign competition in their markets, or including only those sectors for favored consideration in government purchases of these goods.
- Local employment is suffering. By allowing foreign imports local jobs are lost because local domestic producers are losing
  market share. This means a cut back in production or a move to
  labor-replacing capital investment.

Protectionisms's effect on country economies is one of the most
hotly debated economic topics in international affairs. Protectionist
approaches to defend national interests against the effects of a growing
international interdependence will continue because it is easier for
policymakers to blame foreigners for national shortcomings than to
fashion policies to deal directly with the problem. Protectionism yields
immediate short-term relief and hence provides political gains. In the
long-run, however, protection is generally self-defeating because it
leads to a waste of resources, less consumer choice, and slower economic growth.

The implications of protectionism to MNC managers are clear. If
domestic economic interests feel threatened by foreign competition
and government acquiesces to these complaints, then management can
expect the threat of or the actual implementation of protectionist policies. Such policies as quotas, for example, translate directly into increased costs for the firm. Cut off from a reliable foreign supplier, local
management will often be forced to substitute parts from more costly
domestic suppliers. They may also incur higher transportation costs,
financial transaction costs, and labor costs. The result is a more costly
product that drives profits down and often leads to loss of market
share. Recent complaints by the U.S. semiconductor, computer chip,
specialty steel, and copper industries, and the lone remaining U.S.
producer of motorcycles (Harley-Davidson) have led to protectionist
policies for these industries.

Given this, international managers have two options. First, in
their own domestic market they can seek to influence government policy by lobbying in legislatures or by testifying at public hearings. The
goal of these activities is to create a more friendly political environment towards open trade. Secondly, they can develop a local scanning
capability and prepare contingency plans for responding to the effects
of protectionist policies. For example, awareness of a government's intention to put a tariff on imported industrial materials could be offset
by early strategic stockpiling or investment in local production of the
needed materials.

It is important to note that the trend is not necessarily towards protectionism. There also are actions taken to open up borders. For example, since 1984 Japan made some major policy adjustments that allow foreigners to more actively participate in Japanese capital markets. Recently, under great pressure from the United States and Europe, Japan also has made concessions to reduce its nontariff barriers against foreign agricultural products, cigarettes, and other consumer products. Similarly, the U.S. passage of the 1980 Deficit Reduction Act successfully modified the DISC (Domestic International Sales Corporation) legislation to allow for a new entity, the foreign sales corporation (FSC) to replace it. The passage of the Export Trading Company Act in 1982 similarly encouraged further U.S. export activity. These actions translate into opportunities for more business abroad.

Governmentalism

By "governmentalism" we refer to an increase in the tendency for governments in market oriented economies to intervene in markets rather than allowing the mechanism of markets to direct the patterns of economic activity. Governments have always played a major role in providing the framework within which economic activity takes place. But, it is a matter of the degree to which governments control economic activity that distinguishes different countries in their treatment of production, consumption, and income distribution. To do this the economies of Western Europe, Japan, and Latin America use "indicative planning." By this we mean a planning process whereby government gives general indications of the goals and directions it would like to see the economy take, and provides limited financial and programmatic support for the private sector to move in the indicated direction. This includes government decisions to privatize business firms that were formerly nationalized, as in the case of the British telephone system, or decisions to allow government-run firms to fail, as in the case of the French metals industry.

Even with the recent conservative governments in the United States and England, it seems that the practice of governmentalism is on the rise. In the United States for example, there is a growing pressure for having some kind of a national industrial policy. Industrial policy appears to go a step beyond indicative planning since industry policy often calls for active government programs. Proponents aim to target specific industries for support and restructuring bolstered by government-backed financial support. Further support would be provided for programs to retrain employees and to enlarge export activities.

This interest in industrial policy appears to have its roots in a number of developments, including: (1) the material success of the Japanese industrial policy model; (2) the relative decline of traditional industries in the developed economies; (3) the increased level of international competition; (4) the increased frustration with past policies of economic adjustment that reflect neither an appreciation for the large-scale systems nature of industrial structure nor an acceptance of the possible need for major change. In many cases it represents a reaction to what appears to be willy-nilly ad hoc protectionist policies.

Foreign Direct Investment Review.   One area where governmentalism exerts an influence is that of formal review of foreign direct investment (FDI). Like free trade, the free flow of the factors of production (e.g., capital, technology, human skills) has always been defended in terms of allocative and comparative advantage efficiencies. However, regulation of investment flows was partly stimulated by the concern that MNC investment was not always beneficial. Among the investment decisions labeled "not in the national interest" are:

- The substitution of capital for labor in high-unemployment regions.
- The use of local capital that had the dual effect of reducing capital supplies for local firms plus raising local interest rates.
- The investment in simple production operations such as parts assembly that represented an end-of-the-line, low level technology, with no new upgrading of local skills or manufacturing sophistication (which is often perceived as a low-to-no-risk investment and commitment for the company).
- Foreign participation in industries affecting national defense capabilities.
- Adverse effects on the balance of payments either because of little use of domestic supplies or too large a dependence on importation of raw materials.

The foreign investment review process has both positive and negative aspects. First, the review process has given governments a more effective negotiating position on investment decisions because of improved information on which to base decisions. Costs can be more clearly balanced against benefits in the negotiation process. Secondly, the decision process is somewhat more open and rational (as opposed to closed and political) since the rules, criteria, and methods of calculations are more public. Thirdly, the process does not always cast the MNC as the "bad guy." Benefits of MNC investments, once hidden or thought inconsequential, can now be highlighted more readily. Lastly, the investment review process provides countries with a managerial tool to actively monitor, review, and adjust investment programs according to their effective contribution to national economic development plans. In conjunction with other national economic control strategies (e.g. protectionist legislation, monetary policy), it could provide a more effective method of offering incentives and posing constraints to FDI activity than the relatively ad hoc, politicized methods of the past. At least that is the hope.

The costs of an investment review program can be significant. Among the more common complaints are the following: existence of another barrier to international transmission of resources and the subsequent opportunity costs to countries as firms decide to locate elsewhere; increased delay and loss of competitive advantage in investment start-up due to bureaucratic review slow-downs; the creation of "nonissues" because formerly unimportant issues grow in importance as more constituency groups have access to the process; use of investment review as a tool of foreign political policy.

Change in Canadian government policy reflects a concern for the barrier effect the investment review process can present. The recently elected conservative government blamed the lack of economic growth in Canada on the decline of foreign investment. The Foreign Investment Review Board was seen as a major obstacle to the investment process and has subsequently had its role reduced to that of monitor rather than as reviewer and decision maker. Whatever the net results of investment reviews, it is probable that some form of foreign investment review process has become a permanent part of strategies to regulate MNC activity.

A CHANGING PERSPECTIVE ON MNCS

As noted earlier, a chorus of criticism has been aimed at the activities and perceived ill effects of MNCs. It appears, however, that the earlier harsh criticism of MNCs has given way to a less ideological and less strident view. This was noted recently in the *World Handbook on MNCs*:[4]

> In summary, then, while the search for economic autonomy and political sovereignty still goes on, and criticisms of MNCs continue to abound, our reading of the situation in 1982 is that, the environmental climate facing MNCs is more relaxed than it was seven to eight years ago and that governments are taking a more positive and rational approach to their impact on economic development. We believe the 1980s augur considerably better for a more conciliatory and mutually rewarding relationship between MNCs and host countries than the 1970s. The rules of the game and lines for negotiation have now been quite firmly drawn: in most cases, the parties know what to expect from each other and, although

changes of leadership of both governments and MNCs may modify
—and even drastically change—attitudes and policies, and individual MNCs may still be arraigned for particular actions perceived to be against the public interest, we would not expect any
wholesale return to the kind of confrontation which marked the beginning of the 1970s.[4]

The reasons for the apparently more balanced view include more
equal capabilities in negotiations, less radicalism in economic and political policies, increased acceptance of interdependence, recognized
benefits of MNC activity, and some host government dissatisfaction
with contractual arrangements that do not reflect a real commitment
like foreign direct investment does. Of particular importance to this
are the relationships of technology to economic development and the
role the MNC can play in restructuring an economy.

A country's development goals are highly dependent on the country's technology base. To increase industrial productivity, to make industries more competitive, or to restructure the economy from basic
raw material to higher value industrial products, a country needs access to modern technology. Technology, in turn, is a strong point for
the MNCs. Through their R&D efforts and global scanning capability
they are able to create or buy the best technology. Furthermore, the
creation and ownership of a specific technology often gives firms their
unique competence and competitive edge. As such it will not be readily
shared unless the firm gets very specific guarantees and benefits for its
proprietary rights. Since the know-how and technical capabilities of
the firm are not easily copied, those who want that knowledge must be
willing to meet the conditions put on its use by the owning MNC. Thus,
the MNCs' strengths in technology creation and transfer has increased
its bargaining strength vis-a-vis, governments and non-MNC firms. In
addition to this, the competition among countries to attract modern
technology has further increased its value. One result of this favorable
attention to the MNC is a changed attitude and a more positive assessment of its role.

A second influence on the changed perceptions of MNCs stems
from the positive roles MNCs might play in the policy of industrial
restructuring. However, restructuring has international effects. One
country may benefit while another may lose. One author points to this
as follows:

---

[4] John U. Stopford and John H. Dunning, *The World Directory of Multinational Enterprises, 1982–83* (Detroit, Michigan: Gale Research Company,
1983).

Although the different forms of MNC can make a variety of contributions toward the achievement of the criteria of acceptability in a restructuring of industry internationally, they will not automatically do so in the ways in which each host country desires. Therefore, negotiations are required not only at time of entry but also throughout the period of operation and in the event of termination of investment. During such negotiations it is important that governments recognize the limitations of the different forms of MNCs and that the MNCs themselves recognize the priorities of the host countries in achieving various criteria and goals. Both must recognize the necessity to make trade-offs in the pursuit of their mutual or conflicting objectives. Under such an approach, MNCs can be guided to help achieve desirable restructuring, but governments must first agree on the nature of the new industrial structure and on the criteria of acceptability if it is to achieve greater industrial integration. Greater disintegration requires no agreement at all.[5]

We can expect the MNC to continue playing an important role in the globalization of industries. However, the ability of MNC managers to make decisions freely and autonomously will be reduced by direct government action and by home-office policies that are intended to reduce potentially antagonistic situations between countries and firms.

MANAGING INTERDEPENDENCE EFFECTIVELY

From this book's environmental perspective, management is concerned with how country/market environments can result in opportunities or threats for the company. Interdependence is one such general environmental condition.

The implications of increasing interdependence suggests a more turbulent future. Increased requirements for change and adjustment will result from faster technology-driven rates of change. More complex arrangements, structures, and institutions will be required to coordinate the activities of a larger number of parties to management problems. Perhaps we may see a movement toward more centralized management and well-developed management information systems as firms attempt to better coordinate and control their policies and operations.

Given the pressures of population, economic growth, and technological development, the trend towards interdependence is likely to

---

[5] Jack N. Behrman, *Industrial Policies. International Restructuring and Transnationals* (Lexington, Mass.: D. C. Heath, 1984).

continue unabated. For management the implications are clear: There will be an increased need for understanding and effectively responding to the complex set of demands placed on the private firm as a result of this.

The actual response by management depends on the strategic problems and options faced. One obvious choice for a firm is either to "not go international," or if it has gone international to reduce the international content of its business. A firm that makes a strategic decision to not go international may be able to control its output dependencies (not rely on foreign markets). However, the issue of controlling its input dependencies (e.g., logistical support, purchasing, capital), the firm may have less choice. This has resulted from the shifts of competitive advantage in industrial materials and machine technology from domestic to foreign producers in both developed and newly industrialized countries. Such firms may then still be dependent on foreign suppliers.

Furthermore, deciding not to go international does not shield the firm from foreign competitors that may decide to locate their investments in the domestic firm's home market grounds or export into the firm's domestic market. The near disaster for the U.S.-based Talon Zipper Company is a case in point. Having failed to develop an international strategy, Talon was not prepared for the very successful penetration and near takeover of Talon's own domestic market by YKK of Japan. This suggests that active management-by-avoidance of internationalization is not really an option even for domestic firms. In fact, it may call for the opposite: conscious though reluctant entry into a foreign competitor's market as a "preemptive" strike against them.

The real difficulties in managing interdependence effectively is based on two conditions. First, management of interdependence is essentially a long-term strategic process. Temporary strategies to reduce interdependence via controls on transnational flows by firms (e.g., transfer pricing tactics, introduction of "zero-based" inventory practices) and by governments (e.g., interest equalization taxes, new residency requirements for skilled workers) are often successful in the short run. However, they involve inefficiencies that the local domestic economy or the firm's operations must absorb. The net result may be that the benefits of a reduced interdependence may become more costly than effectively managing it. From a government's perspective the maintenance of an "independent" automobile-, steel-, or even clothespin-making capability reduces dependence on foreign sources. However, the cost in terms of higher consumer prices and postponed adjustments are nearly always higher than the benefits of employment and local economic stability. For example, in the case of foreign direct investment the reduction of capital investment by substituting an older technology may reduce a firm's local dependence and risk level but it may also affect its competitive position because of low quality products, disruption of delivery capability, and increased costs of maintenance. Similarly, the failure to seriously develop a human resources strategy to improve local worker and managerial skills may allow competitors to receive advantageous treatment when government contracts are opened for bidding. Failure to recognize the strategic and systems nature of managing interdependence will lead likely to increased long-term costs.

The second condition that makes interdependence management difficult is the fact that once developed, dependence relations are difficult to break. Trading relations are highly social relations. The establishment of a business relationship is an exchange relationship with expectations of returned favors, fairness, and even friendship at times. This applies as well to regular business-government relations. Thus dependence is not a "bad" situation per se. It provides a sense of certainty and reduced risk even if at times at a higher cost. There is a certain comfort in the predictability of the relationship. In this case the search for alternative trading partners may seem to be a high price to pay for a reducing dependence. Furthermore, MNC managers and governmental decision makers alike often have personal stakes in maintaining present relations. This makes the issue of autonomy a less central concern for them. For example, a marketing manager who has come to depend on one or two foreign sources of supply may prefer to avoid the disruption of a satisfactory supply relationship to gaining some independence by developing alternative suppliers.

However, dependence has its problem side for both the dominant and the weaker parties. The case of a manufacturer demonstrates this. Since international competitive conditions are so dynamic, the manufacturer's search for lower-cost substitutes is constant. Comfortable dependencies on traditional suppliers and distributors might be an effective strategy under conditions of stable market conditions where reliability is the main concern. However under changing conditions of competitive advantage the need to maintain cost and quality advantages require that suppliers not just be reliable. There is a need for them to also remain competitive. Thus the manufacturer is forced to break off relations with an established trusted supplier or they can require the supplier to become more competitive in price, quality, and other performance measures if they wish to maintain the business relationship. If they continue the relationship as is, they themselves face consequences of higher costs or lost market share.

This appears to be the case in the U.S. auto industry. Japanese practices of zero-based inventory have been successful because of the way interdependencies with parts suppliers have been managed. U.S.

firms like GM and Chrysler Corporation have realized that for them to compete effectively against Japanese imports they too must manage their supplier and dealer relationship differently. GM, for example, has announced that it is planning to establish a completely different distribution system with dealers for its new Saturn project cars. Similarly, Chrysler has made public goals of reducing costs by one third, part of which will be achieved through redefined relations with its suppliers and dealers.

Dependence however is more of a problem for the subordinate partner in a business relationship. Dependence means less power to affect changes in conditions of sale, price, and timing of transactions and it tends to create a more passive business relationship. In this situation, dependence leaves a firm more vulnerable to change and the whims of others. It also contributes to the creation of a defensive strategic response rather than a proactive approach to interdependence management.

The management challenge of interdependence then becomes one of developing a way to balance a "portfolio" of dependency relationships. How much dependence is good? At what level does dependence on a foreign supplier or market become a problem for management? What approaches are useful in assessing the impact on business operations? What advantages are gained by increasing another firm's dependency on us? Or decreasing our own dependence? How do we manage our relations with firms and groups that have become dependent on us?

These questions are of critical importance to governments as well as firms. Since economic development is a long-term process, governments appear to be more willing to accept dependence relations with MNCs in exchange for jobs, access to technology, and increased export opportunity. As noted before, the Egyptian willingness to allow a joint venture in auto production with GM in part is motivated by a reassessment of the value of having an independent national auto manufacturing operation. While producing Egyptian cars is a symbol of industrial development, the fact that it was a money-losing operation probably helped make the costs of dependence on an MNC like GM seem less costly. In fact, the lesson in this might be the opposite of what is expected: In an independent world the dogged pursuit of independence can be a costly and maybe a foolish path to follow. This applies to firms as well as countries.

The recognition and acceptance of interdependence as a state of the world is probably the necessary first step to achieving more effective international management. Implicit in this recognition is the realization that neither the relentless pursuit of independence nor the passive resignation of dependence serve well the interests of management in firms or government. Interdependence suggests a balanced set of relationships where dependencies in some interest areas are balanced by independence in other areas. It also suggests that firms both win and lose in the course of doing business, but, neither losing big nor winning grandly is usual. The present trade imbalance between the United States and Japan exemplifies this. Nature may abhor a vacuum but it also dislikes imbalances. Finally interdependence suggests that the nature of relations is a negotiated order of things. In an interdependent world, where decisions bump into each other with increasing regularity, autonomy is less a symbol of power than a cherished resource and privilege that should be wisely used. In the end, interdependence requires a mature management, one capable of respecting the limitations of a single planet, but one which also pursues the search for more dimensions in a three-dimensional world.

SUMMARY

Governments are increasingly interested in making their economies more productive and competitive. To achieve these goals governments need infusions of technology, capital, and human skills from abroad. In their role as profit-seeking enterprises, MNCs provide these needed inputs in return for economic opportunities and favorable business conditions.

Thus, firms and governments need each other and must cooperate to achieve their own goals. However, working together involves real costs, one of which is the partial loss of autonomy in decision making. One result of this dynamic interdependence has been an often antagonistic and ambiguous relationship between the MNC and the nation-state. However, the realities of economic development and an internationally competitive business environment are forcing both governments and MNCs to reassess their relationships. Thus, an era of ideological differences may be giving way to a policy of "real economique" and more tolerance for differences. The management of interdependence may be the next great challenge for today's managers as national economies and firms become more internationalized.

DISCUSSION QUESTIONS FOR CHAPTER TWELVE

1. In what ways are multinational business firms and nation-states interdependent?

2. The interdependence between the MNC and national governments has been described as a "love-hate" syndrome. Why might that be so? How does this affect the management of interdependence?

3. The general business literature has generally lauded the MNC for its contribution to economic growth and development. Yet there are some significant costs to having MNCs set up operations in an economy. What are some of those costs? Why are they considered "costly?"

4. What are the three "isms" of government control and how do they interrelate?

5. How does nationalism become a problem for a firm operating abroad?

6. If the world is served best by a free trade system, why is the practice of protectionism so prevalent? What do countries gain and lose via protectionist policies?

7. Governmentalism (or industrial policy) is a way of describing an active government role in the planning and coordinating of national economic development. Japan, France, Sweden, not to mention all the socialist countries, have active roles for the government in the management of an economy. The United States, for the most part, does not define a similar role for its government. Does this put the United States at an advantage or disadvantage in competing with other economies?

8. The review of foreign direct investment by government is designed to assess the contributions and costs a potential foreign investment has for an economy. What are some of the positive and negative aspects of the foreign review process itself?

9. What accounts for the changing perspective on the role of the MNC in the 1980s as opposed to the 1970s?

10. One way to manage the interdependence problem is to "not go international." Is this a realistic option? How would you argue against a managerial colleague who claimed that, "it was a big mistake for our company to go abroad in the first place. We should have stayed home and developed our market and competencies more fully in the home market?"

11. Dependence is not a "bad" situation per se. What are the trade-offs a manager must realistically deal with in a dependent relationship?

Bibliography

This bibliography represents a listing of some of the major contemporary sources of information on international management. Many of the ideas expressed in this book are more fully developed in these materials. The majority of sources are relatively recent books published within the last 10 years. Since the academic field of international management is also of recent origin, the sources represent, on the whole, a fair sample of the major works in the field. They also reflect specific sources cited in the text. A roughly similar sample of articles were chosen. These represent both "classic" articles and articles on topics covered in the text. There is also a listing of the major journals in which articles of general international management interest appear.

Since this book focuses on strategic management issues, the sources will cover general management function and operational issues in international management. References to special topics such as foreign exchange management or taxation issues in accounting can be found in the other books in this Irwin series.

BOOKS IN INTERNATIONAL MANAGEMENT

BLAKE, DAVID H., and ROBERT S. WALTERS. *The Politics of Global Economic Relations.* 2nd ed. Englewood Cliffs, N.J.: Prentice-Hall, 1983.

BUSINESS INTERNATIONAL CORPORATION. *New Directions in Multinational Corporate* Organization. New York: Business International, 1981.

CARBON, JOAN P.; W. H. DAVIDSON, and R. SWVI. *Tracing the MNC: A Sourcebook on U.S. Based Enterprise.* Cambridge, Mass.: Ballinger Publishing Co., 1977.

CAVES, RICHARD E. *Multinational Enterprise and Economic Analysis*. New York: Cambridge University Press, 1982.

COHEN, R. B. et al. *The MNC: A Radical Approach*. New York: Cambridge University Press, 1979.

CONTRACTOR, F.J. *International Technology Licensing: Compensation Costs and Negotiation*. Lexington, Mass.: D.C. Heath, 1981.

DANIELS, JOHN D., and LEE H. RADEBAUGH. *International Business: Environments and Operations*. 4th ed. Reading, Mass.: Addison-Wesley Publishing Company, 1986.

DAVIDSON, WILLIAM H. *Global Strategic Management*. New York: John Wiley & Sons, 1982.

DAVIS, STANLEY M. *Managing and Organizing Multinational Corporations*. Elmsford, N.Y.: Pergamon Press, 1979.

DIEBOLD, WILLIAM, JR. *Industrial Policy as an International Issue*. New York: McGraw-Hill, 1980.

DUNNING, JOHN. *International Production and Multinational Enterprise*. Winchester, Mass.: Allen & Unwin, 1981.

FAYERWEATHER, JOHN. *International Business Strategy and Administration*. 2nd ed. Cambridge, Mass.: Ballinger Publishing Co. 1982.

FAYERWEATHER, J., and ASHOK KAPOOR. *Strategy and Negotiations for the International Corporation*. Cambridge, Mass.: Ballinger Publishing Co., 1975.

FRANKO, LAWRENCE G. *The European Multinationals*. Stamford, Conn.: Greylock Publishers, 1976.

GARLAND, JOHN, and RICHARD N. FARMER. *International Dimensions of Business Policy and Strategy*. Boston, Mass.: Kent Publishing Company, 1986.

GHADAR, F.; STEPHEN J. KOBRIN and THEORDORE H. MORAN, eds. *Managing International Political Risk: Strategies and Techniques*. Washington, D.C.: School of Foreign Services, Georgetown University, 1983.

GORDON, ROBERT J., and JACQUES PELKMANS. *Challenges to Interdependent Economies*. New York: McGraw-Hill, 1979.

HAERDEL, D. *Foreign Investments and the Management of Political Risk*. New York: Westview Press, Inc., 1979.

HEENAN, D. A., and H. V. PERLMUTTER. *Multinational Organization Development*. Reading, Mass.: Addison-Wesley, 1979.

HOOD, NEIL, and STEPHEN YOUNG. *The Economics of Multinational Enterprise*. New York: Longman Publishing, 1979.

HURONYNIS, OTTO, ed. *The New Economic Nationalism*. New York: Praeger Publishers, 1980.

HYMER, STEPHEN H. *The International Operations of National Firms*. Cambridge, Mass.: MIT Press, 1976.

KENEN, PETER B. *The International Economy*. Englewood Cliffs, N.J.: Prentice-Hall, 1985.

KINDLEBERGER, CHARLES P., and DAVID B. AUDRESTCH. *The Multinational Corporation in the 1980s*. Cambridge, Mass.: MIT Press, 1983.

KOBRIN, STEPHEN J. *Managing Political Risk Assessment: Strategic Response to Environmental Change*. Berkeley: University of California Press, 1982.

KOTLER, P.; LIAM FAHEY and S. JATUSRIPITALS. *The New Competition*. Englewood Cliffs, N.J.: Prentice-Hall, 1985.

KRAMER, ROBERT J. *New Directions in Multinational Corporate Organization*. New York: Business International, 1981.

LEONTIADES, JAMES C. *Multinational Corporate Strategy: Planning for World Markets*. Lexington, Mass.: D.C. Heath, 1985.

McCLELLAND, DAVID C. *The Achieving Society*. Princeton, N.J.: Van Nostrand and Company, 1961.

MORAN, THEODORE H., ed. *Multinational Corporations: The Political Economy of Foreign Direct Investments*. Lexington: D.C. Heath, 1985.

OTTERBECK, L., ed. *The Management of Headquarters–Subsidiary Relationships in Multinational Corporations*. Brookfield, Vermont: Gower Pub. Co., 1981.

PERLMUTTER, H. V.; T. SAGAFI-NEJAD; and R. W. MOXON *Controlling International Technology Transfer*. New York: Pergamon Press, 1981.

ROBINSON, RICHARD D. *Internationalization of Business: An Introduction*. Hinsdale, Ill.: Dryden Press, 1984.

ROBOCK, STEFAN H., and KENNETH SIMMONDS. *International Business and Multinational Enterprises*. 3rd ed. Homewood, Ill.: Richard D. Irwin, 1983.

ROOT, FRANKLIN R. *International Trade and Investment*. Cincinnati: South-Western Publishing, 1984.

RUGMAN, ALAN M. *Inside the Multinationals: The Economics of Internal Markets*. New York: Columbia University Press, 1981.

RUGMAN, ALAN M., ed. *New Theories of the Multinational Enterprise*. New York: St. Martin's Press, 1982.

RUTENBERG, DAVID P. *Multinational Management*. Boston: Little Brown, 1982.

SOLOMON, LEWIS D. *Multinational Corporations and the Emerging World Order*. Port Washington, N.Y.: Kennikat Press, 1978.

STAFFORD, J., and J. H. DUNNING. *The World Directory of Multinational Enterprise 1982–83, Vol. 3*. Detroit, Mich.: Gale Research Co., 1983.

TERPSTRA, VERN and KENNETH DAVID. *The Cultural Environment of International Business*. 2nd ed. Cincinnati: South-Western Publishing, 1985.

TSURUMI, Y. *Multinational Management*. 2nd ed. Cambridge, Mass.: Ballinger Publishing Co., 1984.

UNITED NATIONS CENTRE ON TRANSNATIONAL CORPORATIONS. *Transnational Corporations in World Development: Third Survey*. New York: United Nations, 1983.

VERNON, RAYMOND. *Storm Over Multinationals.* Cambridge, Mass.: Harvard University Press, 1977.

VERNON, RAYMOND, and LOUIS T. WELLS, JR. *Manager in the International Economy.* 5th ed. Englewood Cliffs, N.J.: Prentice-Hall, 1986.

WORTZEL, HEIDI V. and LAWRENCE H. WORTZEL, eds. *Strategic Management of Multinational Corporations: The Essentials.* New York: John Wiley & Sons, 1985. [readings]

YOSHINO, MICHAEL Y. *Japan's Multinational Enterprises.* Cambridge, Mass.: Harvard University Press, 1976.

ARTICLES IN INTERNATIONAL MANAGEMENT

BARTLETT, CHRISTOPHER A. "How Multinational Organizations Evolve." *The Journal of Business Strategy 3,* (Summer, 1982), pp. 20–32.

BEHRMAN, J., and W. FISCHER. "Transnational Corporations: Market Orientations and R & D Abroad." *Columbia Journal of World Business,* Fall 1980, pp. 55–60.

CALVET, A. L. "A Synthesis of Foreign Direct Investment and Theories of the Multinational Firm." *Journal of International Business Studies,* Spring/Summer 1981, pp. 43–59.

DAVIDOW, JOEL. "MNCs, Host Governments, and Regulation of Restrictive Business Practices." *Columbia Journal of World Business* 15, no. 2, Summer 1983, pp. 14–19.

DAVIDSON, WILLIAM H. and RICHARD HARRIGAN. "Key Decisions in International Marketing: Introducing New Products Abroad." *Columbia Journal of World Business.* Winter 1977, pp. 15–23.

DOZ, YVES. "Strategic Management in Multinational Companies." *Sloan Management Review* 21, no. 2, 1980, pp. 27–46.

DOZ, Y., and E. K. PRAHALAD. "How MNCs Cope with Host Government Intervention. *Harvard Business Review,* March–April 1980, pp. 57–65.

GLADWIN, T. and I. WALTER. "How Multinationals Can Manage Social and Political Forces." *Journal of Business Strategy,* Summer 1980, pp. 46–57.

HARVEY, MICHAEL C. "The Other Side of Foreign Assignments: Dealing with the Repatriation Dilemma." *Columbia Journal of World Business,* Spring 1984, pp. 53–59.

HAWKINS, ROBERT G. and BERTRAM FINN. "Regulation of Multinational Firms, Foreign Activities: Home Country Policies and Concerns." *Journal of Contemporary Business* 6 Autumn 1977, pp. 14–30.

HAYS, R. D. "Expatriate Selection. Insuring Success and Avoiding Failure." *Journal of International Business Studies* 5 (1974), pp. 25–37.

HEENAN, DAVID and WARREN KEEGAN, "The Rise of Third World Multinationals." *Harvard Business Review*, January–February 1979, pp. 53–61.

HEFLER, D. "Global Sourcing: Offshore Investment Strategy for the 1980s." *Journal of Business Strategy*, Summer 1981.

HELLER, JEAN E. "Criteria for Selecting an International Manager." *Personnel*, May–June 1980, pp. 67–74.

HOUT, T.; M. PORTER; and E. RUDDEN. "How Global Companies Win Out." *Harvard Business Review*, September–October 1982, pp. 98–108.

JAEGER, A. M. "The Transfer of Organization Culture Overseas: An Approach to Control in the Multinational Organization." *Journal of Business Strategy*, Fall 1983, p. 93.

JOHANSON, J., and J. VAHLNE. "The Internationalization Process of the Firm —A Model of Knowledge Development and Increasing Foreign Market Commitments." *Journal of International Business Studies*, Spring-Summer 1977, pp. 23–32.

LORANGE, PETER. "A Framework for Strategic Planning in Multinational Corporations." *Long Range Planning*, June 1976, pp. 30–36.

MAZZOLINI, R. "Government Policies and Government Controlled Enterprises." *Columbia Journal of World Business* 15, no. 3, Fall 1980, pp. 47–54.

POYNTER, THOMAS. "Government Intervention in Less Developed Countries." *Journal of International Business Studies*, Spring–Summer 1982, pp. 9–25.

PRAHALAD, C., and Y. DOZ. "An Approach to Strategic Control in MNCs." *Sloan Management Review*, Summer 1981, pp. 5–13, Fall 1981, pp. 15–29.

RAJAN, DAS. "Impact of Host Government Regulation on MNC Operations." *Columbia Journal of World Business*, Spring 1981, pp. 85–94.

RAPP, W. V. "Strategy Formulation and International Competition." *Columbia Journal of World Business*, Summer 1973, pp. 95–106.

RUMMEL, R., and D. HEENAN. "How Multinationals Analyze Political Risk." *Harvard Business Review*, January–February 1978, p. 69.

SORENSON, R. Z., and U. E. WIECHMANN. "How Multinationals View Marketing Standardization." *Harvard Business Review*, May–June 1975, pp. 72–80.

STOBAUGH, R. B., JR. "How to Analyze Foreign Investment Climates." *Harvard Business Review*, September–October 1969, p. 101.

STOBAUGH, R. B., JR. "Where in the World Should We Put That Plant?" *Harvard Business Review*, January–February 1969, p.129.

TEECE, D. J. "Technology Transfer by Multinational Firms." *The Economic Journal*. June 1977, pp. 242–261.

TUNG, R. "Selection and Training Procedures of U.S., European, and Japanese Multinationals." *California Management Review*, Fall 1982, pp. 57–71.

TUNG, R. L. "Selection and Training of Personnel for Overseas Assignments." *Columbia Journal of World Business*, Spring 1981, p. 68–78.

TUNG, R. L. "Strategic Management of Human Resources in the Multinational Enterprise." *Human Resource Management* 23, no. 2 (Summer 1984), pp. 129–43.

VERNON, R. "The Product Cycle Hypotheses in a New International Environment." *Oxford Bulletin of Economics and Statistics*, November 1979, pp. 255–269.

MAJOR U.S. BUSINESS JOURNALS WITH INTERNATIONAL MANAGEMENT ARTICLES

Asia Pacific Journal of Management

Business Horizons

Business International

California Management Review

Columbia Journal of World Business

Harvard Business Review

International Executive (abstracts of current international management literature)

International Management Journal

International Marketing Review

International Studies of Management and Organization

Journal of International Business Studies

Journal of International Marketing

Journal of Business Strategy

Management International Review

Management Japan

McKinsey Quarterly

Multinational Business Quarterly

Sloan Management Review

The International Trade Journal

INDEX